·MAR '07

Bridging the Divide

Bridging the Divide

My Life

Senator Edward W. Brooke

Rutgers University Press

New Brunswick, New Jersey, and London

Second printing, 2007

Library of Congress Cataloging-in-Publication Data

Brooke, Edward William, 1919–
    Bridging the divide : my life / Edward W. Brooke.
      p. cm.
    Includes index.
    ISBN–13: 978–0–8135–3905–8 (hardcover : alk. paper)
  1. Brooke, Edward William, 1919– 2. Legislators—United States—Biography.
3. African American legislators—Biography. 4. United States. Congress.
Senate—Biography. 5. Attorneys general—Massachusetts—Biography.
6. Massachusetts—Politics and government—1951– I. Title.
E840.8.B76A3 2007
328.73092—dc22

                                       2006005715

A British Cataloging-in-Publication record for this book is available from the British Library.

Manufactured in the United States of America

To Anne, with love

Contents

Acknowledgments

Undertaking the writing of an autobiography is not for the faint of heart. Even John Adams, according to David McCullough's masterly biography of the nation's second president, expressed frustration with writing his memoirs: "To rummage trunks, letter books, bits of journals and great heaps of bundles of old papers is a dreadful bondage to old age, and an extinguisher of old eyes." Massachusetts's most venerable son was right about this, as he was about so many things.

No individual can take full credit for the weaving of one's own memoirs. Memory is a decidedly fickle mistress, and reliance on the research, experience, recollections, and expertise of family, many dear friends, and supporters has made an appreciable difference in the accurate retelling of my life story. This book could not have come to fruition without the assistance of too many to recount.

My wife, Anne, who has shared nearly three decades of my life, has been the inspiration behind this endeavor. Her insistence that I tell my story for the benefit of my children, grandchildren, and others has kept me going when the tedious nature of recounting past struggles, disappointments, and triumphs almost caused me to throw up my hands in despair. Anne not only provided encouragement but carefully read, reread, and corrected countless drafts, astutely identifying potentially embarrassing oversights and incongruities. A poorer document would have emerged without her intelligence and insight.

In pulling together the threads of my life I have been indebted to professional wordsmiths who have helped me shape my story. Andrew Szanton, a talented literary scholar and writer, worked with me at the very beginning of the book. I am grateful to Andrew for his support during the early stage and his all-out effort in doing research and interviews under the happy but difficult circumstance of having a newborn son and trying to work from his home in Somerville, Massachusetts, with a newborn author five hundred miles away.

Marie Lanser Beck belongs on a pinnacle in that category of people "without whom this book could not have been written." With a strong background in journalism and history and a broad intellect, she has worked tirelessly and with unrelenting drive to get it done. Marie's supreme optimism has inspired us all. She has been my confidant and catalyst.

Patrick Anderson, a well-recognized journalist, editor, and author, on his first reading liked the book but thought it too long and used his talents to bring it down to size. Ronald Goldfarb, my agent, gave me confidence along with his professionalism, patience, and perseverance, and with the support of his associate Charles Younger, found a comfortable home for my book.

Marlie Wasserman, director of Rutgers University Press, enthusiastically embraced the project together with Ross K. Baker, professor of political science at Rutgers University. Marlie's assistant, Christina Brianik; the prepress director, Marilyn Campbell; and gifted copy editor Beth Gianfagna worked with her diligently and expertly to translate the manuscript to the printed page. I am indebted to talented artist Robert Anderson, who generously lent his technical expertise to transferring the image of the full portrait he completed to the jacket cover of the book.

Special appreciation goes to Marilyn Dexheimer Lawrence, author and former legislative assistant. She found time to help immeasurably in editing and in a variety of other ways. Marilyn is the one who says: "It's too long—cut it! It's repetitive—cut it! It's insignificant—cut it!" And, "Why don't you say so? You won't get another chance." But Marilyn's talents and her contribution to this book are by no means limited to her cutting.

Roger Woodworth was my close confidant and political adviser for most all of the years of my political life. He spent days with me on my farm in Virginia talking about people, issues, campaigns won and lost, political allies and adversaries, and one of his greatest loves, the Republican Party—his other loves being the Boston Symphony Orchestra and the Boston Red Sox. Many of our conversations were tape-recorded, and his words are a constant reminder of the wonderful years we shared in politics.

Although my beautiful, talented, and committed Senate case worker Maura O'Shaunessy did not live long enough to see the publication of this book, the example of her all-too-brief time on earth, in which she gave so much of herself in service to our constituents and others, was quiet inspiration.

Other staff members offered invaluable assistance in the crafting of this work with remembered anecdote and insight. For their dedication and continuing friendship I am indebted to Vivian Beard, Eileen Belford, Jeremiah Buckley, Levin Campbell, Patricia Caroleo, John Collins, Caryle Connelly, Ruben Dawkins, Meg Eisenberg, Harry Elam, T. T. Fernandez, Alton Frye, Caroline Gainan, Jacqueline Goodspeed, Kathleen Hagan, Stephen Hand, William Hayden, Claire Alfano Hill, Barbara Hurley, Michael Jones, Ann Keep, Mary Claire Kennedy, Martha King, Brian Lees, Gael Mahony, Joseph McMahon, Ralph Neas, Glendora Putnam, Thomas Reid, Eileen Riley, David Rossiter, Jerry Sadow, James Schuyler, Janet Sjolund, Dorothy Smith, Robert Waite, Betsy Werronen, and John Wright.

My dear cousin Adelaide Cromwell, in addition to making countless suggestions, corrections, and contributions, graciously endowed the book with the rich benefit of a scholar's eye and the impassioned recommendation that I drop the hyphen in the term *African American*.

Dean Ronald Cass and Margo Hagopian of the Boston University School of Law filled in critical details from my law school days; Jeffrey Conley of the Boston Finance Commission dusted off ancient files to secure details from my tenure there; and F. Lee Bailey, Julian Soshnik, and Ron Wysocki provided helpful information and insight, particularly with the chapter dealing with the Boston Strangler.

With warmest appreciation I wish to acknowledge those who have played a decidedly important role in bringing this book to life. By mail, e-mail, telephone, over breakfast, lunch, dinner or snack, in all four seasons and at all times of the day they have been helpful to the production of the book: Frank Arrindell, Thomas Bennett, David Benson, Dorothy Bethel, Linda Black, Roberta Brundrett, John Bynoe, Carlyn Carter, Norman Cohen, Angela Consoli, Sheila Crowley,

Milton Davis, Horace Dawson, Ruth Dendy, Annette Duke, Herbert Feld, M. J. Flatley, Peter Fuller, Stanley Gaffin, Joan Gormalley, Evelyn Gray, Robert Hannan, Margaret Henson, Marjorie Hewlett, Anthony Hill, Charlotte Holloman, Cyrus Honesty, Sewell Horad, Nancy Kincaid, Prentice Kinser, Paul Knight, Constance Koeford, Julian Kulski, Stew Leonard, Susan Lewis, Terry Lierman, Martin Linsky, Michele Lipscomb, Aaron Manaigo, Douglas Marshall, Jean Maza, Sandra McElwaine, Sherri McFarland, David Montague, Sherma Munger, Zygmunt Nagorski, Joyce Osborne, Gloria Pope, John Rector, Reid Rector, Marie Rhone, Henkie Rivers, Jeremy Ruskin, Jaye Whittier Sands, Ann Schiro, George Scurlock, John Simms, Mary Smick, Dina Stanley, Carolyn Stewart, Louis Stokes, H. Patrick Swygert, Donna Sylvester, Ellen Ternes, Harriet Elam Thomas, Harold Vaughn, Dave Wilson, and Catherine Yerkes.

Among any accomplishment that may be attributed to my tenure as Massachusetts attorney general, one of the most stellar is hiring William Cowin and his future wife, Judith Arnold, as members of my staff. I still smile at the memory of their budding office romance while they were young assistant attorneys general, and I take undue credit for their long and happy marriage. Today Bill is an associate judge of the Massachusetts Appellate Court, and Judith is an associate justice of the Massachusetts Supreme Judicial Court. Their combined review and counsel regarding the manuscript was invaluable.

The tremendous resources and staff of the Library of Congress, Archives; the Military History Institute at Carlisle Barracks, Pennsylvania; and the National Archives, Silver Spring, Maryland, were instrumental in providing documentation for the book.

I am most grateful to my son, Edward W. Brooke IV, for suggesting the title *Bridging the Divide*, passionately arguing, "Dad, this is what your life has been all about." He also says that after more than eighty years of inhaling and exhaling that I have never breathed properly, obviously a lesson he learned in the ancient Tibetan art of Boabom, to which he is a devotee.

As the history of our republic has demonstrated, almost anyone who works hard, exudes boundless energy, has staked out some portion of political ground, and is favored by that curious alchemy of circumstance and luck can achieve success in politics. But no one can do it alone. In politics all accomplishment is the result of group effort. For this reason I would like to thank my colleagues in the Senate, along with the many unheralded individuals who diligently and professionally went about their duties as staff members of the Boston Finance Commission, Attorney General's Office, and the United States Senate in service to city, state, and nation, and the thousands of individuals who devoted their treasure, time, and effort to my election campaigns. No greater badge of honor can be bestowed on an American than having earned a fellow citizen's vote.

For this reason, my deepest appreciation goes to the voters of Massachusetts who accorded me the highest privilege of my public life: representing the great Commonwealth of Massachusetts in the United States Senate.

Edward W. Brooke
April 2006

Bridging the Divide

Introduction

As I look back over my life and political career, I am struck by a paradox: that so much has changed, and yet so little. As a young man, I grew up in a highly segregated Washington, D.C., attended segregated schools, and served in a segregated unit of the U.S. Army during World War II. It was beyond my wildest dream that I might go on to become the first African American attorney general of a state—Massachusetts—and then the first popularly elected African American U.S. senator. Yet that is what happened, and it is a dramatic reminder of how America has changed in my lifetime.

Yet in so many ways, little has changed. We have made progress on civil rights, but so much remains undone. I spent many years working for voting rights, but we still see sophisticated efforts, led by white officials, to disenfranchise black voters in local and national elections. We see unemployment rates above 25 percent for black males and more young black men in jail than in college. We see outbreaks of violence—drive-by shootings, for example—that were unknown in black communities when I was growing up. We see levels of inadequate housing and homelessness that grow worse instead of better. The rhetoric of the American dream continues to be far from its reality for millions of our citizens.

As a young man, I was proud to fight in "the good war" against Hitler, but twenty years later I opposed our dubious adventure in Vietnam, just as others and I today oppose our dubious invasion of Iraq. I see young Americans dying—my fellow African Americans disproportionately among them—for goals that are not clear and may not be attainable, and I wonder: "When will we learn?"

In the Senate I fought to protect a woman's right to choose—in accordance with the Supreme Court's historic *Roe v. Wade* decision—and yet today that right continues to be imperiled by antiabortion activists and politicians who pander to them. We can go right down the line, on issue after issue—women's rights, gay rights, medical care, safe and affordable housing, education, employment security, the minimum wage—and find that the political battles I fought are still the burning issues facing America and the world.

Politicians write books for many reasons. When I left the Senate in 1979, several publishers approached me about writing my autobiography, but I was not ready. My story was far from over. Although the specifics were not clear, I knew that a new life lay ahead of me. I went on to have a new career, a new marriage, and a new child—now grown to manhood. I also had time to reflect on my life and to see it whole.

Now, at eighty-six, with most of my life behind me, I have embarked on this book, hoping it will be of interest to others, hoping there are lessons to be learned from it, hoping it can provide insight into American politics, and knowing that the process would give me both pleasure and pain. Believing, with Plato, that "the unexamined life is not worth living," I have attempted to offer an honest and frank accounting of my personal and political life. As the reader will learn, the two became all too entwined.

My life has been richly blessed from the beginning, with a comfortable upbringing in a loving home, religious guidance, a good education, and a rewarding life of purpose, achievement, and love. Even so, as an African American in the tumultuous twentieth century, the blessings have been counterbalanced by perils. Having known war as a young man, I worked for peace; having known racial prejudice, I worked for racial justice.

I am proud to have been a politician. It was a privilege to serve the people of Massachusetts and of all America. Today politicians are too often disparaged. While some have earned public skepticism, I regret the media's increasingly reckless invasion of the private lives of public servants, an intrusiveness that has deterred young men and women of promise from entering public service. The battle for justice and equality is an unending one, and I hope my story will encourage others to take up arms—to join, as Justice Oliver Wendell Holmes said, in "the actions and passions" of their time.

It is my fondest hope that some readers of this book, reflecting on my role in our nation's long political struggle for equality, opportunity, and justice in America, may be moved to continue that battle in their own lives and their own eras. The torch must be passed from generation to generation if America is ever to achieve its full promise.

Let me make one stylistic note. When I was growing up, people of my race were called—and called ourselves—*colored* or *Negro*. (We were called other, worse things, too, but those need not be repeated.) In the 1960s, to be called *black* became a symbol of racial pride. Later, the term *African American* came into favor. In this memoir, I have mostly used the word that fits the period under discussion. I was the same person, decade after decade, whatever I was called. I have often thought how ridiculous these distinctions are. My entire life has been devoted to breaking down barriers, to finding common ground. Labels applied to people of any race are inherently offensive. We can only begin to live together in harmony, to appreciate our common humanity, when we look beyond the skin-deep distinctions that separate us and accept one another as children of God.

1

Inside the

Cocoon

For young people growing up in America today, stories of my youth will seem almost incomprehensible. It will require the suspension of their sense of reality to picture a time when large areas of Washington, D.C., were truly safe, when families stayed together, neighbors helped one another, students were encouraged to study, and there were no drugs or drive-by shootings. But I grew up in such a time, and these are my recollections. I grew up black in the segregated South, yet I never knew the poverty or overt racial discrimination that might suggest. My hometown was Washington, D.C., where my father was a government lawyer. I attended good schools and lived in a neighborhood that was attractive and crime-free. My life was dramatically different from that of a young black man in the Deep South. The segregation in Washington was no less real, but it was more subtle and, in my experience, not violent. I was raised in a cocoon, surrounded by other middle-class Negro Americans, rarely dealing with whites, accepting the written and unwritten laws that declared much of my hometown off-limits to me. I knew that some of my ancestors had come to America in chains, and I knew that lynching and race riots still occurred, but the blunt realities of racism did not really penetrate my life until I went off to serve in World War II.

My parents, Edward William Brooke Jr. and Helen Seldon Brooke, were very different people. I loved them both deeply, but I was more like my outgoing mother than my reserved, brooding father. They had two daughters before they had me: Helene, then Edwina. They expected their second child to be their last and hoped for a boy, but of course they adored the little girl who arrived instead. When the girls were six and three, Edwina developed an upset stomach. A doctor prescribed the wrong medicine, and she died of blood poisoning. The doctor's behavior, in my opinion, amounted to criminal negligence, but there was no thought of a malpractice suit. My parents were not the sort of people to make trouble. They rarely spoke of this tragedy; I do not even know if the doctor was black or white or whether it mattered. Edwina's death plunged my mother into a severe depression. She later told me that without my father's love and support, she might have died. Her doctor urged her to have another child to combat her depression, and my mother prayed that she could. My birth, at our rented home on October 26, 1919, was literally the answer to my mother's prayers. She named me Edward W. Brooke III, as much for my dead sister Edwina as for my father.

Some of my ancestors on my father's side were slaves on farms around Falmouth and Fredericksburg, Virginia. As a child, my grandfather, Edward William Brooke Sr., had been a slave on the Brooke plantation near Fredericksburg, from which he derived his name. He was a tall, strong man with copper-colored skin, high cheekbones, and straight black hair. His ancestors were African, Cherokee Indian, and English white. He met and married my grandmother, Dolly Jefferson, in Fredericksburg, and my father was born on August 14, 1889. In those days, many ambitious young Negro men in the South were moving up to Washington, D.C. It was still "Mr. Lincoln's town," and Negroes believed there were better jobs and less discrimination there. When my grandfather made that move, he was the first of his tight-knit family to leave Fredericksburg's rich farm country. He found a job as a trainman for the Pennsylvania Railroad.

My mother, Helen Seldon, was born on April 19, 1892, on a farm outside Petersburg, Virginia, the ninth of ten children. Her mother, Eliza Seldon, died when she was three, and my mother had no memory either of her mother or her white father. Her older sister, Addie, and her husband, William Mavritte, took her to Washington and raised her as their own. Uncle William was a bricklayer, a part-time Baptist preacher, and a strict disciplinarian. My outgoing, fun-loving mother grew up in a family where no one was permitted to drink, smoke, dance, or play cards. She was only fifteen when my father came courting. He was eighteen, a neat, quiet, rather formal young man. When he came to call, Uncle William would never leave the room, and after a brief visit he would escort the young man to the door. After a year the young couple married and escaped to Atlantic City for a honeymoon that my mother talked about for the rest of her long life.

My father worked his way through Howard University Law School while supporting his wife and children and with no help from his family. On May 18, 1918, he took the D.C. bar exam. He did not pass it, nor did most of the Negroes who took it with him. He never blamed discrimination, but my mother said that considering his good grades, hard work, and ambition, she had to believe that was the reason. He never took the bar exam again, perhaps because he did not want to expose himself to that cruel rejection a second time.

Racism caused great pain in my father's life. As a boy, he was not protected by a middle-class cocoon the way I was. As a man, working in the Veterans Administration, he encountered segregated facilities, even segregated toilets, for black and white employees. Year after year he was passed over for promotion, as the good jobs with higher pay went to whites. It took him years to reach the exalted position of attorney reviewer, and he never came close to matching his ambitions or his potential. When he retired after fifty years, he was given a Distinguished Service Award, but he left a bitter man. We never discussed his frustrations or why he never took the bar exam a second time. He did not want to burden me with his problems. He suffered in silence.

My father was a Republican, as almost all Negroes were then; they rallied around the party of Lincoln and Emancipation. He blamed the Democrats for segregation and racism. Because residents of the District (Negroes or whites for that matter) could not vote in the District, he never missed a chance to return home to Fredericksburg and vote Republican. Despite his disappointments, he rejected radical political solutions. He would say of Marcus Garvey's "Back to Africa" movement: "Back to Africa? Why would I go back when I have never been there? I'm an American and I'm going to stay right here." He was a good listener and a wise counselor, imparting some of his favorite aphorisms to me, such as "the quality of a man's judgment is only as good as the quality of his information." I loved him and never had cause to fear him, but we were never as close as my mother and I.

Given all his frustrations, perhaps it is not surprising that my father, like countless other Negro men, sought solace in alcohol. He never went on a binge or missed a day's work. He was never loud or abusive or profane. But he drank too much, night after night. My mother and sister and I left him alone. Perhaps we were all in denial. My father loved his family, but quietly. He took pleasure in my mother's popularity, in her work at church and in the community, and in her many friendships, but he had few close friends of his own and kept his feelings inside.

When I was born, we lived in a rented row house at 1938 Third Street NW, in the LeDroit Park neighborhood. Many of our neighbors owned their homes. Grass was neatly trimmed, the streets were clean, and there were no abandoned homes or deteriorated housing. People left their doors unlocked. We had no fear of crime or the "drive-by shootings" that plague black Washington today. My childhood was a happy one. My mother would take Helene and me on picnics in Washington's long, meandering Rock Creek Park. At Easter we would roll eggs down the hills there. In the summer the park's huge trees provided welcome shade in an era before air conditioning. On unbearably hot nights, Mother would pack blankets, sandwiches, and soft drinks, and we would go down to Hains Point and spend the night beside the Potomac River. For us kids, this was high adventure.

For today's young people it would be insanity. But those days, women did not work outside the home. My mother was always there for us. She was my buddy, my booster, my best friend. She attended every school play and ceremony that Helene and I took part in. She taught me that friendship is an art. When guests came to our house, she lit up with warmth and hospitality, and I learned to do the same. She taught me to thank people and to make them feel special. She was just trying to make me a good, outgoing human being, but her lessons were also useful training for a politician. The thousands of thank-you notes I have written over the years were inspired by her warm and loving personality.

She had an independent, objective mind. If a friend and I got into a scuffle at our house and each began telling his side of the story, she would say to me, "Don't just tell me what he did wrong. Tell me the whole story. Tell me what you did wrong." Then she would sit like a judge and resolve the dispute. At first that bothered me. I thought my mother ought to take my side. But as I came to understand her belief in fair play, it made me proud of her. She taught me the value of honesty and that the world is a complex place with conflicting interests. Most of all, my mother believed in me. She said that if I worked hard, there was nothing I could not do. She told me over and over, "You've got to keep fighting," and her words still ring in my ears.

Advice my mother gave me regarding women has stayed with me all my life, too. Boys then as now often bragged to one another about their sexual conquests. Once my mother overheard one of my friends bragging about having slept with a girl. When my friends left, she called me aside. I could tell she was really upset about something. She told me what she had heard and said that she hated this kind of talk. "If a girl thinks enough of you to give you her body, you should respect her enough not to tell anyone about what you have done." She went on to lecture me, saying "all women should be respected, even prostitutes. Remember, your mother is a woman."

When it came time to start school, young Negroes in Washington were blessed. The District had segregated schools and teaching staffs, but they paid the white and black teachers the same. This meant that teaching was one of the best-paying jobs for Negroes. It also meant that our teachers were often overqualified for their jobs—scholars with advanced degrees, who today would be teaching at great universities, in those days wound up in the black public schools of the District. White colleges would not hire them, and black colleges could not pay them as much as the District did. There were three high schools open to black students in Washington. I attended Dunbar, named for the great Negro poet, Paul Laurence Dunbar, which we believed to be the best Negro high school in America and as good as any white high school. Many Dunbar graduates went on to do well at Ivy League colleges, and its graduates have been leaders in many fields.

When I was at Dunbar, I thought I wanted to be a doctor. In our community, doctors were the men who made the most money, earned the most respect, and had the prettiest wives. Most of the young women I knew viewed marrying a doctor as their most important goal, or at least their mothers did. For all the wrong reasons, I focused on premed courses such as chemistry and biology, ignoring the fact that I had no aptitude for them. I made better grades in civics, history, and English. My favorite English teacher, Miss Bertha McNeil, taught me how to write and organize my thoughts—skills that were invaluable in law and politics. My civics teacher, Cyrus Shipley, a Yale graduate, told me I was wasting my time in the sciences and should focus on political science and history, but I shrugged off his good advice.

I was a good but not outstanding student. Much of what I learned I learned outside the classroom. My mother taught me to love opera, the theater, and classical music. If the best theaters in our hometown, the capital of this proud democracy, would not admit us, she did not let that defeat her. She took me to New York to hear Mozart's works at Carnegie Hall and to see *Carmen* and *Cavalleria Rusticana* performed by the San Carlo Opera Company. In high school and college, I listened to the Saturday afternoon radio broadcasts of the Metropolitan Opera while I studied. We also took advantage of the great Negro theaters in Washington, including the Lincoln, the Republic, the Booker T and the Howard, which rivaled Harlem's famous Apollo Theater as a showcase for the leading black artists of the day. I grew up listening to Ethel Waters, Lionel Hampton, Cab Calloway, Duke Ellington, Count Basie, Jimmy Lunceford, Ella Fitzgerald, and Louis Armstrong. My parents taught me that racial prejudice is a sin, one that robs the world of great minds and talents. They confronted it and persevered.

My early life centered on our large extended family. I spent many of my summer vacations with my mother's oldest brother, Uncle Henry, and his wife, Aunt Carrie, and their seven children on the Seldon family farm outside Petersburg. The farm had a red barn, cows, four plow horses, two riding horses, two mules, and a little store with a tin roof that sat near the road. There they sold vegetables and flowers they grew and bottles of preserves and honey from the bees they kept. As far as I could see, the family lived entirely off the products of their farm. Those were joyous times, feeding their chickens and pigs, hunting rabbit and possum with Uncle Henry, and attending Sunday school, church, and occasional revival meetings. But the funerals at their country Baptist church were what I remember best. People would come from miles around, often on horseback or mule-drawn wagons, bringing with them a cornucopia of cakes, pies, fried chicken, ham, sweet potatoes, and other delicacies. My "country cousins" and I did not focus on the fact of death, just on the people and the treats. A wedding, a funeral, a barn raising—they all meant good times to us.

As I grew older, I spent very different vacations in Harlem with my mother's younger sister, Aunt Ruth, and her Cuban husband, Uncle Alexander Pompez. My mother and Aunt Ruth never got along; she was a difficult woman, although Uncle Alex loved her dearly. Everyone liked Uncle Alex, who was a funny, good-natured, kind man who for a time controlled the numbers racket in Harlem. (My father liked him despite his occupation.) Sometimes I watched in fascination as Uncle Alex and Aunt Ruth counted thousands of dollars in small bills on their dining room table. If I ran an errand for my uncle, he would sometimes reward me with a twenty-dollar bill, a fortune in those days.

Uncle Alex and Aunt Ruth had a luxurious apartment overlooking Yankee Stadium, and they drove their cream-colored Packard convertible to vacations in exclusive New Jersey resorts. Aunt Ruth had no children of her own and often said she wanted Helene and me to come live with her and Uncle Alex. Failing that, she was happy for us to visit during summer vacations. She would buy expensive dresses for Helene and nice clothes for me, too, and take us to Asbury Park in New Jersey and to New York's famous Coney Island.

Uncle Alex loved sports. He owned the Cuban All Stars baseball team and built a ballpark in the Bronx for them to play in. The All Stars drew big crowds and made him a lot of money. Many of those Cuban and Negro players would have been playing in the major leagues if they had been integrated then. I loved our visits to Harlem. I belatedly learned a lot more about Uncle Alex's life when I read a fascinating article by Daniel Coyle in the December 15, 2003, issue of *Sports Illustrated*. The story told how Fritz Pollard, a black all-

American football star at Brown University in the 1910s and later a star in the National Football League, helped start the New York Brown Bombers after the white NFL owners unofficially banned black players from their league. My Uncle Alex was involved because he owned the stadium where the Bombers played. Coyle has this to say about him:

> Pompez was a criminal in the eyes of the police and a crown prince in the eyes of Harlemites. From his cigar store, the soft-spoken Cuban ran a numbers bank—a lottery that filled his pockets to the tune of $8000 a day—which he used to fund his Negro league baseball team, the New York Cubans. Courtly, suave and scrupulously honest with his clients, Pompez was beloved in Harlem for his civic generosity.
>
> All went swimmingly for him until an evening in 1931 when the Bronx-based gangster Arthur Flegenheimer, better known as Dutch Schultz, employed his .45 revolver to persuade Pompez to hand over control of the numbers game. Needing another source of income, Pompez turned to sports enterprises. In 1935 he leased a vacant field at Dyckman Oval from the city and transformed it into one of the finest sports palaces in Manhattan.

This was the stadium in the Bronx where both the Cuban baseball team and the Brown Bombers football team played. Coyle goes on to say that Uncle Alex regained control of the numbers racket after Dutch Schultz was killed by other gangsters in 1935 and that in 1937 New York's crime-busting District Attorney Tom Dewey led a raid on his office. Uncle Alex escaped to Mexico for several months but later returned home and became a prosecution witness against some gangsters who were on trial. He thus kept his freedom, but the city, perhaps as a punishment, tore down his stadium. Uncle Alex went on to a new career as a baseball scout for the New York Giants. According to Coyle, he was "the scout who opened the Latin pipeline to the big leagues" by helping sign such stars as Orlando Cepeda and Juan Marichal. As I recall, he also helped recruit Willie Mays. Not long before his death, Uncle Alex served on the committee that selected Negro league players for inclusion in the Baseball Hall of Fame, and he himself became a member in a special election on February 2, 2006.

Even as a teenager, I knew that Uncle Alex was special, but I did not fully appreciate his saga until I saw that article. In the 1960s, when Tom Dewey was a Republican elder statesman, having run unsuccessfully for president in 1944 and 1948, I met him at two Republican national conventions, but I never told him that he had tried to put my uncle in jail. I was a United States Senator when I went to Uncle Alex's funeral in the 1970s.

When I was leaving Harlem to return home, Uncle Alex and Aunt Ruth would always buy me a first-class train ticket. In those days, the first-class cars were the height of elegance. I loved to sit in the parlor car in a big swivel chair of rich dark green velour and twirl about as the landscape raced by. In first class, the conductors and the maitre d' were always white, whereas the Pullman porters and waiters in the dining car were always black. I could see what a kick they got out of seeing a young black kid enjoying the luxury of first class. Once, one of the waiters told me that the distinguished-looking gentleman across from me was General John "Black Jack" Pershing, a great hero of World War I. A little later, the general spoke to me, asking my name and where I went to school. I was thrilled to have even a brief exchange with a famous man. Already I dreamed of growing up to know important people and visit exciting places. Years later, I was saddened to learn that in 1917 General Pershing had issued a strongly worded directive to prevent contact between French officers and the few black American officers. This was necessary to avoid "spoiling the Negro," he explained.

In 1929, three days after my tenth birthday, the stock market crashed and the Great Depression began. Thanks to my father's government job, we were spared the economic devastation that so many Americans suffered. But we did see, in our neighborhood, homes being sold at foreclosure sales and the people whose belongings were suddenly stacked on sidewalks or in the street. I never knew of any government relief helping the many thousands in need. For many families, the bad situation was made worse by the stigma attached to working women. You never heard sympathy for single mothers, only that if a woman took a job she was stealing it from a man "with mouths to feed."

My parents were raised as Baptists. When I was growing up, my father rarely attended church, but he began each meal with a prayer of thanksgiving, a practice I've carried on all my life. Mother was an enthusiastic churchgoer. My parents never hated anyone, no matter how cruel or racist, and they taught me to trust in prayer and to love everyone. My father's brother, Clarence Brooke, had joined St. Luke's Episcopal Church, Washington's first independent Negro Episcopal Church. He served on the vestry for many years and was superintendent of the Sunday school. Because of him, my parents became members. Helene and I were baptized and confirmed there, as were our children years later.

I loved church and rarely missed a Sunday service. I was an acolyte when I was seven and later served as crucifer, carrying the cross at the front of the procession at each service. Many people thought I would someday become a clergyman, but I never felt I had a calling. I became a politician instead, and my supporters often said my speeches sounded like sermons. Religion meant deeds, not just words, to our family. When my father's younger brother, James, died at the age of thirty-seven and left his wife Betty with six children, my parents did not hesitate to bring two of the children, James Jr. and Yvonne, the only girl, to live with us and go to school. Yvonne was like a younger sister to me, and we are close to this day.

Despite the Depression, Dad managed several summers to rent a cottage for our family in Highland Beach, Maryland, near Annapolis on the Chesapeake Bay. Many middle-class Negroes from Washington vacationed there, and for teenagers it was a wonderful time of swimming, catching crabs, dancing, and enjoying moonlight walks and picnics on the beach. At home, I was expected to share in the chores and to earn my spending money. I shoveled snow off sidewalks and coal into neighbors' coal chutes, mowed lawns in the summers, did chores for a doctor's family up the street, and delivered the *Washington Tribune* and the *Baltimore Afro-American* newspapers. I was dating a good deal in high school. Often I would meet a girl for a movie at the Lincoln Theater on U Street. I always arranged to meet her inside the theater, a none-too-subtle ploy to ensure that the girl would buy her own ticket, which I could not afford.

I loved sports, too. When I picked up the *Washington Post* each morning, the first thing I read, before the front page, was Shirley

Povich's great sports column. I played sandlot football, baseball, and basketball, but I was too light and too slow for the varsity teams. My best sport was tennis. As a senior at Dunbar, I captained the tennis team and won a few trophies. I learned to play on the city's segregated public courts, often playing many sets a day despite the city's brutal summer heat. But tennis in those days was not a sport for Negroes; we were barred from playing on most courts or, even if we were good enough, in the U.S. Lawn Tennis Association's tournaments.

I never knew my father to engage in sports, but he loved them, particularly horse racing. Horse racing was in Dad's blood, although he never owned a horse, much less raced one. He went to the races on Saturdays when he could. I suspect, although he never told me, that he occasionally wagered with bookies. All this, of course, was much to my mother's chagrin. Once when I was in high school he took me to the Pimlico track in Baltimore to see a running of the Preakness, and thanks to him, in 1938, when I was in college, I saw the "race of all races" between Seabiscuit and War Admiral.

My father had the notion that any horse with "war" in his name was a sure winner, and War Admiral was his favorite horse of all time. He had eagerly awaited the race between "his" horse and the people's choice, Seabiscuit. For my part, I was excited to see Dad so excited as he strode up to place his bet—and then place a second bet for me. It was a sunny, warm November day, and we stood below the grandstand and could barely see the finish line as people elbowed and jumped in front of us. As the world now knows—reminded by Laura Hillenbrand's book *Seabiscuit* and its movie version— Seabiscuit won by four lengths. Dad was deeply disappointed, but he never gave up his penchant for horses with "war" in their names, and he aroused in me a love for horses that has lasted a lifetime. It was in his blood, and in mine, too, as I later found.

When I graduated from Dunbar in June 1936, it was understood that I would go to college, and there was never much doubt that it would be Howard University. My father had graduated from Howard's law school, and Helene had received her bachelor of arts and master's degrees there and went on to a teaching career. A few of my friends were headed for the Ivy League, but my father could not have afforded to send me there, and I had neither the grades nor the athletic skills to win a scholarship. In truth, I was not ready to leave home. So in September, I entered Howard, walking the twelve blocks to school and back, sleeping in my own bedroom and eating meals with my family. Hitler had by then come to power in Germany, but like most young Americans, I paid little attention.

One of my big concerns was joining a fraternity, for campus social life revolved around the fraternities and sororities. Several approached me, but I had my heart set on Alpha Phi Alpha, the oldest Negro fraternity in America and in many minds the best. I admired its history, its distinguished alumni, and its high ideals. I was only briefly tempted by Omega Psi Phi when it brought the gorgeous young singer Lena Horne down from New York to sing at an Omega Psi Phi smoker. We freshmen were bowled over by her talent and beauty, but my commitment to Alpha Phi Alpha was unshaken. In time I served my fraternity as chapter president, as an undergraduate member of its national executive council, and as a national officer. Alpha was full of talented, ambitious young men; if you could advance in its politics you could do well in politics anywhere.

While I was at Howard, Dr. Charles H. Wesley, a history professor and dean, was our fraternity's national president. I came to know him well, not only as a teacher, but as a friend and brother. His intelligence and curiosity encompassed the whole world. He deplored racism, but he never talked in terms of what America owed the Negro. Wesley spoke, rather, of what we owed ourselves and could do for ourselves. His philosophy left a lasting impression on me.

During my sophomore year, my father bought the first car our family had ever owned: a new 1938 Buick sedan. Prior to that, we had sometimes caught rides to places with friends, and about two years earlier my godfather, Charles Harris, had given me an old Jordan automobile which I had driven. "Roll, Jordan, roll!" I would cry. Needless to say, I encouraged Dad's purchase of the Buick. I went with him to the dealer to pick it out. Dad had never learned to drive and did not intend to. I became the family chauffeur, and when my parents did not need the car, which was most of the time, it was mine. I loved that car.

My father made it clear that if I wanted to drive the car, I had to buy my own gas, so I took an evening job as a bus boy at the Chalfonte

Restaurant, off Sixteenth Street in Washington. It served only whites, and all of the help was white, too, until I was hired. The owners considered hiring a Negro bus boy a major experiment, and some of their diners seemed shocked to see me, particularly after I was promoted to waiter. To me, it was just a way to buy gas for the car that was so vital to my social life. To drive a handsome new Buick made me quite popular. I dated a lot and for a time discussed marriage with Dr. Wesley's beautiful daughter Charlotte, a music major and gifted soprano.

I was still a premed student, but then I failed organic chemistry, a prerequisite for medical school. After a brief period of denial, I realized that the professor had been right to flunk me. I had missed labs and neglected to turn in papers. I was far more concerned about my social life than chemistry. I had no great urge to be a doctor. I wanted a doctor's prestige, not a doctor's responsibilities. So I switched my major to social studies and focused on history, economics, political science, and literature. I soon felt better about school and made much better grades.

I never visited the U.S. Senate where I would one day serve, although it was only a couple of miles from my home. Had I gone there, I would have found the separate bathrooms for "whites" and "colored" that existed almost everywhere in the city. I did take part in my first civil rights demonstration while I was attending Howard. Two of my campus friends were Walter Washington, the future mayor of Washington, and Otto Snowden, young activists who were followers of the pioneer civil rights leader Mary Church Terrell. They recruited me to join a march outside a People's drugstore that did not open its lunch counters to Negroes. I was glad to participate, but it was an exception to my general acceptance in those days of the world as I found it.

I knew that New York Governor Franklin D. Roosevelt had defeated President Hoover in the 1932 election, and I knew from my father that Hoover was a conservative Republican, but that meant little to me. My political experience was limited to marching with other Dunbar cadets in a Roosevelt inaugural parade. I heard talk at home that Roosevelt reached out to Negroes, and my parents came to respect him even though he was a Democrat. They respected even more his wife Eleanor, who always seemed to be doing the right thing for the right reason for people in need. But I cannot say that politics seemed relevant to my early life. Our overwhelming reality, as much as we tried to ignore it, was segregation. Our parents tried to shield us as best they could. We were free to dream and to pursue happiness within our safe, segregated cocoon. We had little contact with the world outside, except what we read in the papers or heard on the radio, and they had little to say about us. I was taught in school that America was a melting pot, unique in world history, but we never saw the amalgamation that implied. All we knew was that there were white people and colored people, in our city and in our land, but we never met on common ground.

At Howard, I heard many distinguished guest speakers, including George Washington Carver, the famed agriculturalist; A. Philip Randolph, the courageous leader of the Brotherhood of Sleeping Car Porters; and the emperor of Ethiopia, Haile Salassie, famous then as the "Lion of Judah." But the visitor who made the greatest impression on me was the world-famous contralto Marian Anderson, who came to receive an honorary doctorate in music in 1938. I knew enough about music to appreciate her greatness.

It was the next year, 1939, that the Daughters of the American Revolution refused to let Miss Anderson sing in Constitution Hall, a short distance from the White House. First Lady Eleanor Roosevelt, with her customary courage and compassion, resigned from the DAR in protest. Moreover, she encouraged the secretary of the interior, Harold Ickes, to invite Miss Anderson to sing in a free concert on the steps of the Lincoln Memorial. A more beautiful symbolic moment, or a more devastating rebuff to the DAR, would be hard to imagine.

My mother and I were among the seventy-five thousand people who attended her concert on the chilly Sunday afternoon of April 9, 1939. The huge crowd was strangely quiet, even reverent. People wanted to express not only their outrage at the DAR but their love for one of the world's greatest singers. As soon as she sang the first notes of "My Country 'Tis of Thee," I felt pride rush through my body. Tears came to my eyes. I held my mother's hand, and we were spellbound by this elegant Negro woman, standing straight and tall, her head held high and eyes fixed on the sky. I was inspired and yet, as she began "Nobody Knows the Trouble I've Seen," I felt a sense of anger rush through me, that this great woman had to suffer from racism. I had never felt such anger for myself, but it was unthinkable that this noble, brilliant woman should suffer at the hands of ignorant, bigoted people.

War clouds continued to gather in Europe, but for a long time my friends and I ignored them. I had joined the ROTC when I arrived at Howard. That meant that if I successfully completed the course, I would be commissioned as a second lieutenant in the U.S. Army Reserve Corps. Hitler kept seizing more of Europe, but it was not until September 1, 1939, when his troops entered Poland, that my friends and I began to realize we might be facing war.

By the time I graduated from Howard in June 1941, I knew I would be called into the army, and I had arranged a temporary job at the government's Bureau of Printing and Engraving. That fall, our family became homeowners for the first time. Dad purchased a fine, two-story, detached house, with a lovely porch and backyard, at 1262 Hamlin Street NE, in the Brookland neighborhood, which had an almost country feel to it. Unfortunately, that November my mother took to her bed with a serious gastric attack. She had a lacerating pain in her abdomen and severe fever and headaches. She could barely eat or tolerate the slightest noise. Our family doctor could do nothing for her, and all my father and I could do was keep our house quiet as a tomb. We kept a pillow over our telephone and wrapped a towel around our doorbell. We admitted no visitors except our immediate family and the doctor. We stopped playing the radio.

On Sunday, December 7, I was sitting on our front porch, talking quietly to some neighbors, when a Western Union messenger arrived with a telegram for Second Lieutenant Edward W. Brooke. The army ordered me to report immediately to the 366th Infantry Combat Regiment at Fort Devens in Ayer, Massachusetts. When I expressed shock, the delivery boy explained that the Japanese had bombed Pearl Harbor that morning, and President Roosevelt had declared war. It had been on the radio for hours, but at my house we no longer listened to the radio.

I told my father the news. His great concern was that my going off to war might do serious harm to my mother. After a long talk, we decided that I should request a postponement because of her illness. I made the request, and the army delayed my arrival for twenty-six days, until January 2, 1942. We still had to consider my mother. We agreed to break the news in stages. First we told her the United States was at war. A few days later we explained that I must go serve. Despite our efforts, she was upset, as millions of other mothers were at that point. My father accepted my departure more easily. Duty was something he understood.

In those early days, the army was highly selective about who it took—that would change in time. I was six feet and one inch in height, but weighed only 132 pounds, and to qualify for my commission, I had to reach 135 pounds. I went on an emergency diet of milk and bananas and just made it. I would later think that my ROTC training, which won me my commission, had saved my life. Far more privates died in the war than lieutenants. I guessed that I owed Howard University my life, as well as my gratitude for more than four wonderful years and a fine education. As I made my final preparations to leave, I promised my parents that I would return healthy and well. They promised to be waiting for me. With those loving and optimistic vows, I left my cocoon and moved into the larger world.

2

Captain

Carlo

On January 2, after an emotional parting from my parents, I boarded a train for Boston at Washington's Union Station. It was so crowded with soldiers that I stood up most of the way. In Boston, as I changed trains and headed for Ayer, home of the 366th Combat Infantry Regiment at Fort Devens, I found myself increasingly excited. The 366th was one of only three Negro regular army regiments created by the mobilization plan of the Selective Service Act of 1940. I knew that some of its officers had been my fellow students at Howard. I was eager to join them and do my part in winning the war.

As I climbed off the train at Ayer, I had never in my life been so cold or seen so much snow. As soon as I could, I bought my first pair of long johns. I reported to the officer of the day, First Lieutenant Samuel Wilbert Tucker of Virginia. After the war, Sam Tucker would become a celebrated civil rights lawyer. U.S. District Court Judge Robert R. Merhige Jr., the equally courageous white man who ordered busing to desegregate Virginia's schools in 1968, said that he and Sam Tucker "were two of the most hated men" in Virginia and added that Sam was "the bravest man I had ever met." When I met him, Sam was just a harried young officer trying to keep up with the influx of soldiers. He assigned me to an officers' barracks and gave me orders to report the next morning to an antitank company.

My barracks, smelling of floor polish and coal heat, was one of scores that housed thousands of new soldiers, with bunks lined up on either side of a center aisle. As an officer, I shared a small room on the second floor with another officer. Upon arrival, I dropped my belongings in my room and headed for the showers. In the bathroom I received my first culture shock. The toilets were lined up very close to each other with no panels between them or in the showers. For a middle-class youth who had always had his own bathroom, the lack of privacy was jarring. Soon, of course, I thought nothing of it. My roommate, Samuel Jackson, had been a year ahead of me at Howard. We became fast friends, despite his habit of dropping his clothes wherever he took them off. Compulsively neat, I often found myself cleaning up after Sam.

Our training intensified as summer arrived. We began to take thirty-seven-mile hikes with full field packs weighing thirty-five pounds on our backs. We officers were supposed to keep the men moving, but as the summer sun beat down, soldiers began to collapse. I often felt like dropping myself, and several of my fellow officers did. My feet were like raw meat. Breathing was agony and my body ached, but pride kept me going. Back at the mess hall, I ate heartily, gained weight, and was soon in the best shape of my life. Sometimes our commanding officer, Colonel Howard Donovan Queen, drove by to observe our marches. This was supposed to be good for our morale, although in fact many of the men muttered unkind remarks at him under their breath. The colonel was a career officer and a veteran of World War I, but they resented these grueling marches. Yet he was right. Physical conditioning could be the difference between life and death during real wartime conditions. Moreover, as a black officer, Colonel Queen knew how many white officers scorned Negro soldiers, and he must have been determined to produce the best troops he could.

I was often shocked by the lack of education in black soldiers from the South. Many came from extreme poverty and had never received a chance to develop their native intelligence. They had known nothing but a savage inequity between the races; only when it came time to die for their country was there a hint of equality. Several of our officers were dentists and did what they could to help men who had never owned a toothbrush, much less visited a dentist. Others had never taken a shower or more than an occasional sponge bath. We encouraged them to take advantage of the showers—we had plenty of soap and hot water—and if all else failed, we would toss them into the showers in the hope it might be habit-forming. One day I read a letter written to our antitank company commander by a Mississippi farmer. He asked that a certain soldier be returned home to his farm. "Since this Nigger went off to the army, I had to get myself two mules to do his work." I showed the letter to the soldier, expecting him to be angered, but he only said softly that he would like to get back home. He spoke warmly of the farmer and said the army life was not for him. The incident made me think of Tolstoy's remark that man's inhumanity to man is not only what he denies his fellow man but what he keeps him from even wanting.

In the army I felt racial discrimination more keenly than ever before. I could not ignore that our government's policy endorsed blatant inequities in the treatment of black and white soldiers. The segregation was total. The whites had their part of the post, and we had ours. Their facilities were far superior. The Post Exchange, where soldiers could buy personal items at bargain prices, was off-limits to us. To leave the post by the main gate we had to pass through the white area and could glimpse the all-white Officers' Club and Noncommissioned Officers' Club that were barred to us. There were no clubs for us. The base swimming pool and tennis courts were also white-only. Because Negroes were not welcome in the small towns around the post, we had to travel more than thirty miles to Boston's Roxbury or South End for any kind of social life or recreation. In every regard, we were treated as second-class soldiers, if not worse, and we were angry. I felt a personal frustration and bitterness I had not known before in my life.

We junior officers, although we were not lawyers, were called on to defend our men at court-martial hearings. Many officers shunned this thankless task, but I came to enjoy the challenge. I read up on military law and fought hard for my men. In most cases, I thought their biggest offense had been the color of their skin. I had a good success rate and became known as a "soldier's lawyer" who fought for his men. It began to dawn on me that, if this war ever ended, I might become a lawyer.

My courtroom work led to a friendship—one that lasted a lifetime—with a court stenographer and noncommissioned officer named Clarence Elam. Clarence was a bright, friendly young man whose home was in Roxbury. I often went home with Clarence, where I met his close-knit family and began to explore Boston. Unlike Washington, D.C., there was no discrimination in its restaurants, theaters, or public places. I could go where I pleased. After the indignities of a segregated military base, I felt a wonderful sense of freedom when I could escape to the city for a weekend. I often walked through the Boston Common and the Boston Gardens, along the Charles River, and up to the State House. I attended concerts at Symphony Hall and went to the High Hat Club on Massachusetts Avenue for jazz. I fell in love with the city, although I did not imagine that it would one day be my home.

My first command assignment in the summer of 1942, on orders from First Lieutenant Cyrus "Mike" Honesty, the demanding regimental transportation officer, was to take a convoy of thirty men to the tiny, all-white community of Onawa, Maine. The army, not sure what to do with its Negro troops, and reluctant to give us combat duty, assigned us to noncombat missions, such as guarding bridges or air force bases. The 366th had been given responsibility for protecting installations from Cape Cod to Canada. Onawa was located several hours northwest of Bangor, and our mission was to protect a Canadian Pacific Railway trestle and bridge there. We lived in converted railway cars and kept our eyes peeled for saboteurs. The Germans did not invade, and we got to know the people of Onawa. It was an isolated place, occupied mainly by French-Canadians who had never traveled far from home and had never seen a Negro before. We were a curiosity to them, but we never felt the slightest hostility. Rather, they invited us to their homes for dinner and picnics. Their kindness was in sharp contrast to our treatment back at Fort Devens.

I sometimes said, not entirely in jest, that when the army learned I could read and write, they resolved to send me to every school they could. I spent most of 1943 receiving advanced military training. First I was sent to Sturbridge, Massachusetts, for a combat training course, with emphasis on infiltration behind enemy lines. That was where I learned to crawl under a barrage of live machine-gun fire. Next, at Fort Benning, Georgia, I received advanced infantry officer training as well as a motor maintenance course in which, to my amazement, I learned how to take apart and reassemble a two-and-a-half-ton truck in record time. While at Fort Benning, several of us were told that we could apply for pilot training in the air corps. Some of us gave the offer serious thought, and the next time I called my mother, whose health had somewhat improved, I asked for her opinion. Mother, who had never flown on an airplane, was horrified. So I did not join the air corps. Later, under enemy fire in the mud and snow and ice of Italy, I reconsidered my decision. The "fly boys," as we called them, were often envied by foot soldiers, and they were never known to envy us.

Leaving Fort Benning, I rejoined my regiment, which had relocated to Camp Atterbury, Indiana. Here again Negro soldiers were barred from the PX and the Officers' Club and could only see movies at post theaters at designated times. Colonel Queen protested that German POWs confined there were treated better than his men. Finally, on March 28, 1944, our regiment boarded a troop ship carrying almost five thousand men, bound for North Africa. A long, uncomfortable voyage was made worse by the zigzag route we took to avoid German submarines. We did not even throw our garbage overboard for fear of attracting a U-boat. I was seasick for most of the crossing, as were many others.

We landed in the fabled Moroccan city of Casablanca on April 6. Humphrey Bogart and Ingrid Bergman were nowhere to be seen. Instead, we gazed on half-starved Moroccans who waited by our ship to fill their pails with our garbage. Their eyes betrayed their bitterness at having to beg for our swill. We set up tents on rocky terrain outside the city. At night we watched movies in the open air. They included a cautionary film about the dangers of sexual intercourse with local women or prostitutes. The graphic close-ups of advanced cases of syphilis were enough to make anyone think twice about sex.

We then traveled by boxcar to the seaport of Oran, Algeria. As soon as we arrived, our commanding officer was summoned to a meeting with the base commander, Colonel George W. Pense, from Alabama. Pense urged Colonel Queen to set up a separate soldiers' club for Negro soldiers, or "these people," as he called them. His request was poorly timed, because Queen was still fuming from his treatment on the trans-Atlantic voyage, where he had been relegated to a shared cabin while junior white officers occupied staterooms. He angrily informed the Alabaman, "I am not a 'colored officer,' but a colonel in the United States Army. My answer to your request is absolutely, irrefutably, no!" Pense relented, and our men used the soldiers' club with whites, but he issued an order that all dancing in the clubs would stop. Negro soldiers were taking local women to the clubs, which angered white soldiers. During the remainder of our time there, our enlisted men were charged by white officers with a variety of violations and often put in jail. I thought this a campaign of harassment. The 366th had an excellent record for discipline and had just received a commendation for its deportment on the trans-Atlantic voyage.

When the 366th disembarked in Naples on May 3 with 151 officers and 3,095 enlisted men, we expected to enter combat. Instead, we learned that the army had never intended for us to fight in Italy. We had been sent there to provide airbase security. From then until November, our units were scattered from Sardinia to the Adriatic coast and assigned to the tedium of guard duty. We were second-class soldiers, and we bitterly resented it. The army's refusal to let us fight was an insult to our dignity, our courage, and our patriotism. It was a catch–22 that Joseph Heller did not discover: we were accused of being unfit for combat, and we were not permitted to enter combat to disprove it. But if there was to be protest against our treatment, which many of us considered, it would have to come from above, from the officers in command, and probably they were as helpless as we were against the system.

With our morale at an all-time low, Colonel Queen appointed me the regiment's special services officer. My job was to organize activities that might raise the men's spirits. I staged boxing matches, softball games, and track meets. I brought in the Lucera Symphony and a USO "French Follies" show complete with acrobats. I found some talented singers who became the 366th's choral group and traveled about entertaining our fragmented regiment. They even performed in the stately Garibaldi Opera House in Lucera before a packed house of soldiers and civilians, singing "Land of Hope and Glory," "Old Man River," "Smoke Gets in Your Eyes," and "The Lord's Prayer."

On August 29, Staff Sergeant Joe Louis, the undefeated heavy-weight champion of the world, visited us and spoke to our boxing team. His visit reminded me of the time my father had run an extension cord and put our radio outside the house so the whole neighborhood could hear the broadcast of Louis's dramatic knockout of the German champion Max Schmeling. Seeing this great Negro American hero buoyed our spirits, but we were still angered to be combat soldiers who were guarding airbases instead of doing the job we had been trained to do.

We were not alone in our indignation. Two leading Negro organizations, the NAACP and CORE, had pressured the Roosevelt administration to let Negro troops fight, as had many Negro newspapers. Their demands echoed in the background when, on November 15, the 366th was attached to the 92nd Infantry Division, which was part of General Mark Clark's 5th Army. This put us under the direct command of Major General Edward M. Almond, a Virginian and graduate of the Virginia Military Institute. We had been told that he held racist views, but we were so overjoyed to be given a chance to fight that we felt we could stomach General Almond.

On November 26, when we reached a staging area, we were stunned by our new commanding general's "welcoming speech." He stood before us with one hand on his hip and the other holding a bullhorn. In an angry and condescending tone, what he told us was essentially this: "Your Negro friends and your Negro press back in the States have been clamoring for you to go into combat. Well, since you asked for it, let's see how you like it. You can believe I will make you fight and suffer your share of casualties." This was a general who, after the war, would blame his 92nd Division's unsatisfactory performance on "the undependability of the average Negro soldier." His speech left our men furious at him and the entire racist military establishment. Some said they would shoot him if they got the chance. Tragically, that is what racism can do to you.

General Almond was true to his word. Three days later, without the usual prebattle indoctrination, several companies of the 366th were sent directly into combat under the command of officers of the 92nd Infantry Division. Our regiment was fragmented, and orders from the 92nd command for the most part bypassed our commanders and staff. But, despite everything, we were elated to be seeing combat. In our first major clash with the enemy in late December, many of our soldiers were killed. I missed that fighting because, in early December, Colonel Queen had assigned me to a special unit to work with Italian partisan fighters behind the German lines, but there was plenty more fighting when I returned to the regiment in February 1945.

We were positioned high in the Apennines, a chain of mountains and tall hills in the interior of northern Italy. The Germans knew the terrain far better than we did; they had placed their guns strategically and concealed them well. They subjected us to periodic artillery shelling from their mountain strongholds. Mortar shells rained down on us, filling the air with shrapnel. Units of the 366th occupied the ground southeast of the town of Gallicano. The Germans had an artillery battery and observation post on a 1,500-foot peak west of Gallicano called Mount Faeto. To move forward, we had to take that peak. General Almond's plan of attack was to shell Mount Faeto with heavy artillery fire each morning about six. Then we would send our troops down into the valley separating us from the enemy and up their steep slope for the attack. We suffered high casualties because the Germans knew exactly what we were going to do, and we never altered our strategy. Day after day, the Germans would wait for our shelling to end, then come out of their foxholes and embankments and start killing our men. After our soldiers were forced to fall back, the Germans could rest. We were sending our troops to die in a German killing machine. General Almond's strategy devastated our men's morale and troubled me deeply.

We now had a new regimental commander, Colonel Alonzo Ferguson. Colonel Queen had returned to the United States because of illness and perhaps in part because of increasing friction with General Almond. I went to Colonel Ferguson and suggested that we change our failing strategy and conduct a surprise attack in the middle of the day. I recommended that a platoon move up the enemy's hill without artillery shelling to announce the attack. I suspected that many of the Germans would be sleeping during the day, not expecting us to vary our routine, and the element of surprise might bring victory.

Colonel Ferguson took my plan to the 92nd Division, where it was rejected by General Almond's deputy, Brigadier General John E. Wood, who told the colonel to tell me he would "never send a boy to do a man's job." I didn't know precisely what that meant, but I did know that General Wood sometimes sauntered among Negro troops yelling, "Pick up that piece of paper, Nigger!" Perhaps he had legitimate questions about the ability of a platoon to succeed against an entrenched enemy, but I thought he disregarded the element of surprise. Nothing, I thought, could be worse than the strategy we were pursuing.

When Colonel Ferguson told me my plan had been rejected, I offered another. I would lead a small reconnaissance patrol on the mission, instead of a platoon, because I thought we could achieve the same objective. "I can't give you authority to try your 'revised' plan," the colonel told me, "but . . . " I took his long pause to be his unofficial blessing. However, he insisted on one major change in my plan: I would organize and plan our attack from our vantage point on the hill facing the enemy, but I would not lead it. He told me to send another lieutenant, and I chose Lieutenant Francis Chung, a brave and rugged young African American with reddish hair who I thought was ideal for the job and who jumped at the opportunity to lead the attack.

At high noon on February 23, with the sun shining brightly, Chung led a patrol up Mount Faeto as we covered him and his men every step of the way from across the valley. At the top, they found the enemy off-guard, many of them drowsy or asleep. The Germans retreated in confusion, and our men followed them a short distance, guns blazing, before digging in and securing our position. We later learned that the enemy believed they faced a major attack and therefore withdrew along a broad front. The result was that Company E of the 366th Infantry now occupied this strategic peak that we had shed so much blood trying to capture. Colonel Ferguson later told me he had recommended me for a promotion and a Silver Star. I was eventually promoted to captain, but I never got the medal.

Our siege of Mount Faeto—and many similar incidents elsewhere—confirmed in my mind that our men had been used as cannon fodder by racist commanders who did not want Negroes under their command and were willing to send us to our deaths to teach us a lesson. In wartime, many men of all races die in battle, often pursuing dubious or desperate strategies, and what motivates their commanders cannot be proven. But at Mount Faeto, the persistent use of frontal attacks in the face of an entrenched enemy that could count on our regularly scheduled forays left no doubt in my mind that, at the very least, our commander did not place a high value on the lives of our men. It saddens me that there were so many Negro soldiers in that war whose bravery will never be known or recognized. Many died, many had their lives shattered, and they were all heroes. They fought and died for our country, and to free Europe, even though they had little hope that the discrimination they faced would at all lessen when the war was won and they went home. They, too, were part of "the greatest generation."

Although I take pride in our success at Mount Faeto, I believe the highlight of my service in Italy had occurred back in December and January, when I led twenty-nine Italian partisans and ten of our noncommissioned officers and enlisted men behind enemy lines. My high school Latin had helped me gain a rudimentary grasp of Italian. I carried an army knife and a Baretta pistol and wore a fur cap and whatever clothing the partisans could provide. For some reason, they christened me "Captain Carlo."

We were scouts, a roving patrol, gathering information in hostile territory. We mapped roads and ammunition dumps, located minefields, assessed enemy troop strength—and then sent what we learned back to help our intelligence officers plan attacks. To an extent, we were grown men playing a game, taking reckless pleasure in our work, feeding our masculine egos, but it was a deadly serious game. Discovery and death were always close at hand. We had been told that the Germans summarily executed captured partisans, often by slitting their throats. We lived like wild animals, hunting and being hunted. We worked mostly at night, using darkness as our cover. Some of the fields we mapped were filled with mines, and we had no instruments to detect them. We slept in the open air, chilled by the cold, tormented by lice. When we returned to our own lines, we stripped naked and were deloused, and our clothes were burned.

Sometimes, Italians took us into their homes. Once, one of the partisans and I were in a stone farmhouse near Barga, a small town in the Serchio Valley, north of Pisa. The elderly couple who lived there hated the Germans. Suddenly we received a warning from a neighbor: a German patrol was coming. The man and woman rushed us down some wooden steps to their "wine cellar," which proved to be a filthy, dirt-floored basement with rats scurrying about and no wine that I could see. Soon we heard the thud of boots on the floor above us and Germans demanding to know if the couple had seen any Americans or partisans. The old folks played dumb. They kept saying, "Gesu e Dio! Gesu e Dio! Non capisco!" The soldiers were not convinced. They knocked the furniture around and threatened the couple. Downstairs, the partisan and I were cornered animals, drenched in sweat, nervously fingering the triggers of our guns. If discovered, we would try to shoot our way out, but the odds were not good. We did not move a muscle; the only sound was the rats skittering about our feet. The soldiers finally left, but we stayed in the cellar for a long time, for fear they might return.

Another time I stayed in the farmhouse of a different elderly couple. The room they gave me was bitterly cold, but they wrapped up a hot iron and put it at the foot of my bed. They were enormously generous, and I will never forget the meal they served. By then I had resigned myself to army food. C-rations were not appetizing, but they kept you alive and were far better than living off the land. Now this old couple, in their modest home, were feeding me mouth-watering pasta and salad with a red wine vinegar such as I had never tasted before. Most of all, I savored their Italian bread—dark, thick, crisp, and delicious. For a young man raised on Wonder Bread, real Italian bread was a revelation.

The war was brutal as the Germans withdrew and left ravaged towns behind them. The Italians were seeking peace, and their one-time partners were determined to lay waste their land so nothing of value would be left for the Allies. The Germans had taken silver and gold, horses and mules. They had taken cars, machinery, and weapons. They had taken able-bodied men for their labor and girls and women for their pleasure. When they left, only the town's old people remained. The young men were either fighting with the Germans, serving as partisans against the Germans, in POW camps, or dead. The partisans I supposedly commanded had seen brutality against their parents, the rape of their wives and sisters and sweethearts, the looting of their homes, and the destruction of their villages. They had a reckless and sadistic bitterness that comes to men who have seen such horrors and been helpless to stop them. They did not want to take prisoners. They wanted revenge. They wanted to kill.

A major part of our mission, however, was to take prisoners for interrogation. Farmers or townspeople would give us a tip: a German was coming to their house or shop at such-and-such a time to get a haircut or collect food. We would ambush the German, carry him off for initial questioning, and then turn him over to higher echelons behind the lines. But it was not always that simple. One bitterly cold night I came upon several of our partisans who had captured a German soldier. He was in his early twenties, slight of build, with blond hair and blue eyes. He was frightened and for good reason. The partisans had tied his hands behind his back. They took his wallet, found a picture of his girlfriend, and mocked her in graphic terms. A flush of anger colored his cheeks.

They had been hitting the German, and I knew they wanted to kill him. I ordered them not to harm him further. I said he might have valuable information. But as I walked away, I heard a horrible scream. I raced back and found the German bleeding to death from a savage knife wound; his blood stained the snow. The partisans claimed that he had tried to escape. I knew they were lying, and I accused them of murder and reported them to headquarters. But I realized nothing could be done: there were no witnesses, no evidence. This was one killing among millions in a vast and terrible war. As a legal and military issue, the matter was closed. But it was not closed for me. For many years, I would wake up at night and see the boy's face and hear his scream. On my watch, a fatal vendetta had been carried out on a helpless young man who could have been anybody's son. It is a memory I will never completely put out of my mind.

I have lived long enough to see a glorious mantle surround World War II. It was a "good war." I would say it was a necessary war, but war is never good to those who fight it or those who live through it. War is dirty, gruesome, and horrible. Most puzzling to me is to hear those who claim to have fought this or that war "in the name of God." I do not think God ever sanctioned any war. God must weep to see the folly and cruelty carried out in His name.

3

Romance

in Italy

On March 28, 1945, the 366th Combat Infantry Regiment was abruptly disbanded. Its personnel were transferred to scattered quartermaster units and to two engineering services battalions. For a regiment that had won two battle stars and whose men had won nine Silver Stars and eighteen Bronze Stars and suffered more than 1,300 casualties, this was a terrible blow. We were a proud unit. We had overcome prejudice and delay to prove ourselves. To be broken up, scattered to the winds, was hard to accept. Battle-hardened men wept at the news that our 366th was no more. To me, it was another day of infamy. I was hurt and humiliated; I could not believe it.

I was assigned to the 224th Engineering Battalion, which was stationed near Pisa, and told to prepare my men to be sent to the Pacific Theater for the invasion of Japan. Mostly we sat around camp playing cards, pitching horseshoes, and otherwise passing the time. The days and nights were humid and hot, long and lonely. Whorehouses and freelance prostitutes were easily found. Several times I saw a long, serpentine line of GIs leading to a single prostitute. Our officers sometimes fired their guns into the air to drive away the women and their pimps. Officers, of course, did not have to wait in lines. Pimps would bring a woman directly to the officers' tents, where she would move from cot to cot. For my part, lonely as I was, I could not bring myself to engage a prostitute. Partly it was a matter of pride, and remembering my mother's advice about respecting women, and partly my memory of those graphic films on the horrors of syphilis.

On August 6, the United States dropped the first atomic bomb on Hiroshima, and the war was soon over. Once we no longer faced the possibility of being sent to invade Japan, boredom became the enemy. I sought diversion by exploring Italy's towns and countryside in a jeep. I was thrilled to make several visits to the extraordinary city of Florence, where I admired the perfection of the Duomo and walked the narrow streets once trod by the Medicis.

The prejudice Negro soldiers faced in the army was underscored by the friendliness of the Italians, who were colorblind with regard to race. We were simply American soldiers who happened to be black. It was maddening to be given lectures on the evils of Nazi racial theories and then be told that we should not associate with white soldiers or white civilians. When Negro soldiers paired off with Italian girls, they were sometimes attacked by white GIs. Other times, they were attacked for no reason at all.

One Saturday afternoon, I decided to visit the nearby resort of Viareggio, on the Ligurian Sea, part of the Italian Riviera. My friend and former roommate from Fort Devens, Sam Jackson, now also with the 224th Engineers, joined me. On reaching the town, we rode around in our jeep for a while, admiring the sea view and taking in the sights. We stopped at a corner hotel restaurant facing the beach and took a table overlooking the sea. As we ate delicious lasagna, we noticed two nicely dressed Italian young women on the beach, engaged in animated conversation. One had dark hair and fair skin; the other reddish-brown hair and a darker complexion. We finished our lunch and went down to where they were sitting on a bench by the sea wall. I saw that the dark-haired one was the younger of the two and pleasantly attractive. But the woman with the reddish-brown hair was far more than that. She was radiantly beautiful with sparkling brown eyes, lovely olive skin, and perfect white teeth. Her clothes were stylish. Even though she was seated, it was clear that she had a good figure.

In my best Italian, I introduced myself as Carlo, my partisan name, and Sammy as Lieutenant Rinaldo, the Italian name he had adopted. The younger woman gave me a warm smile and said something in

Genovese, a dialect I did not know. The elder one ignored us, and they continued to talk to each other. Finally, I looked squarely at the older one and asked if we could sit down. She replied, as best I could make out, "This is a public place, so I cannot ask you to leave. But if you don't go, I will." Undeterred, I sat down and kept talking.

I learned that the younger woman was Mina Ferrari-Scacco, and her older sister was Remigia Ferrari-Scacco. As I gazed at the gorgeous Remigia, I thought that she looked a lot like pictures of my mother as a young woman. And when she stood up, I saw that her figure was not just good but great. Sammy asked the young women what they were doing in Viareggio. Remigia said she had come with her husband and that her sister had come to be with her. I asked where her husband was, and she replied that he was asleep. "At this time of day?" I asked with a smile.

Remigia said her husband was a pianist who performed in the restaurant-bar at the hotel across from the beach. He worked late and sometimes slept in the afternoon. Mina asked what we were doing in Viareggio, and Sammy explained that we were stationed in Pisa and had come to see the town. When Remigia rose, as if to leave, I declared that I wanted to see her again. She reminded me that she was married. Smiling, I told her I was a lawyer and could help her get a divorce. Could I at least visit her, if not here, maybe at her home? Remigia said that her mother was too sick for her to entertain visitors at home. I told her I was a doctor and could help her mother. She gave me a suspicious look. "Ah, but you are much too young to be both a doctor and a lawyer," she replied. The two of them laughed and said goodbye, then crossed the boulevard and disappeared inside the Hotel Principe di Piemonte.

Back at camp that night, I could not stop thinking about Remigia. She had been haughty at first, but later she had been friendlier, almost flirtatious. She apparently spoke no English and enjoyed my rough Italian. I wanted badly to see her again. Sammy and I returned to Viareggio a couple of nights later and went to the Principe di Piemonte. In the bar, a man of about forty was playing the piano, with Mina and Remigia watching from a table nearby. They saw us and seemed both surprised and apprehensive. I returned to the lobby and asked the clerk if either of the two young ladies was married to the pianist. The man said no, but the older of the two was the piano player's girlfriend.

This was becoming an adventure. We caught the women's eyes and signaled that if they did not come outside, we would join them at their table. Mina, came out, grinning; Remigia stayed at the table. Mina said they had looked for us all day, but Remigia could not come out because her husband was very jealous. I said I knew Remigia was not married and I did not intend to leave until she came out and talked with me. Mina reluctantly returned to Remigia with my ultimatum. Sammy and I took a table near the door. Soon, Remigia whispered something to the pianist, then she and Mina walked out of the bar and crossed the boulevard to the beach. We joined them. I asked Mina to sit with Sammy while Remigia and I walked down the beach. The night was cool with plenty of stars but no moon. We could hear the waves rolling onto the shore. It was not long before I drew her close and kissed her, first tenderly, then with passion.

Remigia responded nervously. She admitted she was not married and that although she was engaged to the pianist, she did not love him. She said he was very jealous and insisted she had to return before he began to ask questions. I told her that she had been constantly on my mind and that I had to see her again soon because I might be shipped out any day. Remigia told me that she and Mina would be returning home to Genoa on Tuesday, and she invited me to visit her later that week. I eagerly agreed. She asked me to wait there on the beach so she could send Mina back with her address and telephone number. She asked if I would come the next Saturday, and I replied that if I was still in Italy nothing could stop me. She asked if Sammy could come too, an indication that her sister was interested in my friend. With a final kiss on the cheek, Remigia rushed off. Sammy and I waited for what seemed an eternity until a smiling Mina came back, reveling in the intrigue, looking over her shoulder as if she were on a spy mission. She handed me a piece of paper with their address and phone number, then kissed Sammy and me on the cheek and was gone.

Six days later, Sammy and I drove in a jeep to Genoa on roads choked with soldiers and refugees. We found that Remigia lived in an apartment in a stone building in what looked to have been, before the war, a prosperous neighborhood. Mina opened the door, all smiles, and ushered us into a spacious apartment. She called out to Remigia, "Carlo and Rinaldo are here." Remigia came to meet us. She was as beautiful as ever, and attractively dressed, but her manner was more reserved than I had expected.

She shook hands with us and led us into a parlor filled with faded draperies and many photographs. A man in his late thirties entered the room. Remigia introduced him as a friend of the family, living with them temporarily. Then Remigia and Mina took Sammy and me in to meet her bedridden mother. Remigia had already told me that her mother had been strafed by U.S. aircraft fire and was confined to bed by her injuries. Teresa was a youthful looking woman, with dark hair, dark eyes and a dark complexion. She greeted us with a cheerful smile. I felt guilt that our warplanes had caused her injuries, but her warmth put me at ease.

Teresa's daughters helped her into a wheelchair, and she joined us for a sumptuous lunch that Nana, their young maid, had prepared. The pasta was delicious, and I ate it slowly, to savor every bite. When Remigia saw how slowly I was eating, and wrongly took that as distaste for their pasta, she told Nana, "Take it away. The lieutenant doesn't like it." Over my protests, my plate was whisked away. It was clear that Remigia ruled the house. The next course was veal scaloppini. I hadn't eaten veal since leaving the States, and I knew it must have been hard to obtain in Genoa. Lunch concluded with salad, cheese, fruit, and cake, all delicious.

The language barrier hampered conversation, but Teresa did manage to ask if I was married. When I said no, she smiled and said, "Va bene" ("That's good"). Mina giggled and punched Remigia, who tried to suppress a smile. I later learned that Remigia's mother had little fondness for her pianist boyfriend. When the meal was over, Remigia suggested we take a walk. As soon as we reached the street, she told me that she "just *had* to get out of that house." The "family friend" I had met was really her mother's lover, and Remigia hated him. She said that he was spending whatever money her mother had left and that he had made advances toward her.

She began to tell me about her family. Her father was forty years older than her mother. He was a wealthy Italian count and paper merchant who had owned a publishing house in Genoa but had lost his fortune in the war and was now living in the country. The family had been forced to spend much of the war in the countryside. Remigia's brother, Pino, who served on an Italian submarine, was believed to have been lost at sea. Her father was at the family's country villa and had been living apart from his family for some time.

When we returned from the walk, Mina and Sammy had gone off by themselves, Teresa was resting, and the boyfriend had left. Remigia and I had some quiet moments together, and as my time of departure drew near, she seemed on the verge of tears. She suddenly asked if I could send for her to come to America. I was stunned. I told her I did not know where I would be living or what I would be doing, but that I would send for her if I could. I told her I could not believe this was the end for us. I gave her my home address and phone number and urged her to learn English so we could correspond. She promised that she would. She said that she wanted to join me in America and that she loved me. That she wanted to come to America I had no doubt. That she loved me I had a lot of doubt. All she knew was that I was an American officer, and a gentleman, or what passed for one in wartime. Twice she told me I was "full of life" and that this quality appealed to her.

I was infatuated but I did not believe I was in love, or what I imagined love to be. I told her how hard she would find it in America without English and how difficult it would be to adjust. She promised again to learn English. We kissed for a long time before saying a tearful goodbye. On the drive back to camp, I was deep in thought recalling all that Remigia and I had said and done that day. I was wary but also saddened by the prospect of not seeing her again. I wondered whether she should come to America. Did she want to join me there for the right reasons, or was she just trying to escape an unhappy home in a ravaged land? All this had happened so fast. We had seen each other only three times. There was still much about her that I did not know. And she knew almost nothing about me.

Suddenly, in the midst of the romance, my world was turned upside down by tragic news from home. Back in Washington, my sister Helene, who had married her longtime boyfriend Ernest "Bun" Amos before the war, now had three small children. Helene was working as an English teacher and Bun was a D.C. policeman who would later rise to detective sergeant. One day Helene was sitting on her front porch with Patsy, her three-year-old daughter while eight-month-old Peggy slept in her crib inside. When the phone rang, Helene told the child not to leave her chair, then went inside. Instead, Patsy ran down the steps to join her five-year-old brother, Michael, who was playing across the street. She darted out between two parked vehicles and was hit by a passing car. Patsy died the next day. The phone call had been a wrong number.

I received the news indirectly from a soldier who had learned it in a V-Mail letter from his family in Washington. It was not possible to call home. I think my family was too much in shock to write to me immediately. Sick with worry, I wrote to my mother begging for more information. I did not even know which child had been killed. Helene's letter finally came. "This is undoubtedly the hardest letter I have ever had to write," her V-Mail began. "My darling little girl Patsy was struck by a car. . . . Patsy, who was so lovely so very sweet and so full of life, is dead." This terrible news was one more reason I found it maddening to be in Italy when the war was over and my family needed me.

At last we received orders to return to the United States. I sent word to Remigia in Genoa, but it was impossible for us to meet again. We departed on a "liberty ship" five decks high, with most of the soldiers in raucous high spirits. But I was grieving over Patsy's death and still uncertain what I should do about Remigia. It became a nightmare voyage. The ship was so crowded that soldiers were battened down and sleeping on the deck. The food was awful. We encountered major storms. Everyone was sick, and the stench was terrible. For five days, I managed to perform my duties, but on the sixth day, I surrendered to the worst sickness I had ever known. I threw up everything. No medicine helped. Sleep was impossible. I stayed in my bunk as the ship tossed endlessly. At times I wanted to die—they could bury me at sea. Finally, on the fifteenth day, the cabin boy asked if I thought I could eat a sour pickle. The thought of it made my stomach heave. But he insisted it would help, and I was ready to try anything. I ate a quarter of that pickle, and when it stayed down, the cabin boy brought me more. On my twenty-first day on that ac-

cursed ship, I was able to eat a little food. Slowly, my strength returned. I never saw the cabin boy again, but I have always thought he
was God's answer to my prayers.

On the twenty-seventh day, the ocean grew calm, and on the
twenty-eighth day we came into New York harbor and passed the
Statue of Liberty. I had seen it before, but its majesty, and what it had
meant to millions of immigrants, had never fully struck me until I
saw it from the upper deck of a troop ship returning home from war.
We were home! We were triumphant warriors, proud soldiers victorious in a righteous cause. We had helped save the world from tyr-
anny. We fell to our knees on the deck, heads bowed, as Captain
Charles Fisher, our chaplain, led us in a prayer of thanksgiving. We
prayed too for our brothers, the brave soldiers we had left behind. In
that silent moment, the world turned from darkness into light.

On that cool day in late October, we docked in New York and
were taken, in two-and-a-half ton trucks, to Camp Kilmer in New
Jersey. I felt an overwhelming desire to run all the way home to embrace my mother and father. Instead, we stayed at Camp Kilmer for
three days, while the army conducted a battery of physical and mental examinations on us and calculated how much money they owed
us. Finally we were allowed to call home. Long lines formed, as hundreds of servicemen stormed the few telephones available. Those
waiting yelled for those on the phone to hurry up. When my turn
came, the phone seemed to ring for an eternity before my mother
answered. I had never stopped hearing her voice in my mind, but this
was the first time in nineteen long months that we had spoken.

"Mother?"

"Oh, Baby!" she cried. "Thank you, God. Thank you, God."

Then, just to make sure, she said softly, "Edward?"

I said, "Yes."

"You're safe! Thank Jesus! Oh, my baby, where are you?"

Hearing the clamor of the men waiting in line, I cut short the
conversation. I told Mother that I loved her dearly and could not
wait to see her and Dad. Finally it was time to leave the base. Those
of us headed south would be transported to Fort Meade, Maryland.
Anxious as we were to get started, we felt another emotion too. Soon,

men we had lived with, faced death with, shared our innermost thoughts and fears with, would be out of our lives, in most cases forever. It was a family breaking up and it hurt. When I reached Fort Meade, I called my mother and said I was on my way home. One of my senior officers, Major Clinton Burke, gave me a ride to Washington, which enabled me to arrive earlier than I had expected. He and his wife dropped me in front of my house, and carrying all my belongings in a single duffel bag, I bounded up the porch steps and rang the doorbell. My father opened the door. While he and I were hugging and kissing, my father, with tears in his eyes, yelled, "Helen, Helen, it's Edward!"

Mother ran down the stairs screaming, "Thank God!" and "My baby!" She ran into my outstretched arms and smothered me with kisses and tears. All three of us hugged and cried together. I had arrived home earlier than expected, and Mother had not yet changed into her best dress. Her hair was still partly in rollers. Modestly, like a young woman, she told me that she had wanted to look beautiful for my homecoming. I assured her that she was more beautiful than ever. "You are still full of stuff," she teased.

Soon, my mother showed me to my old room. She had put fresh flowers in a vase and spruced it up, but it was unchanged. Dad called Helene and her husband Bun, to tell them I was home, and they rushed over. Mother, Dad and Helene prepared a homecoming feast. Dad made his specialty, Southern fried chicken. Mother roasted my favorite leg of lamb, with mashed potatoes, sweet potatoes, and collard greens. Remembering my letter raving about Italian red wine vinegar, Mother made a salad with lettuce, tomatoes, and cucumbers, and tossed it with oil and red wine vinegar, instead of the apple cider vinegar she had used all of her life. Helene brought rice pudding with lots of raisins and a big, tasty chocolate cake. We ate vanilla and chocolate ice cream, too, which neither my mother nor I could ever resist.

All through the meal, they bombarded me with questions. But they soon sensed my reluctance to talk about the war. After dessert, Mother said I looked tired and thin and ought to go up to bed. Indeed, I had barely slept the past five nights. After two emotional reunions and a huge dinner, I was ready for bed. I went upstairs and opened the windows to let the cold air in so that I could sleep. As tired as I was, I would not be able to sleep unless I could feel cool air blowing through the room. After living and sleeping outside for months, I found it hard to move indoors. The bathtub made me squirm, my bed felt cramped and hot, and my once-comfortable bedroom was confining, claustrophobic. Mother poked her head in to say goodnight and asked if I was cold. I told her I was comfortable. But I really was not comfortable, and soon we all knew it.

After months of living day to day, I felt the future looming ahead. I knew that at twenty-six I was a different person from the naive boy who had gone straight from his cocoon into a world war. It was hard to pick up the thread of my old life. War had taught me self-discipline. I was a more serious man, with more pronounced opinions. I was now, even more than before, deeply opposed to violence. I hated to see even two cats fight on the street. After all the people I had seen die, I hated any kind of explosion, even fireworks on the Fourth of July. Yet I was a man now and had to decide what do to with my life. Should I go to law school, something I had again begun to think about? Or, having been promoted to captain, should I stay in the army and accept a promotion to major that was open to me? I wondered how this war, fought and won in the name of freedom and democracy, would affect racial discrimination in our nation's capital and in the country at large.

My parents were alarmed by this son they did not entirely know. Sometimes, I would catch them observing me, and I would wonder if I really was acting strangely. In truth, my thoughts were often on the uncertainties of the future, including Remigia, and dark memories from my past in Italy. I had lost what little interest I ever had in making money. The sacrifices of war made the pursuit of money seem petty, absurd. Two of my army friends, Corporal Al Brothers and Sergeant Clarence Elam, said we should start a business together in their hometown, Boston. Life was better for Negroes in Boston, they said. I knew how much I had enjoyed that city and that nothing had changed in my hometown, and I sensed that after all I had been through, Washington would be too confining, despite the fact that my parents dearly wanted me to stay. My father was working on the side with a small real estate company, and he wanted me to work there with him while I attended law school at Howard University. Al and Clarence talked about starting a small construction company or opening a Howard Johnson's franchise in Roxbury, and they encouraged me to join them. I was intrigued, but in the end, I chose to study law. In Boston.

4

Law and

Politics

I was accepted into Boston University School of Law's accelerated program, which was intended to turn veterans into lawyers in the shortest time possible. By going to school twelve months of the year, I could earn my law degree in two years instead of three. My studies were made possible by the GI Bill of Rights, the visionary legislation passed by the postwar Congress that made higher education possible for millions of veterans and helped build a more open, more prosperous America.

On my first day of law school it dawned on me that I had never before been in an integrated classroom or had a white teacher. I was one of seven Negroes in a class of more than three hundred. At first, I felt a tinge of insecurity, having come from exclusively Negro schools, but I worked hard and had no academic problems. I began to make friends with my white classmates—integration was new to them, too. One fellow came home to study with me one day. I have no idea what he expected, but he found that I was compulsively neat. When he left he said, "Ed, you're not so different after all."

The GI Bill paid for my tuition, books, and school fees, and I lived on very little money. I briefly shared an apartment in Roxbury with my cousin Adelaide Hill and her husband Henry, who had been among those encouraging me to come study in Boston. Adelaide's father was a teacher and scholar, and she followed in his footsteps. She was like a sister to me, and she and her family were always a good influence on me, urging me to read and expand my mind in every way possible. After a short time with Adelaide and Henry, I found a twenty-five-dollar-a-month apartment close to the law school at 198 Chambers Street in the West End. My father helped me with the rent, food, and other miscellaneous costs, giving me the freedom to focus exclusively on my studies. I also had savings from my army salary, which I never touched. I found the study of law fascinating, and I liked my classmates, many of them fellow veterans who were as serious about their studies as I was.

My neighborhood was perhaps three-quarters Italian. I loved its narrow streets and friendly people and the small shops with their aroma of Italian sausages and cheese. I learned many of my neighbors' names, and they loved to hear me talk in my broken Italian. There was actually an organ grinder with a pet monkey who sometimes played beneath my second-floor window. I shopped for groceries at the open-air North End Market near Faneuil Hall. The vendors cut their prices just before closing on Saturday nights and sometimes would even give me fruit and vegetables for free. By shopping carefully, I could buy a week's supply of food for three dollars. When I could afford to eat out, it was almost always at Durgin Park, a restaurant famous for its cheerfully brusque service, huge servings, and low prices. A late lunch at Durgin Park, costing less than half a dollar, would last me all day.

My Italian neighborhood intensified my thoughts of Remigia. I knew that here her lack of English would not be unusual. Besides, she sent me colorful postcards that showed her sense of humor and growing skill with English. The fact that she was making the effort touched me. She always asked if I really would send for her. I had promised to seriously consider it, and I intended to honor my promise. I talked to my parents, who expressed doubts about the relationship. Finally, in May 1947, after much soul-searching, I filed the necessary papers and sent her money to cover her passage. I was careful to make no promise of marriage in my letter, but I knew this was a large step in that direction. Remigia's sister, Mina, was herself about to marry an American GI, Staff Sergeant Samuel Jones, an outstanding young Negro who would stay in the army and rise to colonel.

Remigia received my letter in Genoa and left for New York the next day. She asked Mina to send me a telegram about her arrival, but it never reached me. To further complicate matters, Remigia forgot to bring my phone number with her. Thus, there was no one to greet her in New York, and she wound up spending two days in a dormitory on Ellis Island. Fortunately, she called Mina, who had my friend Sammy Jackson's number in New York, and Sammy called me, picked her up, and put her on a flight to Boston.

I asked my parents to come to Boston, and we had an intense discussion about whether I should marry Remigia. My father was strongly opposed. He pointed out that I was still in school and could barely support myself, much less a wife. He called my romance with Remigia "a wartime situation" and noted the enormous cultural differences between us. He was also worried about the racial difference. When I said that race had not mattered during our courtship in Italy, he reminded me, "You won't be living in Italy, you'll be living in America." But his primary reservation was that we barely knew each other. My father urgently wanted me to pursue a career in law, and he saw marriage as a threat to my future.

Mother and Dad went with me to welcome Remigia at Logan Airport. As each young woman stepped off the DC-3, my mother would ask, "Is that Remigia?" I kept saying, "No, you'll see her when she comes. She looks like you." Finally, Remigia emerged from the plane, smiling, dressed in a tailored suit, and carrying a brown bag. She looked about the same as I had remembered, but thinner, tired, and more fragile. Her reddish-brown hair fell below her shoulders. When I hugged her, she was trembling. My mother liked her instantly. She kept saying, "She looks like she could be my daughter." For the rest of my mother's time in Boston, she tried to teach Remigia how to cook the food I liked and to help her learn English. My mother's concern had been our compatibility, but once she met Remigia, she took up her cause. She asked me to put myself in the place of this young woman who was giving up her home and family, her friends, her language, and her country to come to a strange land. Mother said she would be disappointed in me if I did not uphold my promise and marry her. I had completed a year of law school by then, and I told her I had made no promise actual or implied to marry Remigia. Mother proved herself a better lawyer than I, by arguing that sending for her was in itself an implicit promise of marriage.

There is a euphoria that comes at such a moment, and Remigia and I both felt it. We had met by chance in the aftermath of a terrible war, shared a brief and intense romance, and now she had crossed the ocean to be with me. All that, and my mother's feelings, pushed me toward marriage. Yet on our first day together, Remigia confessed that a friend of hers had written all those endearing postcards and letters for her. She still knew no English. I told my parents that I felt tricked, even betrayed. My mother was adamant. "You can't send that girl back to Italy! You've got to go through with it." Mother prevailed, as she usually did. A few days later, on June 7, 1947, Remigia and I were married. It was a small ceremony in the Roxbury apartment of my cousins Henry and Adelaide Hill, presided over by the Reverend Kenneth Hughes, Rector of St. Bartholomew's Episcopal Church in Cambridge. My parents were there, of course. My childhood and lifelong friend Raymond Savoy was my best man, and Sammy Jackson, alias Rinaldo, gave away the bride. It was a joyous event. Remigia and I would soon have more than our share of problems, but on that day, like all newlyweds, we faced the future with love and hope.

As we started married life, sharing my small apartment, I was preoccupied with my legal studies, and Remigia was often alone and lonely. I was at law school almost all day. On lunch breaks, weather permitting, I would grab a tuna salad on rye and a soft drink and sit on a bench behind the Robert Gould Shaw Memorial on Boston Common. There I would study my cases, eat my sandwich, and feed crumbs to the pigeons, just as I had before we married. At home, after dinner, I studied long into the night. I studied on weekends, too, and rarely found time to take Remigia to the movies that she loved. She met other Italian war brides, but most of them worked and lived in outlying towns, and she could not see them often. Life with a struggling law student could not have been everything she had hoped.

There were good times, of course. My friends always liked her. Although our apartment was small, it was cozy, and we entertained a few times. In the summer, we would walk down to the bottom of our street and swim in the chilly waters of the Charles River, something you would not dream of doing today. We shopped for groceries together, and Remigia prepared wonderful lasagna and homemade focaccia. One weekend, we went to Washington, where Mother gave a party for us. My bride was warmly received by our friends. Although she was embarrassed by her broken English, I assured her that it did not matter. Probably her embarrassment and insecurity were worse than I realized at the time.

On June 7, 1948, my first wedding anniversary, 204 classmates and I received our bachelor of law degrees during commencement exercises on the banks of the Charles River. Remigia and my proud parents were on hand, and it was a glorious day in every regard. I immediately enrolled in a bar review course given by Bernard A. Marvin, who taught at the law school. I took the bar exam very seriously. I could not forget my father's terrible experience with the D.C. exam. I even asked Remigia to spend a month with my family in Washington so that I could devote myself full time to study. As it turned out, I passed the written bar exam with a grade sufficiently high to exempt me from taking the oral exam.

My father had hoped that when I graduated from law school, he and I might work together in law and real estate in Washington, but I did not want to return there. Instead, I set out to find a job in Boston. Some of my professors wrote letters of recommendation emphasizing my academic record and work on the *Law Review*. I applied to a number of old-line, high-prestige Boston firms but received no offers. My only offer came from a small Jewish law firm, as a legal researcher at thirty-five dollars a week. I turned it down. The GI Bill would pay me twenty dollars a week for another fifty-two weeks (the 52/20 Club, it was called), and if I could not make up the difference of fifteen dollars on my own, I was in the wrong profession. I saw no alternative but to open my private practice.

I learned that Necco Wafers, a candy company, owned an old, boarded-up theater in Roxbury. I asked the president of the company if I could use part of the second floor of the building as an office. He said he would like to help me, but I would only occupy a small space and he would have to heat the whole building, theater and all. I told him I would find other tenants and that perhaps his engineers could put up partitions and heat only the offices. He was a kind man and agreed to my plan.

After painting my new office and purchasing secondhand office furniture, I opened my law offices, sharing a two-room suite with Al Brothers, who had gone into the real estate business. Later my old Howard University friend Otto Snowden, and his wife Muriel, became tenants and started Freedom House, where they worked for civil rights. Another tenant I was able to attract was Amelia Gourdin, wife of Colonel Ned Gourdin, a Harvard Law School graduate and later the first Negro Superior Court judge in Massachusetts; she opened an employment agency. I also hired my first assistant, Mrs. Marguerite McKinney, who became a cherished friend.

My law practice was slow at first. I was only twenty-nine and looked younger. Some clients came into my office, looked right at me, and asked to speak with the lawyer. I bought a long-stemmed pipe, which I never filled with tobacco, much less lit, but which I held between my teeth hoping it made me look older. Many days I was glad to get a call from Remigia, just to hear the telephone ring. My office was in Roxbury, which had once been inhabited by Yankees, then by Jews, and now increasingly by Negroes. My clientele were overwhelmingly Negroes who did not have a lot of money for legal fees. Another problem was that most of them would not hire Negro lawyers. They thought that a white lawyer would be more successful in a legal system in which virtually everyone was white.

Business slowly picked up. I had a few criminal cases, but mostly I handled probate, wills, divorces, automobile accident cases, and real estate law. Because many veterans were buying homes under the GI Bill, I did many property conveyances, usually after making my own title searches. Probably 35 percent of my work was real estate law. For the first few years, I did not make a lot of money, but I supported my family, learned a lot, savored the freedom of being my own boss, and enjoyed the practice of law immensely.

On April 15, 1949, Remigia gave birth to our first child, who we named Remi Cynthia, after Remigia, and my mother, whose middle name was Cynthia. Soon Remigia and I would proudly walk down the street pushing the baby carriage that held our daughter. Remi was so adorable with her blue-green eyes and golden curls that complete strangers would stop to admire her.

Also in 1949, with help from the GI Bill, we bought our first home, for $10,000. It was a four-decker at 26 Crawford Street in

Roxbury. The house had a large yard and was located in a middle-income area, where some African Americans and families from Barbados were moving into what had been a Jewish neighborhood. We were thrilled to have a place of our own. Remigia, Remi, and I lived in the apartment on the first floor, and we rented out the other apartments to a Jewish widow who wanted to remain on the second floor, and to James Mahoney, an army buddy of mine, who took the basement apartment. Soon Remigia's brother, Pino, who turned out to have survived the war, came over from Italy with his wife, Germanna, and their two children, Carla and Bruno, and they lived on the top floor. Income from the three apartments helped pay the mortgage, taxes, and repairs, so we actually lived almost for free while building equity.

This same year, Remigia, tiny Remi, and I made our first trip to Martha's Vineyard, the magical island just off the southeastern coast of Massachusetts, to visit Lionel Lindsay, president of the Boston branch of the NAACP, and his wife, Edna, at their home in the town of Oak Bluffs on the eastern side of the island. We drove to Woods Hole and boarded the ferry that crossed Vineyard Sound several times a day. I held Remi in my arms so she could see the boats and the whitecaps and the gulls that followed along to seize the bread and popcorn that passengers tossed to them. By the time we reached the wharf in Vineyard Haven, I had fallen in love with the island. This was my first real vacation since the war ended, and I thought I had discovered heaven on earth. I fell under the spell of the island's sandy beaches, tall sea grasses and sand dunes, weather-stained wood-shingled houses, and the clay cliffs at Gay Head rising up from the beach. Soon I was house hunting, and I found one on Canonicus Avenue in Oak Bluffs. It had a view of the ocean, a fine stone fireplace, three bedrooms, two baths, and a large living room. What's more, it was completely furnished—the seller was a widow who could no longer make the trip from Indiana each summer. The price, $4,500, was astonishingly low. I withdrew that amount from my savings account where my wartime pay had been gathering interest for several years and bought this lovely bungalow. During the summer months, almost every Friday evening after work I would drive to Woods Hole, catch the ferry, and be met in Vineyard Haven by

Remigia and Remi—and then, on Sunday nights I would reverse the process.

Our second daughter, Edwina Helene, was born on April 10, 1952, and was named for my two sisters. She resembled her adoring grandmother, Teresa, who having recovered from her war injuries, came from Genoa to live with us shortly before her birth. Edwina was beautiful, with dark hair, dark eyes, and an olive complexion. Our daughters grew to be very close, but from their appearances, one would never have thought Remi and Edwina were sisters. We swam with the girls and countless times took them to ride the Flying Horses in Oak Bluffs, the oldest merry-go-round in the United States. The girls spent practically all day at the beach. The Vineyard was unspoiled in those days: there were few celebrities, not many cars, and the beaches were never crowded. We delighted in such pleasures as the Sunday band concerts in Ocean Park. As fathers have done for decades, I would carry the girls on my shoulders around the bandstand.

Although I was overjoyed with Edwina's arrival, loved Martha's Vineyard, and had developed a profitable law practice, my marriage was a source of increasing concern. Remigia and I had not been married long when I realized we had little in common. I liked candlelight; she wanted bright lights. I loved opera and was wrong to assume that, being Italian, she did too. I was a day person; she was a night person. I hated cigarettes, and she was a chain-smoker. The smell of stale tobacco filled our house, and it pained me that she would not stop smoking even during her pregnancies. Her confession when she first arrived in America that someone else had written those postcards and letters from Italy was an early example of an enduring problem: Remigia had little regard for the truth. In fairness to her, I am sure our life did not turn out as she expected, either. She had enjoyed a life of privilege in Italy before the war. She must have expected that by marrying an American officer, her old lifestyle would be restored. Nothing in her experience prepared her for life with a struggling law student and fledgling lawyer, or for coping with prejudice and discrimination.

Remigia, Teresa, and Pino often argued. Pino's wife, Germanna, was a mild-mannered woman who was wise enough to stay out of the fray. When I went home, it often seemed as if a war was going on, with endless outbursts of heated language and yelling. In search of peace, I would retreat to my bedroom and close the door. Our relationship was further encumbered by a lifelong language barrier. My rudimentary Italian, learned during the war, was insufficient for anything but the most basic daily exchanges. Her refusal to learn English meant that we were never able to discuss such essential matters as our own feelings and needs. Marriage must be based on trust and sustained through regular, open communication. We had neither.

I encouraged Remigia to go to school to learn English, but she insisted that the language was too difficult to learn. The public library offered books in Italian, but her reading was limited to a few Italian magazines. The other Italian war brides she knew had mostly found jobs, but Remigia was not interested in working. My parents knew of our problems. My father, having opposed the marriage in the first place, had little to add. Both parents loved our daughters and hoped they were a bond that would help us transcend our differences. My mother would remind me, "You are married, and marriage is forever."

As my practice continued to grow, I added three bright young associates: Harry Elam, brother of Clarence Elam and later a distinguished Superior Court judge; Louis Johnson; and Cecil Goode. I moved my office out of Roxbury and into downtown Boston, first to the corner of Tremont Street and Massachusetts Avenue and later to 10 Pemberton Square, a building directly across from the Boston Municipal and the Supreme Judicial Courthouses. But law was not the only thing on my mind. From the earliest days of my practice, living and working in Roxbury, I was concerned about the deterioration of services there. My friends and I would discuss how to address the problems of urban decay. We were concerned about crime, poor lighting, inadequate police protection, backed-up sewage systems, and the lack of playgrounds. As we deliberated about how to deal with these problems, our talk turned inevitably to politics. The Irish had long controlled the city's politics, and it was clear that because of the challenges facing Roxbury there was a need for new, black leadership.

In 1949, several of us who had served together in the war, including Joe Williams, Reuben Landrum, Clarence Elam, and Al Brothers, formed the 366th Infantry Regiment Veterans Association. I was elected its first president and coined the motto "good soldiers, better citizens," as we sought ways to improve conditions and race relations in Roxbury. At first, no thought was given to getting involved in politics. This was true even though Clarence and Al had also joined the New Boston Committee, a good-government organization, to help reformist mayoral candidate John Hynes. Although the bookish, soft-spoken Hynes was not typical of Boston politicians, people wanted change, and he defeated the legendary old warhorse, James Michael Curley, in his last race for the mayor of Boston.

Our 366th Veterans Association was courted by the Negro posts of the American Legion and Veterans of Foreign Wars, and by AMVETS, a newly formed national veterans organization dedicated to promoting world peace and helping veterans help themselves. We liked what AMVETS stood for, and after many discussions we became the 366th Infantry AMVET Post #128. I was elected its first post commander. Veterans' organizations were particularly important in the years immediately following World War II. The powerful movie *The Best Years of Our Lives* dramatized what veterans faced in forging a new life in peacetime while still grappling with the trauma of war. For many of them, all over America, banding together to serve the community helped heal the emotional scars of war.

By 1950, many of my friends from Boston's NAACP, Urban League, and Roxbury ministers, and particularly Al Brothers and Clarence Elam, were urging me to run for political office. An election for state representative from Boston's Twelfth Ward in Roxbury was coming up. At first, the idea was foreign to me. I had grown up in Washington, D.C., where I never even had the right to vote. I did not even know if I was a Republican or a Democrat. I simply had never thought about it. Still, the idea of running for office began to intrigue me. I had learned about politics in high school, at Howard, in my fraternity, in the army, and in law school. The army had shown me something of the world, had forced me to confront racial injustice, and had taught me what horrors can occur when politics fails and produces monsters like Hitler. As an officer, I had learned what motivates men, how to take orders, and how to lead. I believed fiercely in the rule of law, and I believed law was a good background for politics.

As a Negro, I understood the aspirations of Negroes and other minorities, and I thought I had learned the aspirations of whites as well. My mother had taught me social skills that could be transferred to politics. I was able to mix easily and talk comfortably with people of all races. I loved meeting people, listening to them, and bringing them together. I asked myself why I was practicing law. Not for the money. I had to support my family, but I had never aspired to wealth. But I liked being a problem solver. I had also always been a bit of a ham, and that could not hurt. Most of all, I loved people, and politics is even more of a people business than law. You not only analyze information, you debate it in public. The world becomes your forum. I liked that. In those days, people were not so cynical about government. We veterans felt that we had sacrificed for a better world, and that meant building a better America—and that meant politics. It was an honorable profession.

One day Al Brothers, while urging me to run for office, called a meeting of about fifteen people, many of them our old friends. We sat in a circle and talked for several hours. We discussed whether the fact that I had not grown up in Roxbury would be a negative factor in my candidacy. We wondered if we could raise money, speculated on which community and church leaders might support me, and discussed ways we could put together an effective campaign. I asked if I could both campaign and practice law, and we confronted the delicate issue of whether my marriage to a white, Italian woman, would be a handicap among the Negro and the Jewish voters in our ward.

Our session was far from unique. All across America in those days, veterans were pondering political campaigns. A few miles from my Roxbury office, a few years earlier, John F. Kennedy had launched his political career by running for Congress. Kennedy and I did not have much else in common, but we were both veterans, were both ambitious, and both cared about the future of America. One day, thanks to politics, a great leveler, we would meet. So, under the watchful gaze of Bill Jackson, Otto and Muriel Snowden, Al Brothers, Clarence and Harry Elam, Arthur and Eunice Williams, and other friends, I sat in a swivel chair, twirling this way and that as different people spoke. As I heard their arguments and looked into their earnest faces, they convinced me, if in fact I needed convincing, that I should take the plunge.

5

"Where the

Huckleberries

Grow"

In 1950, with little money and little understanding of what I was getting into, I jumped into the turbulent waters of Massachusetts politics. In those days, in a state primary election, you could "cross-file," and I was seeking both the Republican and Democratic Party nominations for state representative from Roxbury's Twelfth Ward. Party loyalists disdained cross-filing, but it was something of a tradition in our ward. My friends and advisers urged me to take that route, and I did.

Because I was not associated with either party, cross-filing made it easier for me to reach out across the political spectrum. Members of the ward's Jewish community, who were a majority of the voters, were overwhelmingly New Deal Democrats, but that did not mean they always voted a straight Democratic ticket. Anti-Semitism was a fact of life in Boston Democratic politics, and Jewish voters understood that at least some Republicans were their natural allies. In the Negro community, which formed the second-largest voting bloc, I was accepted as one of their own. So as I knocked on every door I could find, I expressed myself in impartial language and took positions that I hoped would transcend partisanship.

My vote for myself in that primary election, at the age of thirty-one, was the first I had ever cast. And I picked a winner, in that I won the Republican nomination, although I ran behind the two Democratic incumbents I would face in the general election. I had no problem running as the Republican candidate. My parents were Republicans, and I had always admired the party of Lincoln and the Republican virtues of duty and self-help. My father had taught me to believe in free enterprise and to distrust big government. Looking back, I can see how much his "waste not, want not" philosophy influenced my belief in fiscal prudence, a balanced budget, and other issues. Like my father, I admired the conservative regard for history and precedent. I agreed with Abraham Lincoln that "government should do for people only that which they cannot do for themselves." At the same time, I realized that there were a number of things people could not do for themselves and that government must do for them.

The more I learned about Boston and Massachusetts politics, the more comfortable I was with the Republican Party. The Democrats had dominated the state's politics for years, and for some of them corruption was a way of life. Jim Curley once ran successfully for reelection to Congress from his jail cell. I was part of a new generation of politicians, many of them veterans who were ready for a break with the past. We did not accept corruption as inevitable or see the role of government to be primarily the dispensation of patronage.

My friends were the backbone of my campaign. Al Brothers was my campaign manager and Clarence Elam my treasurer. With their help, I enlisted the support of the Negro ministers of Roxbury. Members of the Roxbury Citizens Club helped us to gather signatures for my election petition. James Mahoney, head of the Roxbury Basketball League, drove around with his basketball players, putting up Brooke posters and distributing campaign literature. The Women for Brooke group, under the leadership of Al's mother-in-law, Irene Yates, sold political buttons to help fund our campaign. Dexter Eure, who worked for the *Boston Globe*, generated hundreds of campaign posters in the "Brooke blue" that I continued to use in future campaigns. W. Wentworth Perkins, a master carpenter, made yard signs.

Usually accompanied by my friend William Jackson, I rang hundreds of doorbells. We went in the evening, after people had come home from work. We climbed dimly lit apartment stairs and used a flashlight to read the doorplates so I could greet the tenants by name.

I carried a notebook and jotted down the name of each voter, and what their interests were. That notebook became a gold mine of information. There was a joy about our campaign, an excitement, a spirit of adventure. I was a long shot—why not have fun? I have always been puzzled by the Republican candidates who approach politics as a "duty." There was then, and perhaps still is, an overlay of grimness in Republican politics that scares away potential supporters. Our campaign—and the others that followed—was full of laughter. I do not know why anyone would get into politics if he or she did not love it—even then, it is hard enough.

In those days, it was the Communist Party's national policy to endorse Negro candidates running for office regardless of their qualifications, so they endorsed me. I did not share in the national anticommunist hysteria of that era, and I deplored the behavior of Wisconsin Republican Senator Joseph McCarthy who fanned its flames. Still, I strongly disavowed the support of the Communist Party. Their endorsement may nonetheless have cost me some votes.

I found during the campaign that speaking to groups of voters was not difficult for me. Unlike some candidates, I never enrolled in a public speaking course. If anything, my style was drawn from the Southern preachers of my childhood and Negro orators I admired such as Washington attorney Belford Lawson, Wilberforce University President Dr. Charles Wesley, labor leader A. Philip Randolph, and Howard University President Mordecai Johnson.

On election eve we had an old-style torchlight parade through Roxbury with more than fifty cars in the convoy. The parade ended at Roxbury Memorial High School, where more than 1,500 of my supporters gathered for a rally. Yet for all our hard work, all our enthusiasm, 1950 was a bad year to launch my political career. Democratic Governor Paul Dever won reelection in a landslide and led the Democrats to victory statewide. I finished third in a field of six behind incumbents George Greene and Louis Nathanson. Five thousand and fifty people had voted for me, many of them whites who had ignored my race. I felt that I had scored a moral victory, and professional politicians agreed. When I returned to my law practice, I found that I had new clients and a new respect among my fellow lawyers—and even the judges. People were friendlier, they went out of their way to shake my hand and call my name. The Boston political fraternity is garrulous; my surprisingly high vote in the Twelfth Ward, in a solidly Democratic city and year, caused a buzz. In political circles, I was a man to watch.

I was glad people felt that way, because I had not lost the political bug. My strong showing persuaded me that I should try again in 1952, and my friends and supporters agreed. We thought something was happening, that we had a chance to break new ground. I was further encouraged by the fact that, even as I was losing, a Negro Republican, Herbert L. Jackson, was elected a state representative from Malden, Massachusetts. Jackson's constituency was also largely white, and his election proved that you could be elected on merit.

By 1952, the legislature had ended cross-filing, and I had to declare a party affiliation. I was presumed to be a Republican, although officials of the Democratic city committee were making overtures to me. I chose to remain a Republican—partly out of loyalty; partly because of my admiration for emerging Republican leaders like State Senator Sumner Whittier, who later became lieutenant governor, and liberal State Representative Harold Putnam, of Needham; and partly for purely practical reasons. White Democrats largely controlled Boston and state politics, and they had traditionally offered few opportunities to Negroes.

Over the years I have often been criticized for being a Republican, but I have never regretted my decision. In those days, moderates dominated the Republican Party, both nationally and in Massachusetts. The leading Republicans in our state were men like Christian Herter, who would become secretary of state; Henry Cabot Lodge, who was a U.S. senator and would become United Nations ambassador; and Leverett Saltonstall, a former governor and distinguished U.S. senator. They were joined by Joseph Martin, Speaker of the U.S. House of Representatives, and women like Leslie Cutler, Cybil Holmes, Mary Newman, Eunice Howe, Polly Logan, Harriet Wittenborg, and Georgia Ireland, who would take their places in the State House, in the party leadership, and in the commonwealth. Good people all.

Republicans in Massachusetts struck me as the party of the future. The state Democratic Party seemed devoid of new ideas. There was narrowness, even a meanness to many Massachusetts Democrats. In the era of McCarthyism, it was the Democrats who tried to mount a state investigation of communist subversion at Harvard and the Republicans who stifled that effort. It was a Republican governor and a Republican legislature that enacted antidiscrimination laws, and Democrats who resisted them.

The Republican losses in the 1948 and 1950 elections had been a four-alarm wake-up call for the party leaders. They knew their Yankee Brahmin supporters were not having children at the same rate as the Italians, Irish, and other ethnic groups. To survive, they had to broaden their base, open up their party. They did so dramatically in 1952 with a Republican slate that included for governor, Christian Herter, a classic WASP; for lieutenant governor, State Senator Sumner Whittier, a "swamp Yankee"; for attorney general, George Fingold, a Jew and a rough-and-tumble debater and tireless campaigner; for secretary of state, Beatrice Hancock Mullaney from Fall River, of Irish descent; for state treasurer, Roy Papalia, an Italian selectman from Watertown; and for state auditor, David Mintz, a Jewish accountant. There had never been such diversity in Republican politics, and, as it turned out, the ticket did extremely well. Of course, that diversity did not include a black candidate—that was yet to come.

The great political reality in 1952 was that Dwight D. Eisenhower, the most beloved American hero of World War II, was the Republican nominee for president. Senator Henry Cabot Lodge had played an important role in persuading Eisenhower to actively seek the Republican nomination, and when that decision was made, Lodge became Eisenhower's campaign manager. The problem was that Senator Lodge was also running for reelection against Congressman John F. Kennedy. In his zeal to see Eisenhower become president, Lodge neglected a cardinal rule of politics: never take for granted your own political base. Lodge underestimated the charisma of Jack Kennedy and his family, and having always enjoyed the support of Catholic voters, he wrongly assumed that his attractiveness to them would continue even with Kennedy as his opponent. He failed to appreciate how strongly Catholic voters identified with his young Catholic challenger. Lodge had plenty of money to spend, and most political analysts thought he could beat Kennedy. If Lodge had paid more attention to his own campaign, the Kennedy dynasty might never have been born.

I met John Kennedy for the first time in 1952. The Boston Junior Chamber of Commerce honored us as two of the Ten Outstanding Young Men of Greater Boston. At a dinner given for the honorees, we had the opportunity to talk. I asked him how he liked being in the U.S. House of Representatives. He told me that while he enjoyed serving in Congress, the truly important offices were senator and president. As we talked, Kennedy showed not only warmth and charm, but a sparkling mind. It was clear that his eye was firmly set, even then, on the Senate and the presidency. He seemed a man of destiny. As we parted, he said, "You know, you ought to be a Democrat." I smiled and responded, "You know, you ought to be a Republican."

Henry Cabot Lodge's problem was not just Jack Kennedy but the Kennedy women. Kennedy's sisters and his mother, Mrs. Rose Kennedy, a strong and indomitable woman whom I greatly admired, participated in a series of "teas," for the women of Massachusetts that surely won Jack thousands of votes. They hosted these teas across the commonwealth. The gatherings were big, assembly-line productions, but few invitees seemed to care. For many Irish Catholic women, and others as well, an invitation to tea with the dazzling family was the thrill of a lifetime. They dressed up in their Sunday best, hobnobbed with the Kennedy women, and were charmed by their affectionate stories of their son and brother. Even my wife, at the invitation of a friend, naively attended one of these teas, not realizing that the wife of a Republican candidate does not attend political events of the other party. When Henry Cabot Lodge heard of this, he thought it hilarious. I laughingly insisted that Remigia had only gone to "count the house." Years later, Lodge continued to ask Remigia if she still attended Democratic events and counted the house for us.

With Eisenhower running, the Republicans had their first chance since the days of the state's own Calvin Coolidge to carry Massachusetts in a presidential election, and they pulled out all the stops. On election eve, a sparkling but chilly November day, General Eisenhower's long motorcade wound its way through Boston in a journey that included the Ninth and Twelfth Wards, which had the largest concentration of Negro voters and had not in living memory seen a Republican presidential candidate. Standing in the back of an open convertible, Eisenhower waved and flashed his famous grin. Huge crowds greeted him. I assumed that if Eisenhower had come to Massachusetts on the final day before the election, Lodge was in trouble and Ike was trying to save him.

As the Republican candidate in the Twelfth Ward, I played a small role in this election-eve drama. When the caravan reached my Roxbury headquarters on Humboldt Avenue, Eisenhower's convertible stopped, another minor Republican candidate got out, and I climbed in. I was hurriedly introduced to the general as the car moved on. I joined him in waving to the crowds, proud to be next to this American hero. All too soon, we reached the line where my ward ended. The car stopped. I got out, shook hands with the general, wished him good luck, he wished me the same, and another candidate took my place. If all went according to plan, our brief journey together would have convinced some of my constituents to vote for Eisenhower and some of his fans to vote for me.

That evening the Republicans held a huge rally at Boston Garden, and I was invited to be on the platform with gubernatorial candidate Christian Herter and his wife, Senator and Mrs. Lodge, Senator and Mrs. Saltonstall, and General Eisenhower. I actually stood next to Eisenhower. The powers-that-be saw value in having a Negro Republican on stage. Perhaps they even thought I had a future in politics. For a little-known lawyer who had lost his only campaign for office, I was breathing rarified air. If I was being used, from my point of view I was using them as much as they were using me.

I must have helped Eisenhower more than he helped me, because the next day he won big and I lost. I came closer than before, but the loss still hurt. I thought my career in politics was over. Remigia certainly hoped so. She had been terrified when I said I would run for office. Her political memories went back to the violence of fascist Italy. "You will be killed!" she cried. I reassured her that in America, we did not kill each other over politics. She told someone, "When I married Carlo, I thought he was a quiet, home type. But he is in everything, this man. Never keeping still." As it turned out, Remigia often proved to be an excellent campaigner in the years ahead, although she never really liked politics. She soon noted that at political rallies, women I did not know sometimes hugged and kissed me—as they did other candidates. My mother tried to convince her it was only politics. The irony was that Remigia's fears were misguided. No one shot me in my political career, but I put more and more of my energy into politics and less and less into our marriage.

Not everyone agreed that my loss in 1952 was the end of my career. A few days after the election, James Michael Curley himself sent me a copy of his biography, *The Purple Shamrock*, by Joseph F. Dinneen. It was inscribed, "Ed, Don't get discouraged. You are destined for a successful career in politics." I also received comfort from my old law school classmate Glendora McIlwain, who said, "Next time, Ed, you're going to do better." "There's not going to be a next time!" I replied. "I'm through with politics!"

Although I lost, the Republican "diversity ticket" had done well. Herter had ridden Ike's coattails—more successfully than I—and unseated Democratic Governor Paul Dever by fourteen thousand votes. Whittier was elected lieutenant governor, and Fingold won as attorney general. I was thrilled by Christian Herter's narrow victory, for he was one of the finest and most remarkable politicians I ever knew. He had risen to speaker of the house in the state legislature and then served five terms in Congress and two terms as governor before crowning his career as secretary of state late in the Eisenhower administration.

As governor-elect, he set out to find jobs in his administration for those who had helped his campaign. I had been his Roxbury coordinator, and soon after his election Governor-elect Herter called me in and offered me the job of executive secretary of the Governor's Council. The council, though a relic from colonial days, had considerable powers, including confirming the governor's judicial appointees. Its executive secretary was the liaison between the governor and the council. It was a good job, because you came to know the major players in Massachusetts politics. It was the fast track to becoming an insider. I had been tipped off that this offer was coming, and I had given it serious thought. When Herter made it, I said, "Governor, I am flattered, but I must respectfully decline." What really bothered me about the position was that traditionally it had been a "Negro" job, which was anathema to me. Soon Herter made a second proposal: would I be interested in a district court judgeship? I said, "No, Governor. I am too young for the bench, and I have a young family and a law practice, both of which are just beginning to grow." Herter was entirely understanding.

Having decided to stay out of politics, I resolved to become the best lawyer I could. My decision to move my law office to downtown Boston, with its proximity to the courts, had been a good one. The new location, along with the publicity that my campaigns had inspired, helped me develop a larger, more interracial, and more lucrative practice. One of my most important cases was a suit I filed in the federal District Court on behalf of Daisy Richards, a professional dancer and close friend of the great jazz singer Sarah Vaughan. In 1954, Miss Richards was paralyzed from the waist down in an automobile accident outside of Boston. She was a passenger in a car driven by a member of Sarah Vaughan's band and was returning to Boston after a party in Worcester when the accident occurred. The driver was traveling more than seventy miles an hour when his car hit the raised center strip, veered across the road, and crashed into a tree. Both occupants were thrown out of the car. Miss Richards was hospitalized for more than a year.

I knew it would be a hard case. It was rare at that time for passengers to recover damages from the driver of a car in which they were riding. The injured party, in such a case, had to establish gross negligence on the part of the driver, which is difficult to do. Also, Daisy Richards was a Negro, and in those days Negro plaintiffs did not often receive large jury awards. But this woman had been grievously injured. Just before the accident she had pleaded with her friend to slow down. I found a truck driver who testified that seconds before the accident, the car passed him at eighty-five miles an hour.

I was up against Hubert Thompson, who was considered the dean of Massachusetts trial lawyers and who often represented big insurance companies. After I had concluded the introduction of evidence for the plaintiff, Thompson moved for a directed verdict, on the grounds that the plaintiff had failed to prove gross negligence on the part of the driver. U.S. District Court Judge George C. Sweeney ordered counsel to the bench.

"Hubie, this is a serious case," the judge said. "Have you tried to settle it?"

An uncomfortable feeling swept over me when I realized that the trial judge was calling opposing counsel by his nickname.

"George," Thompson replied, "there is no case, and we see no reason to settle." My heart sank further when I realized opposing counsel was calling the judge by *his* first name.

The two men continued their conversation, totally ignoring me.

"Hubert, I think you just might be making a mistake," said the judge. "I may just have to send this to the jury."

Thompson angrily replied, "Are you sure you have read the cases, George? Clearly there is no gross negligence here."

I could contain myself no longer. "Your honor, I have case after case, and . . . ," I began.

Judge Sweeney waved me down and, looking directly at Thompson, said, "All right, all right, let's move on." Reluctantly, Thompson said, "George, if they are willing to accept five thousand dollars to get rid of this, I'll recommend it to my client. This is a nuisance claim. This case has no value."

Furious at this insulting offer, I said, "Your honor, it's out of the question."

Thompson looked at me for the first time and said to the judge, "George, you should never send a boy to do a man's job."

His scornful remark brought back echoes of my white commanding officer's comments when my proposal for a surprise attack on German positions in Italy was rejected. I was seething as we proceeded with the trial. In the end, the all-white jury, six men and six women, awarded Daisy Richards $135,000 in damages. At that time the verdict was the second-largest ever obtained in Massachusetts in a passenger versus operator case and, as the newspapers reported, the largest "ever secured by a Negro attorney." The Boston papers carried photographs of my thirty-nine-year-old client smiling up at me and my able young associate, Cecil W. Goode, from her wheelchair. To my delight, despite the sizable award, Judge Sweeney chastised the jury for its "not very generous award" and said he would have awarded twice as much. Unfortunately, the insurance company coverage was far from adequate, and Richards did not receive anywhere near a just award.

Throughout the 1950s, my law practice grew, as did my pleasure in engaging in my profession and being able to meet and help all kinds of interesting people. In Roxbury in those days, many people came to me with their problems because the power structure did not know or care about them. Few white city officials or politicians paid much attention to Negroes in Roxbury. I took on their problems and did my best to solve them.

I was increasingly engaged in civic work. I was elected first vice-president of the Boston Branch of the NAACP and to the board of the Boston Urban League. I was also a member of the board of directors of the Hospital for Women and the advisory board of the Boston Public Library. I continued to work with AMVETS, too, helping veterans to get their full government benefits. In 1954, at the organization's tenth anniversary meeting in Fall River, I was elected state commander, the first Negro elected to that position in any veteran's organization in the country. In my later run for a national post at the AMVETS convention in Philadelphia, I addressed as many state delegations as I could. Some of the southern delegations were among my strongest supporters. I was elected national judge advocate of AMVETS and carried every state, including Mississippi, a feat many thought impossible.

Once bitten, you seldom lose the political bug. My law practice did not offer me the challenge I wanted, nor did it fulfill my ambitions. I still dreamed of holding elective political office. In the 1950s, the media portrayed America as a paradise of peace and plenty, but many of us knew that was an illusion. I saw resentments bubbling. There was too wide a gulf between the rich and poor. Urban renewal was destroying homes of the working poor. Fathers, lacking jobs, were deserting their families, causing mothers and children to live on welfare and fostering cycles of dependence. Those who did find work often were paid less than what they could receive on public welfare.

I deplored a system that made it more profitable not to work than to work. I wanted to help change all that.

One more thing spurred my return to politics: my growing distaste for the political corruption in my adopted state. It was common knowledge that in much of state government, to grease the wheels, you had to pay. Dishonesty was practiced not just by the corrupt at heart; good people were led into bribery and pay-offs, told this was the right way to proceed. People who sought jobs in city, county, and state government were told that the salary was "only the beginning." Men who were leaving these jobs actually instructed their successors about how to solicit bribes without detection. In and around some of the larger cities in our state, for an unpaid seat on the local school committee, people were launching $25,000 campaigns, big money in the 1950s and 1960s. Why was a nonsalaried school committee job worth so much? For the kickbacks! And not just on schoolbooks. It was said that some school committee members routinely got kickbacks on everything they ordered, down to the soap and toilet tissue in the school restrooms. It was a shameful mess. And reform was not going to come from the Democrats.

In early 1960, I met Joe Fitzgerald, a smart, energetic man who was close to Governor Herter. Joe strongly felt I should seek public office again and suggested that I become a candidate for the Republican nomination for Massachusetts secretary of state. I sought the advice of my old political advisers. They were unanimous in support of my running. I decided to do so, and Joe became my campaign manager. At the Republican nominating convention in Worcester, we held a reception in Joe's suite. It went so well that he had the hotel staff remove the furniture to make room for all the delegates who were lined up in the hallway. The next day my name was placed in nomination by Senator Saltonstall's niece, Sally Saltonstall, and almost the whole convention stood to second it. Soon I had such a commanding lead that my five Republican opponents conceded. I was the first black man ever nominated for statewide office in Massachusetts history.

I told the delegates, "We will show the people of Massachusetts we are a united party and will destroy the myths of class, race, creed, wealth, antilabor, suburbia, which the Democratic Party attempted to shackle us with. It is not the Democratic Party—it is the Republican Party which is truly the party of the people, the party of Lincoln." Because both parties that year had hotly debated their positions on civil rights, I added, "It is unfortunate in 1960 that so much time must be spent on the fight for a strong civil rights plank, when civil rights are guaranteed by the Constitution . . . and the platform is merely a reaffirmation of our principle, 'with liberty and justice for all.' "

With the nomination won, I faced the challenge of the general election. The secretary of state race and the others at the bottom of the ticket typically got almost no press coverage and aroused little public interest, so many voters reflexively voted straight Democratic for those offices. No Republican had been elected secretary of state, treasurer, or auditor since 1946. The Republican Party put very little money behind its candidates for these minor offices. The problem was intensified in 1960 because Massachusetts's own John F. Kennedy was the Democratic candidate for president. He was expected to inspire a record voter turnout and that could only help all Democratic candidates.

I had another problem: Why did I want to be secretary of state? How could I convince voters that the race for this office was important and relevant to their own lives? The secretary of state supervises vital statistics for the commonwealth, prepares election ballots, supervises elections, and handles the state archives. The job calls for integrity, dedication, and a sense of duty. But there are few volatile issues on which a candidate can run, and the public has only the vaguest idea about what the job requires. Some voters thought I was running against Christian Herter, who by then was President Eisenhower's secretary of state. One asked me in all seriousness how fast I could type and if I took good dictation, because she figured any good secretary should be able to do those things. The truth was that the office was regarded by politicians mostly as a stepping-stone to other offices. Indeed, given a choice, I would much rather have been running for state attorney general, where I believed I truly could make a difference.

The political reality I faced was summed up by one reporter this way: "Brooke is a Republican in a Democratic state; a Negro in a white state; a Protestant in a Catholic state; a 'carpetbagger from the

South' and he is poor." I was guilty on all counts. But I wanted to prove that white voters would vote for qualified Negro candidates, just as Negroes had voted for qualified white candidates. To me, it was logical and it was right.

I continued to have the support of old friends, and new ones rallied to my cause. I met Roger Woodworth, a politically astute young Republican who became a close friend and adviser. I met the brilliant young attorney Gael Mahony and his wife, Connaught, and Sally Saltonstall, who had volunteered to work for my campaign full time without pay. Senator Saltonstall would smile and say, "I can't get my own niece to work for me. She's working for Ed Brooke." Sally became the soul of the large volunteer effort behind my 1960 campaign. Marion Boch, who had previously been a Republican candidate for secretary of state, joined our campaign and was a tremendous resource. Carol Santry, who had just graduated from Skidmore College, came aboard and took on our scheduling. Pat Beck, who later became an aide to Governor John Volpe, ran the sound truck at our rallies that played a song called "Look for Brooke on Your Ballot." Rudy and Kay Sacco literally introduced me to western Massachusetts, an introduction that bore fruit in all of my statewide campaigns. As always, love and joy filled our campaign.

Joseph Martin, the former Speaker of the U.S. House of Representatives, was on the same plane I took back from the 1960 Republican National Convention in Chicago. Joe Martin was no blue blood but a tenacious man with a hard-won education in practical politics. He and his brother Ed had published the *Attleboro Sun,* so he had a newspaperman's feel for issues and people. As we chatted, he gave me some advice. "Ed, when I was a boy, my mother told me, if you want to fill your pail with huckleberries, you go where the huckleberries grow."

When I heard those words, something clicked. He was telling me I had to campaign all over the state, not just in Boston and Cambridge and the South Shore, but wherever the voters lived. I had to explore unknown territory, to move beyond the country clubs and wealthy suburbs and campaign door-to-door in the Democratic cities of Worcester, Lawrence, Fall River, New Bedford, and Pittsfield. That is what I did. My friend Bill Jackson took leave from his job and drove me all over the state. I grew to know and love all of Massachusetts and to appreciate its regional differences.

Western Massachusetts had always complained that the state spent all of its money and talent on problems east of Route 128, the beltway around Boston. They wanted to see political candidates in the flesh. So I went out to the far corners of the state: to industrial Pittsfield, the onion county of Hatfield, and the beautiful towns in Franklin and Hampshire counties. I campaigned along the highways and byways—among rows of middle-class suburban houses, in quiet rural sections, at asparagus farms and casket factories I did not know existed, in the cranberry bogs on Cape Cod, and down at the docks and fish piers along the seaside at Gloucester and the Cape. I discovered that once you moved out of Boston and the big cities, people had time to stop and talk and many were pleased to have someone take the time to ask them for their vote. I never encountered any opposition based on race. People were hospitable and warm. Campaigning was not a chore for me. I loved it, along with the sometimes-religious experience of reaching out to voters, looking into their eyes, and being energized by contact with so many fine, decent people who wanted better government.

I received an unexpected boost from *Look* magazine. Its publisher, Gardner Cowles, liked to encourage promising young moderate Republican candidates. He asked me to come down to New York for a meeting. We had a good talk, and he arranged for *Look* to run a major story on me. It was my first national exposure. But a politician must never forget that, as you grow in popularity, you cannot ignore those who supported you first. There were grumblings in Roxbury that Ed Brooke was campaigning all over the state and forgetting where he came from. I had missed a few weddings and funerals in Roxbury while out campaigning, and my law office, once a major connection to the Roxbury community, was now downtown. And there was still disgruntlement because I had married a white woman.

Actually, Remigia blossomed in that campaign. She had come to accept that politics was what I wanted, and she wanted to help. Although her English had improved somewhat, she often campaigned with Italians with whom she could speak her native tongue. She praised me in both languages, and her sincerity and infectious smile were highly effective. Part of her charm was that she did not know how good she was. On the Sunday before the election, we had an afternoon tea for Remigia, at the Women's Service Club on Massachusetts Avenue, on the edge of Roxbury. My friend Georgia Ireland, then the dynamic vice-chair of the Republican State Committee, made a tough speech, declaring that Negroes had to learn to stick together and support their own, as the Irish and other voting blocs had done. She said bluntly that who one married was of no political consequence and that I should not be penalized for marrying the woman of my choice.

To my dismay, the Communist Party endorsed me again. This time I sent a registered letter to Premier Khrushchev himself, asking him to stop the American Communists from endorsing racial minorities for political office. It was a publicity stunt, but I needed the publicity—and I also wanted to forcefully reject communism once and for all.

My Democratic opponent for secretary of state was an ambitious young Irish Catholic named Kevin White. Kevin was a graduate of Williams College with a law degree from Boston College. He had been an assistant Suffolk County district attorney and was a member of the Boston City Council. He ran by arguing that the powers-that-be in Massachusetts were Democrats, and voters needed a Democrat to do business with them. I countered by saying that with so many Democrats out there, spending the taxpayers' money, the people of Massachusetts needed a Republican minding the store. If that was a reminder of Democratic corruption, so be it.

Kevin and I had met a few times and always been cordial. We never had a real, face-to-face debate; those were just being popularized by Kennedy and Nixon. Kevin ran his campaign; I ran mine. Then his campaign put out a bumper sticker that read, "Vote White." I was surprised and hurt that he had sanctioned what appeared to be a blatant appeal to people to support him—and reject me—on the basis of race. I confronted him. "Kevin, why are you using this slogan?" He insisted it was not racial. He reminded me, as if I did not know, that his name was White and insisted that "Vote White" was a natural phrase for him to use. He said I was the one reading racial innuendo into it. I told my campaign workers to ignore the bumper sticker, and I never made an issue of it. But many of my supporters will tell you to this day that Kevin White's people knew exactly what they were doing with their slogan.

With all of Kevin's connections, and with John Kennedy, the most popular politician in the state's history, leading the ticket, Kevin was expected to win a runaway victory. He won by fewer than 112,000 votes. I had spent just $17,000 on my entire campaign, and I received 1,095,054 votes. I could not afford to buy any television time, and that was too big a handicap to overcome. My concession speech on election night was the first time the voters had ever seen me on television. Looking into a TV camera instead of a crowd of people, I felt myself freeze for a moment, then I spoke from the heart. My supporters were more upset than I was. Many of them, gathered in the lobby of the Somerset Hotel, were in tears. The elevators were so crowded that many had to walk up several flights of stairs to find me and offer their condolences. Some of them were crying out in the hall, because they could not bear to walk into my quarters and face defeat. Over and over I told them, "Smile. We have no reason to cry."

I believed that. Losing is never fun, but for a Republican, able to spend only a fraction of what his opponent spent, yet winning more than a million votes, it was no defeat. Probably only 2 to 3 percent of the Massachusetts voters were black in those days, so I had proved that white voters would vote for a qualified black candidate. I proved that I could overcome the racial and financial handicaps and demonstrate to the newspapers and to the entire political world that I was for real. I had begun to build a strong and loyal statewide following. And I had reinforced my belief that what I most wanted out of life was to be an elected public official.

I knew that in two years I wanted to run for attorney general, the job I really desired. I believed that in 1962 I would have a good chance. Election victories are a harvest. You plant the seeds. For months or years, you water and tend them. In the election season, you reap the harvest. In 1960, I found more than a million voters who, in future elections, were not likely to think they had been wrong in voting for me. I took comfort that I had harvested those million votes, and I intended to keep planting seeds. All those huckleberries would be waiting for the next harvest.

6

The Boston

Finance

Commission

It was a testament to the growing appeal of the Massachusetts Republican Party that in 1960, when favorite son John F. Kennedy won the White House, John Anthony Volpe became the first Roman Catholic Republican to be elected governor of Massachusetts. John, the son of Italian immigrants, began as a hod carrier, one of the humblest jobs in the construction trade, but he and his brother Peter worked hard and built the Volpe Construction Company into a huge firm that made them millionaires.

John's wealth and energetic fundraising made him a player in Republican politics. He entered public life as a federal highway commissioner, appointed by President Eisenhower. He was a hero in the Italian community, a man who was clean living, hardworking, smart, doggedly determined, and unflappable. I got to know John because we were both on the 1960 Republican ticket, but we were not close. He was in many ways an insecure man, wary of politicians like myself for whom banter with strangers came easily. I felt more comfortable with Jennie Volpe, his wife, whose kind disposition and friendly smile helped smooth over her husband's rough edges, and his chief legal adviser, Joseph L. Tauro, later chief of the U.S. District Court in Massachusetts, well known for his sound and courageous decisions.

During the campaign, I had gone out of my way to urge John's election. When he narrowly won and I narrowly lost, he owed me. However, it was not until the spring of 1961, after several months had passed, that the new governor called me into his office to talk about a job. I could not help noting that Christian Herter, eight years before, had been more prompt. After some small talk, he asked me what job I wanted. When I hesitated, he said,

> "Ed, there will be some judicial openings, would you be interested?"
>
> "Governor, I think I am too young to sit and rock," I told him. "I had really thought about something more active."
>
> "Such as what?" he said cautiously.
>
> "I had thought about the chairmanship of the Boston Finance Commission."
>
> "What's that?" he asked. "And how much does it pay?"
>
> When I explained the commissioner's duties and responsibilities as best I could and told him the salary was five thousand dollars, he looked at me in some disbelief but finally said, "Ed, if that's what you want, you got it. I'll tell my staff to work out the details."

I had the feeling that John thought he had gotten off easy, and he was right to be perplexed. No one had ever thought of the "Fin Com" as a political plum or a stepping-stone to higher office. But my savvy campaign manager, Joe Fitzgerald, had seen its potential as a position from which to lead a battle against local corruption and urged me to seek its chairmanship. Joe pointed out that it could be a potent instrument for government reform; it had the power of subpoena, and Fin Com members could only be fired for cause. I could even maintain my law practice. I had scarcely heard of the Finance Commission, but I respected Joe's advice and his idea intrigued me. My own research showed me that the commission not only had subpoena power to expose graft and corruption, it was also authorized to propose reforms. "Joe," I said, "that Fin Com is twice as powerful as you said it was." As its chairman, my powers would be, in a limited way, not unlike those of the state's attorney general.

When I took office in April 1961, the Finance Commission occupied a sparsely furnished suite on the seventh floor of a Boston bank building at 24 School Street. It had three other members, all Democrats, who were uneasy about my coming, and if they had wished, they could have outvoted me. Volpe later appointed another Republican to fill the commission's fifth seat, but we were still outnumbered by the Democrats. I scheduled sixteen meetings of the Fin Com in the remainder of 1961. At the first one, I told the Democrats that I had studied the history of the commission, explained my view of its mandate, and asked for their cooperation in carrying it out. They were at first understandably suspicious of my motives. Years before, the commission had been created by the Republican state legislature to monitor the doings of the Democratic-controlled capital city. But the three commissioners I inherited were not party hacks. They were men of intelligence and honor, and insofar as I acted reasonably, explained my goals, and appealed to their sense of justice, they followed my lead. Sometimes they were reluctant or cautious—and sometimes they clearly were feeling pressure from Democratic officeholders, but in the end we always agreed on the course we should take.

In the 1960s, corruption was commonplace throughout the Commonwealth of Massachusetts. Contractors and others who did business there often bribed state legislators, and the payoffs were not onetime cash payments in a brown paper bag, but brazenly came in regular monthly payments, by check. When people treat corruption as a routine part of the process, you have something far worse than wrongdoing or moral failing. You have a political cancer that breeds cynicism about democratic government and infects all of society.

Although I was not required to do so, I gave up my law practice. The commission had a first-rate staff and a first-rate team of investigators. As the media began covering our work, anonymous tips from government employees and ordinary citizens multiplied, all eager to blow the whistle on the corruption surrounding them. We took our first major step in July, when we informed Boston Mayor John F. Collins that we had uncovered gross inequities in real estate appraisal in land-taking cases. We had found that property owners were being encouraged by unscrupulous city appraisers to set a value on their real estate two or three times greater than the city's appraisal. When the two sides settled in the middle, or split the difference, the "middle" was far too high. That practice encouraged the property owner to make a kickback to the appraiser who had made his windfall possible. With a new Government Center being built, land-taking in Boston was at an all-time high. Millions of dollars of property were involved in the project. Boston needed a single, fair, and objective set of appraisal standards. Property owners subjected to government land-taking deserved real cash value for their land, but not a dollar more; and certainly not the outlandish awards that were being made under highly suspicious circumstances. We urged the mayor to invite local members of the American Institute of Real Estate Appraisers to confer with the Boston Bar Association for the purpose of recommending those new standards. Mayor Collins did not comply.

On another front, I obtained information that the Boston city auctioneer, John J. "Mucker" McGrath, was using sham buyers to acquire municipal property for him at rock-bottom prices that he had set himself. On October 9, I called an emergency meeting at which I declared my intention to investigate McGrath for illegal corrupt practices. I requested that he meet with the Fin Com. He failed to appear and instead hired a criminal lawyer. McGrath did finally appear with his lawyer before the commission, but he refused to produce records that we requested or to discuss matters crucial to our inquiry. We served him with a subpoena; he ignored it. We got a court order requiring his compliance with our subpoena. McGrath then appealed to the Supreme Judicial Court.

On November 28, I announced that I had asked my friend Gael Mahony, one of Boston's most able trial lawyers, to prepare our response to McGrath's refusal to comply with our subpoena and to represent our commission before the state's Supreme Judicial Court. I also announced that I had retained Mahony to serve as-counsel for the commission. The Supreme Judicial Court ruled in our favor, ratifying not only the McGrath subpoena, but the general powers of the commission to investigate city matters and to compel witnesses to produce their federal tax returns. That was a great victory for the integrity of the Finance Commission. Before we were done, we had recommended the firing of McGrath and had also defined the debate about the auction procedures needed when city property was sold.

City property up for auction was often poorly advertised, with small announcements appearing only a few days before the auction was to take place. There was too often no effort to notify those who owned adjacent land of the coming auction, which sharply reduced the number of bidders. The auctions themselves were usually conducted at a whirlwind pace, leaving less experienced bidders bewildered and silent. We worked with the legislature in writing legislation that required the auction of city property to be promptly and prominently advertised. We insisted that the auctioneer describe the parcel being auctioned with care, aiming for the widest possible participation.

In my first year as chairman, the finance commission also found graft and corruption in the municipal fire department and in the building department. Boston's newspapers and television stations gave us a lot of coverage. The *Boston Herald* called me "a young Republican with the toughness of a bulldog and the tenacity of a terrier." Then, on November 30, 1961, CBS-TV aired a documentary called *Biography of a Bookie Joint*. It showed film of customers coming and going from a small key shop in Boston that doubled as a bookmaking parlor. Footage showed uniformed police officers directing traffic past the shop, while other police came and went from it. It even showed a policeman watching as men burned gambling stubs in a barrel on a city sidewalk. The program strongly implied that policemen not only looked kindly on the illegal operation, but were active participants in the illegal acts themselves. The show caused a scandal in Boston and around the country. Illegal gambling occurs in every city in America, of course. I knew that well from my days with Uncle Alex Pompez. But in most cities there is a tacit assumption that gambling cannot be conducted in the open, and certainly not in the presence of police. That assumption did not hold in Boston.

In those days, the appointment of the Boston police commissioner was still made by the governor. Governor Volpe had already directed Police Commissioner Leo Sullivan to clean up gambling in Boston. This television program, seen nationally, put Boston law enforcement in very bad odor. CBS executive Fred Friendly gave Volpe and his legal staff a private preview of the show. Volpe was about to leave on a ten-day golfing vacation in Palm Springs, so he headed for

California knowing he had a serious case on his hands but believing the matter would be handled by his office alone.

I did not accept that. I believed the public actions of the police department were clearly within the purview of the Finance Commission. With the governor out of town, I telephoned his legal office and asked them to tell him that the Finance Commission would be following up on the CBS documentary. A lawyer on Governor Volpe's staff urged me to leave the investigation to the state. I refused. A Volpe staff member then called California, pulling an annoyed governor off the golf course. Volpe reacted bluntly. "Tell Brooke to stay out of it." When this was relayed to me, I insisted on speaking to the governor in person. The aide told me that the governor could not be disturbed again.

I boarded a plane for Palm Springs that afternoon. On arrival, I went straight to the country club where Governor Volpe was staying. I was refused admittance—not because the governor was not seeing visitors, but because I was a black man at the front door of an all-white golf club. Finally, Volpe himself came out and escorted me to his suite. His demeanor could be described as sour. But after a lengthy discussion, we agreed that we would jointly try to find a way to remove Leo Sullivan as Boston police commissioner. I left the country club and caught the first plane home.

At the Finance Commission's December 11 meeting, we discussed the growing police scandal. I handed my fellow members a letter outlining my views: the commission had not just a right but a duty to explore the police scandal. I moved that we engage an independent expert to survey the police department and report back to us. Outside investigations into the operations of a police department were as unpopular with the police then as they are today. My Democratic commissioners were loath to incur the ire of their political friends and associates on this sensitive matter. But after much debate they agreed unanimously to my proposal.

John Volpe could hardly object to our efforts to weed out corruption in the city, but his political instincts told him that we were going too far, too fast. On December 19, the governor called me into his office and asked me to slow down. I told him I would not. At my invitation, Quinn Tamm, the director of the Field Service Division of the International Association of Chiefs of Police, agreed to meet with us in Boston on December 22 to discuss how his agency could help. I sent a letter to Police Commissioner Leo Sullivan, advising him that the Fin Com was having a survey conducted on the "financial and administrative procedures" of the police department. In response, Sullivan told reporters his police department was "beyond the lawful jurisdiction of the Finance Commission" and vowed not to cooperate with us. He also pressured the Democratic commissioners to curtail our investigation, to no avail. Still, removing Sullivan took some doing. Despite public outrage and the governor's call for his removal, Sullivan refused to resign. But after four months he accepted the inevitable and left.

As chairman of the Boston Finance Commission I was able to wield power for the public good. I had never worked harder or loved my work more. But I was still burning inside to hold elective office, to exercise power in my own right, to be responsible directly to the people. I was serious about combating corruption in Massachusetts and was certain, now more than ever, that attorney general was the job I wanted. I understood that I would have to build a coalition in order to win. I knew no black American had ever been elected a state attorney general anywhere in the United States, but I was ready to try. And I also knew that if I was nominated and elected, it would encourage other African Americans to seek state and national offices and not restrict themselves to local elections or to predominantly black constituencies.

Of course, I was only one of many ambitious lawyers who aspired to that office. Buoyed by the million-plus votes I received in 1960 and my successful anticorruption campaign at the Finance Commission, I thought it was a natural next step to seek my party's nomination for attorney general. However, many of my friends worried that it would be another noble but losing effort. They particularly feared the perceived strength of Elliot Richardson, a Republican with a solid-gold résumé who wanted the job just as much as I did. Elliot was a millionaire lawyer in Boston, a partner in the prestigious Ropes & Gray law firm. He had been middleweight boxing champion at Harvard and had served with distinction in the 4th Infantry Division in World War II. As a law student, he had been editor in chief of the

Harvard Law Review. He had clerked for two of the country's most distinguished judges: Learned Hand of the Second Circuit Court of Appeals, and Supreme Court Justice Felix Frankfurter. He had also served as an assistant secretary in the Health, Education and Welfare Department in the Eisenhower administration. As the U.S. attorney for Massachusetts, he had himself been something of a crime buster. In short, he would enter the race with an impressive record, impeccable social credentials, and the backing of important Republican powers in the state, including Governor Volpe. As Volpe faced a re-election campaign, he thought that a Brahmin Yankee as the Republican candidate for attorney general would strengthen his campaign and the entire ticket. Given all of Elliot's strengths, he looked like a good bet to win the Republican nomination.

But I thought my own credentials were solid, too. At the Finance Commission I had brought a sleeping watchdog back to life, barking and biting. I believed that performance had given me momentum that could carry over into the race for attorney general. In late 1961, Elliot got wind of my plans and asked me to lunch at the Parker House, one of the longest continuously operating hotels in America. Boston cream pie and Parker House rolls had been invented in its venerable kitchen. One memorable night, the Parker House served dinner to Henry Wadsworth Longfellow, Ralph Waldo Emerson, Oliver Wendell Holmes, and their English guest, Charles Dickens. Politicians loved the Parker House. James Michael Curley ate lunch there nearly every day. John F. Kennedy had kicked off at least one of his campaigns there. While working at the Fin Com, a little over a block away, I had taken many lunches at the Parker House.

Elliot ushered me into the elegant first floor dining room. He began our lunch by telling me that he, John Volpe, and a few others had already held a meeting—one to which I had not been invited. Then he said, "Ed, we want you to run for lieutenant governor." Without giving me a chance to react, Elliot went on to say that everyone at the meeting had agreed I would be a good member of the team and make "an outstanding lieutenant governor." His condescending tone annoyed me. I did not like the idea that a group of state Republican politicians could privately parcel out our state's top offices months before the election. It sounded like a throwback to the days of smoke-filled rooms. Why not let the voters decide? If such a meeting had to be held, why was I, the "chosen" candidate for lieutenant governor, not invited? They seemed to think they could toss me a few crumbs from the table.

Furthermore, I did not want the office they were offering. Lieutenant governor in most administrations was little more than a ceremonial job. The attorney general was really the second highest office in the commonwealth—a powerful, independent, elected official who was granted broad powers under Massachusetts's law and custom. The attorney general was the people's lawyer.

> I looked him in the eye and said firmly, "Elliot, I don't want to be lieutenant governor."
>
> "What do you mean, you don't want to be lieutenant governor?"
>
> "I intend to be a candidate for attorney general."
>
> After recovering, he said, "But, Ed, I am going to be our candidate for attorney general." He spoke calmly, coldly. "Running for attorney general will cost a lot of money, and I don't think you have it or could raise it. Why not run for lieutenant governor?"
>
> "Elliot, you may have the money," I said. "I'll just have to rely on the people."
>
> Elliot began to recite his qualifications. It was a long litany, and his presumption galled me. I was still seething over the private meeting, not listening very carefully, until Elliot said something that stung me, ". . . and I've got family," he continued.
>
> I took that as a direct insult. I shot back, "I've got family too, and I am proud of it!" Once the flash of anger had passed, I said, "Look, Elliot, I'm going to be a candidate for the Republican nomination for attorney general. So if you want to be attorney general, you're going to have to beat me." I took a final sip of tea, stood up, and left the restaurant. We did not shake hands.

7

One Vote in

Worcester

Within a week of my tense meeting with Elliot Richardson, I returned to the Parker House to meet with my political advisers. Now that I knew that Elliot was going to run, we needed to organize our team and map out a strategy for what I saw as a David and Goliath battle against the establishment's candidate. I asked Roger Woodworth, whose judgment and political sense and timing I had come to admire, to be my campaign manager. I knew that his commitment was total. When time was short, Roger would happily wash his socks in the campaign headquarters men's room, dine on milk and cookies, work around the clock, and sleep on desks. He was a keen strategist who alerted me to what my opponents were doing, praised my staff when I was too busy to do so, and scolded our allies when it was needed. To Roger, no issue was too large and no detail too small. He was soon involved in every aspect of my political life and was indispensable.

One of my great early accomplishments was convincing Harcourt "Courty" Wood of Dedham, a former Richardson backer, to serve as my treasurer and chief fundraiser. Courty, ably assisted by his nephew, Tony Wood, was indefatigable in his forays into Republican "Yankee money" territory. Thanks to Courty, Harvard and other Ivy League alumni dollars began to flow to me as well as to Richardson. Another key aide was Jerry Sadow, who had worked as a reporter and news editor for the *Boston Globe* and for WBZ Channel 4. Jerry walked in the door one day and asked for a job. I hired him as our press secretary, and he worked tirelessly to spread our message across Massachusetts. Harold Appleton, another gem in our campaign, handled campaign public relations and advertising. Harold called former Governor Christian Herter and persuaded him to hedge his endorsement of Elliot, which he had given before he knew I was running.

Nancy Porter, a bright, energetic, young Bryn Mawr graduate, joined the campaign as my administrative assistant after responding to an ad we placed in the *Boston Herald*. Because I could briefly summarize what I wanted to say in a letter, and she could write exactly what I wanted, we were able to eliminate hours of dictation. She soon absorbed the nuances of Massachusetts politics, helped us design our appeal to women voters, lined up meetings with convention delegates, and cheerfully coped with dozens of daily crises. Nancy was unflappable and a tremendous asset in those pressure-filled months.

With these and many other wonderful people working so hard for me, believing in me, how could I not give my all? How could I possibly let them down? My strategy in 1962 was much like that of 1960: I would go where the huckleberries were. Elliot Richardson had money and the power structure, but I did not think he would work as hard as I would. And my 1960 campaign, even though I had lost, was now a blessing. The friends I made then were the nucleus of this campaign. In town after town, I already had friends and organizers, whereas Elliot was often starting from scratch.

Some prominent Republicans continued to urge me to run for lieutenant governor or even to run again for secretary of state. I refused. I officially announced my candidacy in April 1962, but I was starting to campaign late in 1961. Driven once more by Bill Jackson, I went anywhere a half dozen or more potential state convention delegates might gather. I lined up Republican town committees, rang doorbells, and spoke at any Republican function, women's club, Rotary or Kiwanis Club that would invite me.

In those days politicians of both parties often dismissed the counties in western Massachusetts as the boondocks, too small to matter. But each of the wards and towns in those counties had at least one delegate to the Republican convention, and those votes added up. As I went out to these areas, I learned about making the best use of my time. I often scheduled only fifteen minutes at a single stop; I was always looking for just one more delegate-to-be, another reporter to spread our word. Although I had gained a good deal of publicity as head of the Boston Finance Committee and had run one statewide campaign, I was truly not that well known across our big, diverse state. At the outset, our polls showed that about 16 percent of the voters knew who I was and that they were concentrated in the Boston area.

One cold, drizzly day in late 1961 I was invited to address the Worcester Chamber of Commerce. The audience was important, but I also wanted to make my pitch to an influential Worcester Republican state representative, Albert A. Gammal Jr. Al had impressed our campaign team as a dynamic young man. In the 1950s, he had been a deft organizer of Young Republican Clubs. I approached him and said I expected to run for attorney general and wanted his support.

"You don't have a chance against Richardson," was Al's typically blunt reply. "Why don't you run for lieutenant governor?"

"You know, Al, when you were running in the Republican primary, people said you couldn't win because you didn't have the backing of some of the powerbrokers," I told him. "But people knew you, and knew how good you were, so you won. And you're doing a wonderful job. I want to do for Massachusetts what you've done for Worcester."

We had been standing outside in a light rain, but it started to pour. Al said, "Ed, I'm getting soaked here. But I'll promise you this much: I'll deliver you the eight votes in my ward." I said, "That's all I want."

But I got much more. Al threw himself into the campaign, and I asked him to be our field director. He had a natural flair for organization and soon built a superb statewide network of volunteers and molded our supporters into a team that became the envy of every other political camp, the Democrats included.

The highly respected State Senator Leslie B. Cutler of Needham was another key supporter. She was a pioneer, one of the first women elected to our state legislature. She had been an outspoken champion for mental health, public health, and women's rights decades before those issues came into political fashion. In 1946, she had succeeded in overturning the Massachusetts law that kept women off juries. Her support was an immeasurable plus.

On the day in April that I formally announced my candidacy, we held both a breakfast press conference at the Parker House in Boston and an afternoon press conference at the Springfield Sheraton, in the western part of the state. Reporters and delegates came, as did friends and veterans of my 1960 campaign. It was an exhilarating day, but I knew I was in the fight of my life. Republican ward and town committees elected delegates in the early spring. We had begun to pursue potential convention delegates long before. Republican legislators and county officials were particularly important, because they were often delegates themselves and they influenced others. I spent hours on the telephone, and we sent out thousands of letters to delegates and others with influence.

Elliot and I had informally agreed that our campaigns would not deal in slander and innuendo. I honored that pledge, but some of Elliot's zealots, I believe without his approbation, were spreading lies about me, including one that I was a communist sympathizer. That went back to the endorsements of the Communist Party when I was a candidate for state representative. Ten days before the preprimary convention in Worcester, Roger Woodworth, Al Gammal, and several of my supporters met with Philip K. Allen, chairman of the Republican State Committee, and other officials to lodge a strong protest. Allen asked both Elliot and me to come to a meeting to adopt a joint code of ethics. We met a few days later at Republican headquarters on Beacon Hill. With a few senior aides present on both sides, we formalized a joint code of ethics for our respective campaigns. Elliot and I swore an oath to uphold this code.

Two days later, an important Finance Commission story made statewide news just as the convention was opening. Following the commission's recommendation, "Mucker" McGrath, Boston's unscrupulous city auctioneer, had been fired. The news could not have come at a better time.

I reached Worcester on Friday afternoon, June 15, the day before the preprimary convention and checked into the old Bancroft Hotel to attend a last round of meetings, dinners, caucuses, and suite parties.

Everything went smoothly. I retired fairly early to save my energy for the following day. But political spirits were high, and revelry continued far into the night. Young people paraded through the streets carrying banners for their candidates. People honked their horns. In hotel bars and ballrooms, delegates danced the twist and jitterbugged, all the while yelling their campaign slogans.

Saturday dawned a lovely early summer day. I rose before six and looked out my window. Just across the street sat Notre Dame Church, with its lovely steeple. The sight of it, gleaming on the morning of this crucial day, filled me with confidence. I said, "Thank you, God." I knew that I would win that day. Nothing could stop me. At 10 A.M., inside the cavernous Worcester Memorial Auditorium, the convention opened. All the party's business had to be completed in that one day. To no one's surprise, Senator Leverett Saltonstall was chosen as the convention chairman. Many delegates thought the day's most important race was between the candidates for the Senate seat once held by John F. Kennedy. Two Republicans were vying for the nomination: Congressman Lawrence Curtis and George Lodge, son of U.S. Senator Lodge. The winner would face off against the winner of the Democratic primary, then being contested by Ted Kennedy and state Attorney General Edward McCormack. My contest with Elliot was the last business of the day. One of our major challenges was simply to keep our delegates in place. Late in a long day, delegates are tempted to pack up and go home, even if one contest remains. Would those "head-for-homers" help or hurt us?

Elliot had publicly predicted he would win 1,084 delegates, enough for a comfortable victory. We too expected to win handily. I had failed to get the endorsement of the two most important men at the convention, Senator Saltonstall and Governor Volpe, but then they had not publicly endorsed Elliot either. Nothing in our Friday night canvassing dimmed our optimism. We had recorded in a three-ring binder the names of all the delegates and their sometimes-shifting allegiances. The binder, constantly updated, said we had enough solid commitments to win by at least two hundred delegate votes. Remigia, Remi, and Edwina had come to Worcester to be with me. My parents had come from Washington. My father had taken a day off from work, a rarity in his life. He had taken my earlier political losses hard, and

I looked forward to winning this race as he looked on. Everyone in my family was excited and optimistic.

Late in the day Leslie Cutler placed my name in nomination with brief but spirited remarks. Rather than having others praise me, I reserved nine of the ten minutes allotted to my campaign for a speech of my own. Having always spoken for myself, I saw no reason to change now. Dressed in my blue serge suit, white shirt, and blue and white tie, I strolled up on that auditorium stage, made what I thought was a good speech, and sat back down—to watch in amazement as my "lead" fell apart when the roll was called.

Minute by minute, Worcester Auditorium grew ever more hectic, hot, and steamy. Delegates who for months had pledged their support to me now would not look me in the eye. Whole delegations were turning against me and backing Richardson. Rumors and whispers began to fly. Some of my followers, claiming to be acting defensively, were reminding delegates of Elliot's rumored drinking problem, and his partisans were spreading stories that I beat my wife and had communist leanings. Nasty circulars were passed out that read in part: "Negroes voted against the Republican Party in 1960. Negroes will vote against the Republican Party again this year. Why should Republicans vote for Negroes?"

My beautiful day had become a nightmare. The convention was bedlam. Hundreds of people were running around screaming at the top of their lungs. The aisles were congested with frantic, perspiring bodies. But amid the pandemonium our team never stopped working. Representative Mary B. Newman, the parliamentarian of the convention, left the podium to shore up the delegates in her district. Roger Woodworth corralled delegates, trying to stop the defections. Al Gammal was yelling at people, especially in the Worcester County delegation. Joe Fitzgerald, my former campaign manager for secretary of state, always cool, told his three coordinators to move through the Essex and Middlesex delegations and firm up my support. On the other side, Congressman Bradford Morse of Lowell was twisting arms in the Middlesex First District to get delegates to switch from Brooke to Richardson. Things grew ever more frantic. We got reports that Morse was threatening to take people's jobs away who failed to support Elliot.

I sat on the platform, watching our campaign collapse. The convention hall was now even more steamy with sweat and thick with cigarette and cigar smoke. I looked out on all this with a calmness that was strange under the circumstances. I sent a prayer up to God: "I know you're not going to let this happen. I know we're going to win this." Somehow I was confident of our success even at that desperate point, but I doubt that many others in that auditorium would have agreed.

The Richardson forces were playing rough. Brooke delegates in the Brookline-Newton Senatorial District told us that the about-to-be-reported vote was inaccurate, because absent Richardson votes were being recorded as present. When one Brooke delegate tried to reach the microphone to call for a poll of the delegates, he was strong-armed away from the mike. It was ironic—this was the kind of chaos the Democrats were known for, not us civilized Republicans. It was a far cry from the convention two years before that had nominated me for secretary of state by acclamation. Then I was a useful young man, nominated for a minor office to add diversity to our ticket. Now I was challenging the powers that be, and one of their favorite sons, for an important office that could be, for either of us, the stepping-stone to even more important offices. They were doing their best to halt my political career right there. If I lost, I assumed that was the end of the line. I had already lost in 1950, 1952, and 1960. Four-time losers do not get another chance, particularly if they have offended their party elders.

The first-ballot roll call inched forward. Based on the total number of delegates, a simple majority, 854 votes, was needed to win. The lead see-sawed back and forth as each delegation chairman in turn stepped up to the microphone. Several of the delegation votes were challenged, sometimes to stall, sometimes because the vote accuracy was doubted. With all of the pressure and vote switching, and with only one delegation remaining, Elliot and I each had 839 votes. Then came the vote of the final delegation, Middlesex First District. They had passed earlier, unable to resolve a disagreement within the delegation. Now, swayed by their popular and aggressive congressman, Brad Morse, Middlesex First gave most of its votes to Elliot. It was over.

I had won 845 votes, but Elliot had landed right on the magic number: 854. I felt crushed. But I could not believe it. I sat very still, my tongue running mechanically over my dry lips. It was incredible to me that our long campaign had come to nothing. I kept telling myself, "This can't be true." The Richardson partisans screamed and danced and waved their banners. Some of them raced out of the hall to escape the heat and headed home. Some of my disappointed supporters began straggling out of the hall as well. Reporters were running to the phones. Elliot Richardson left his seat and took a chair beside Chairman Saltonstall. John Volpe headed over to shake his hand, as did Brad Morse and other important state Republicans. They all looked delighted. People swarmed to Elliot. Microphones were thrust to his face. Flashbulbs were popping.

Soon Elliot walked over to me and held out his hand. I stood and we shook hands. "Tough fight," he said. "You bet," I said, biting my lip. Just then, amazing events began to unfold. A miracle, some would say. A Richardson delegate from that last, crucial Middlesex delegation asked for recognition. His name was Francis Alden Wood, and because his delegation voted alphabetically by last name, he was the last to vote. As flashbulbs exploded all around, Wood walked to the microphone and said, "Mr. Chairman, I wish to challenge that vote." Middlesex had reported the tally before Wood had actually voted. Knowing his former support for Richardson, he had been counted, prematurely, as a vote for Elliot. But Francis Alden Wood had experienced a change of heart. He wanted to vote for me.

Amid shouts of dismay from Richardson backers—and cheers from my side—Chairman Saltonstall pounded his gavel for order. Weary, laboring to make himself heard, he ordered a new poll of the crucial Middlesex delegation. As Saltonstall explained to the stunned delegates, with Wood's vote now in our column, Elliot was one vote short of the magic number, 854, one vote short of victory. To further complicate matters, there was a third candidate in this contest. Arlyne Hassett, a talented former assistant U.S. attorney, had drawn nine votes before withdrawing from the race and freeing her delegates. Hassett had worked for Elliot in the U.S. Attorney's office and some of her delegates were eager to change their votes to him. Elliot's forces asked Senator Saltonstall to allow this. If he had agreed, Elliot would have won instantly. But Saltonstall knew the rules, and he declared that if these delegates had voted for Arlyne Hassett, their votes would be recorded for Arlyne Hassett. Yet, even this ruling, it seemed, would only briefly delay my defeat.

Elliot still lacked one vote. But surely, in a matter of minutes, some delegate, eager to get home after a long, exhausting day, would succumb to pressure from the Richardson forces and change his or her vote from me to Elliot, thus ending this fiasco and my political career with it. Still, my people were not standing by idly. Through it all, we had been lining up Richardson delegates who might switch on a second ballot. Or earlier, if possible. If the chair had sanctioned vote switching, there would have been a lot on both sides. But Saltonstall ruled that individual delegates could no longer change their votes; only the monitor of one of the forty senatorial delegations could change a vote.

Senator Saltonstall later said he had never seen a situation like this in all of his years in politics. But he felt that his duty was to call for a second ballot. Because Elliot had been a Saltonstall protégé and had served on the senator's staff, and because Saltonstall was who he was, it was impossible to argue that his ruling was anything but an honest parliamentary decision. His integrity could not be doubted. Suddenly, thanks to his rectitude, my campaign had new life.

But where were my delegates? Many had left the hall. My people began scrambling around, rallying our delegates, putting out our appeal over radio stations and telephones: "Get back! Get back! It isn't over yet!" There were no cell phones in those days; we could not know how many would get our message and return. I went onto the convention floor and implored our delegates to stay. I went on the radio and said, "Wherever you are, in the street or in your automobiles on the turnpike, I need you now. There's going to be a second ballot."

Some delegates, both Elliot's and mine, made a U-turn on the Boston-Worcester Turnpike and came roaring back to the convention hall. But 233 delegates never did return, either because they did not get the word or because they did not care enough. As this drama unfolded, my father had said to my mother, "I can't watch Edward lose this election," and had gone up to the balcony to sit by himself.

Representative Harold Putnam found him and gently chided him for giving up too soon. I was going to win, he told my despondent father.

We kept telling delegates that I could win the general election and that Elliot could not. We targeted the delegates who had first pledged themselves to me, then changed sides under duress. We argued that, having duly voted for Elliot on the first ballot, they were now free to vote their conscience on the second ballot. My loyal supporters argued, pleaded, and cajoled, asking wavering delegates to switch back to Brooke. And on the second ballot, our convention floor coordinators convinced eight districts to increase their Brooke vote. In the end we brought enough delegates over to our side to win the nomination by a clear majority of those present and voting: 792 votes to 673.

Now the cheering was for me. Elliot, though obviously shocked, offered me his congratulations. The convention finally adjourned at 9:47 P.M., after nearly twelve hours of nonstop action. My father wept with joy. His son had defeated a rich, powerful Brahmin from Brookline at a Republican state convention in the land of Concord, Lexington, and the Boston Tea Party. One of Elliot's backers, a prominent Boston attorney named Roger Moore, told Gael Mahony's wife, Connaught, "This breaks my heart, but you people deserve the victory, because you cared."

There is no question that the 1962 preprimary convention in Worcester was the turning point of my political life. I had long heard about the power of one vote. But never before had it struck home so dramatically. Ever since that convention victory, for more than forty years now, hundreds of people have pressed my hand and sworn, "I was that one vote in Worcester." And every one of them is right; each of them was the decisive vote that staved off defeat and sent the convention to a second, triumphant ballot.

Traditionally, the candidate who won the Republican convention endorsement was unchallenged in the September primary. With the crowd thundering its applause, I urged all Republicans to get behind our ticket. But that was not to be. Elliot, citing the closeness of the vote, challenged me in the September primary. I understood his frustration with the convention outcome. It was a bitter pill to swallow. But Elliot had openly "deplored the irresponsibility" of delegates who had left the hall. He implied that in choosing Brooke, the convention had flouted the will of the majority. I thought he sounded like a sore loser, and I said so. Later, Governor Volpe and Party Chairman Allen publicly, if reluctantly, advised Elliot to accept the convention result.

My people longed for time to rest, to mend battered Republican fences. Still, as a cold political reality I did not believe that a contested primary was necessarily bad for our campaign. I even wrote a letter to Party Chairman Allen, asking him not to discourage Elliot from running in the primary if that was his wish. I knew that after my name on the ballot would be the golden words: "Endorsed by the Republican preprimary convention." Ever since the reinstitution of the Republican state convention in 1952, the convention's endorsement had guaranteed a primary victory.

Elliot bought a half-hour of television time, appeared with his attractive wife and children, and made a prepared speech announcing his decision to challenge me in the primary. Our campaign raised enough money for me to go on television after him, and we did something we hoped would be dynamic: a no-holds-barred question-and-answer program. We had run newspaper ads that gave a phone number to call with questions for me. Nancy Porter, Sally Saltonstall, and Mary Newman sat at a table answering telephones and gave the questions to Gael Mahony, who sifted out profane questions but not embarrassing or racial ones. I sat next to them in a swivel chair so that I could move freely. As far as I was concerned, the harder the question, the better. In our half-hour of airtime I answered seventeen questions, and the public response was entirely positive.

I also went on a popular early evening radio call-in show hosted by Jerry Williams, the premiere talk show host on New England radio. People had warned me that the questions might be harsh.

One caller asked bluntly, "Why did you marry a white woman?"
    I answered bluntly, "Because I loved her."
    "Why is your daughter, Edwina, working in a soda-parlor in Newton Center?"
    "Why not? She likes her job. She doesn't believe she is too good to work and neither do I. As a matter of fact, I am proud of her."

"Are you a Communist?"

"No, I'm a Republican."

Our question-and-answer format was a big success, bringing more volunteers, more pledges of support, and more financial contributions each time I went on the air. No candidates that year found a better way to reach the electorate, and I have been surprised that few if any Massachusetts candidates have used that format since.

I urgently needed the support of Independents and registered Democrats both in the primary election and the general election in November. We went after them aggressively. Thousands of voters from the Cape to Essex County to the western part of the state went to city and town halls to register as Independents so they could vote for me in the Republican primary. We printed thousands of change of registration forms in our campaign colors, Brooke blue and white. As a result, the 1962 statewide primary experienced a substantial bulge in the Republican turnout—from 237,354 participants in 1960 to 458,425 two years later. Most of these new voters were formerly registered Democrats and Independents who became "Brooke Republicans." They became a vital cadre of support that I took into the general election.

In the September primary, I defeated Elliot by 238,147 votes to 195,791. I was at last the official Republican nominee for attorney general. But I was an upstart Republican, pledged to uphold Republican principles that many Massachusetts voters viewed with suspicion. Voters want to back a winner, and I also had to fight the perception that a Negro could not win a statewide race. In 1962, many experts felt that Massachusetts was not ready for a Negro as attorney general. This was true especially in the small towns, where few white people knew black people except in menial jobs. People never said that they themselves could not accept a Negro; it was always other people who "weren't ready."

In the general election, I faced Democrat Francis E. Kelly. As a former lieutenant governor and a three-term attorney general, Kelly was a household name—an Irish Catholic in an Irish Catholic state, a traditional Boston Democrat in a heavily Democratic state. He was a hard-nosed veteran of statewide campaigns. But in my heart I felt

Kelly was vulnerable. He was a man of the past. Voters already knew him as "Sweepstakes Frankie" Kelly, because of his oft-stated belief that all the financial problems of Massachusetts could be solved by a state lottery, at the time a new and controversial proposal. He was also the Boston Democratic political machine personified. There was no evidence that Kelly himself was corrupt, but he was a symbol of the old system, a man who tacitly heard and saw no evil, who accepted the status quo, who mistrusted reform and reformers.

As if to underscore Kelly's old-school mentality, a few weeks before the election, some of his supporters made sure the voters knew, if they had somehow failed to notice, that I was a Negro. They hired a bunch of ill-kempt Negroes to drive old cars through elite districts of West Roxbury and Wellesley, cars plastered with "Ed Brooke" bumper stickers, yelling that they were moving into the neighborhood as soon as Brooke was elected attorney general. The stunt backfired. Most voters abhorred such tactics, and they cared less about race than reform. They saw me as a serious reformer who owed nothing to the corrupt old order that Kelly embodied. On August 31, I resigned my chairmanship of the Boston Finance Commission and threw myself into the campaign. I drove all over the state with Bill Jackson in a white Ford station wagon marked in Brooke blue "Brooke for Attorney General." I stood at factory gates at 5:30 A.M. to shake the hands of incoming workers and at 3:30 P.M. to shake the hands of outgoing workers. Democratic labor activists like Jay Fialkow and Lee Koretsky, who knew that I was not antilabor and who were less than thrilled with my opposition, used their wiles to get me *inside* factories to the workbenches in Fall River, Boston, and other labor strongholds, where I tried hard to convert working people to my cause. The stereotype was that the wealthy and educated people were above racism, but that the working class wallowed in it. That was not what I saw. When Jay and Lee and I visited garment factories around the state, I approached many white workers sitting at their machines, many of them young women. They were happy to talk, pleased to have the tedium of their day broken by the visit of a politician who was interested in what they had to say. I put aside stereotypes about working people, and I asked them to put aside stereotypes about Republicans.

We built the best field organization in the state. Field Director Al Gammal made it a badge of honor to be a Brooke coordinator. We tapped the zest and talent of Democrats, Independents, or apolitical people who cared little about partisan politics but supported our campaign. We circulated thousands of bumper stickers that read, "Another Democrat for Brooke." They were a way Democrats could publicly join us without abandoning their longtime political allegiance. I made it a point to visit labor union headquarters in every city where I campaigned. I would not concede the labor vote to the Democratic Party and was delighted when the International Ladies' Garment Workers Union endorsed me.

My veteran status and war record were assets. AMVETS members and many individual veterans worked for us. My friend Harold Russell, the real-life amputee who had starred in *The Best Years of Our Lives*, spoke all over the state for me. He was a well-known Democrat, and that added to his value. Another of my volunteers was Leo Martin, a Massachusetts state police officer, whose widowed mother I had helped during my AMVET days to collect her husband's World War I pension. Leo, a popular Irishman from South Boston, joked that if I lost, the morning after the election he would find himself patrolling the New York state border in the distant Berkshires.

I campaigned as a reformer, vowing to expose graft and corruption wherever I found them in state politics. I did not raise the subject of my race. Frank Kelly did that for me. Just before the election, Jerry Williams did an hour-long program, first interviewing Frank Kelly, then me. As I sat in a small room waiting for my turn, I heard Kelly say, "Jerry, you know, if I were not a gentleman, I'd say that my opponent is a Negro man who has a white wife." Exposing the racist intolerance of that statement was the very first thing I did when it was my turn on the air. I simply said, "Jerry, I married the woman I loved. Mr. Kelly's statement is sad." It was hard to believe that Kelly would say something so offensive—not just to me but to the decency and intelligence of the voters. I took it to mean he was desperate.

In 1962, I began a tradition that I continued throughout my political career. On October 26 I celebrated my forty-third birthday with a one hundred dollar-a-plate fundraising dinner at the Sheraton Plaza in Boston. It was the first of many celebrity fundraisers that I would hold, featuring such stars as Roland Hayes, the great Negro tenor, the beloved actress Debbie Reynolds, world-famous pianist and comedian Victor Borge, the beautiful Lainie Kazan, and the incomparable Johnny Mathis. The overflow crowds loved them, and money poured in when I needed it most.

On November 6, I began what would become my Election Day custom of eating cherrystone clams on the half-shell and New England clam chowder at the counter of the North End's Union Oyster House, the oldest restaurant in Boston. That evening I awaited the results in a suite in the Copley Plaza Hotel with family and close friends. It was a long night. The early returns did not look good, in part because communities with voting machines, including Boston, reported first. But just after 1 A.M., when the votes came in from the Republican bastion of Wellesley, we finally pulled ahead. Soon after that, Roger Woodworth and others were telling me we were going to win. The old Democratic strongholds of Fall River, Lynn, and Lawrence were going for Kelly, but even there I was cutting deeply into the normal Democratic majority.

I was the only statewide Republican winner. Governor Volpe was losing to Endicott "Chub" Peabody by a hair. Others on our statewide ticket were being defeated as were many of our candidates for the legislature. A bit uncertainly, I went down to deliver my victory statement to my supporters and scores of TV, radio, and print reporters in the ballroom of the Copley Plaza. I began to speak, then turned away. Francis Kelly had not conceded. I turned to Roger and said, "Are you sure we have won?" "Perfectly sure," said Roger, so I proceeded. Kelly never conceded or offered his congratulations.

The final vote was 1,143,065 votes for me and 883,710 for Kelly. We had lost strongly Democratic Boston by only 29,903 votes; Kelly needed a 100,000-vote Boston majority to be competitive. The voters had ignored race and voted for change and for a spokesman of a new generation. It was a wonderful feeling to look out at the hundreds of people who had worked so hard for me, who now packed the ballroom and were delirious with happiness. I introduced Remigia and my mother and father, who were overwhelmed with the knowledge that their son had made history. Then I introduced my daughters.

"This is Remi and this is Edwina. They are both at least five years ahead of themselves." The crowd roared with cheers and laughter.

I had been up for about eighteen hours, but I had a lot to do before I could think of going to bed. I took a quick shower and went back to my headquarters, to thank the workers there. About 4 A.M., I went with Remigia, Remi, and Edwina to the *Boston Globe* to meet some journalists and ran into Ted Kennedy, Chub Peabody, and Francis Bellotti. Kennedy was the newly elected senator, Peabody the new governor, and Bellotti the new lieutenant governor. We exchanged pleasantries. The winner's circle is always a convivial place.

> Bellotti said, "Ed, we can work together." I smiled and said, "Frank, we'll have to."
>
> On election night, President Kennedy, checking on his brother's race, called a *Globe* reporter. "Teddy's ahead, Mr. President," the reporter assured him. "By the way, Brooke is way ahead. He's practically in."
>
> "My God," Kennedy replied, "that's the biggest news in the country."

Later that morning, after a few hours sleep, I met with my staff to discuss our next steps and how I planned to approach my new job. Then, exhausted, Remigia and I flew to San Juan, Puerto Rico, and then to St. Thomas in the U.S. Virgin Islands, for a few days in the sun.

My campaign confirmed my belief that although there are bigots in America, whose hateful rhetoric seizes the media's attention, the vast majority of people do not harbor such prejudice. Most Americans admire men and women of any race who dare to take the lead in improving our society. In 1962, we proved that.

8

Attorney

General

My fellow Massachusetts Republican, Calvin Coolidge, our thirtieth president, was a notably tight-lipped man. As he returned from church one Sunday, his wife asked him what the sermon had been about. Coolidge is said to have replied with a single word: "Sin." Pressed on what the preacher had said about sin, Coolidge added, "He was against it." Well, much of my work as attorney general was about sin. And I was against it. But I always tried to hate the sin, not the sinner. I had already been exposed to a lot of civic sin in my term with the Boston Finance Commission. In that city and throughout Massachusetts, a cloud of suspicion hung over public officials, good or bad. Rampant corruption, conflict of interest, bribes, and graft still threatened the democratic process. I believed my election was a mandate from the voters of Massachusetts to root out all the corruption I could.

At noon on January 16, 1963, in the overflowing House Chamber of the old Bulfinch State House in Boston, I was sworn in as the thirty-fifth attorney general of the Commonwealth of Massachusetts. I was the first African American to be elected attorney general in any of the fifty states. Sadly, it was another thirty years before another state elected an African American to that post, when Indiana voters chose Pamela Carter in 1992.

The attorney general is somewhat like the most senior partner in a large law firm who has to choose his partners and associates. In the months between my election and swearing in, the office was besieged by applicants, who were drawn by the promise of reform and my stated intention to hire outstanding, full-time assistant attorneys general. I asked Gael Mahony to chair an eight-member advisory committee to review the applicants, not on their political connections, but on their character, legal training, and achievements. This committee worked long and hard to examine every applicant and produce a list of prime candidates for me to interview personally. Fortunately, I had inherited a staff of dedicated civil servants who handled all personnel matters and much more. I relied heavily on the staff, especially the loyal and highly efficient Chief Clerk Russell Landrigan and his able assistant Edward White.

Soon after taking office, I announced the appointment of thirty-eight new, handpicked assistant attorneys general. My predecessors had permitted their assistant attorneys general to maintain their private practices while they worked part-time for the commonwealth, most of them for salaries of about $6,000 a year. The attorney general's job itself paid $15,000 a year. Those who created the political system in Massachusetts were often independently wealthy and believed that public service should not be a path to riches, and it certainly was not. But in 1963, the best lawyers could not afford to work full-time for $6,000. I went to House Speaker John Forbes Thompson and asked for full-time pay for my staff. He and the legislature complied, and I was able to raise the salaries of my top lawyers to a more competitive $12,000 to $15,000. The legislature even increased my salary to $25,000.

Four days after taking office, I served notice that business as usual was over. I acted in connection with a banquet the insurance industry had organized to honor Eugene Farnum, our state insurance commissioner. These banquets were a time-honored practice, designed to bring together the regulators and those they oversaw. Farnum was an honest public servant and a fellow Republican. It was clear to me that he had no nefarious purpose in agreeing to attend. But it was just as clear that the banquet was designed to create a cozy relationship between the insurance industry and its regulatory commissioner. Farnum's office had sent notice of the dinner over to my office for what they expected would be my routine approval. It was not granted. I explained that a statute was on the books prohibiting testimonial dinners of this sort. There was no doubt that such dinners were illegal, but no attorney general in memory had ever invoked the law. Tickets had already been sold, and preparations for the dinner had been completed. Many Republicans were angered by my decision. Democrats and the media were astonished. That was fine; I was sending a message.

On January 29, I vowed vigorous enforcement of a conflict of interest law then pending before the legislature. It covered potential conflicts for all public officials: full time and part time, appointed and elected, at every level of government. The idea was simple: no one should exploit public office for private gain. The law passed, and my office was soon issuing conflict of interest opinions to hundreds of state employees.

Following on my experiences with the Finance Commission, one of the first issues we tackled was misuse of eminent domain by the state, the taking of private land for a public purpose. Even when a state's eminent domain authorities act properly, it can be terribly painful for people to lose their land, and in Massachusetts these authorities were often arbitrary and rude. Moreover, politics often played a role in the decision making. During my campaign, scores of voters had told me horror stories of high-handed behavior by state land agencies. Appraisals and title searches were often hasty, inadequate, done without notice, and conducted after the decision to take the land had already been made. The Massachusetts Turnpike Authority had often seized land from citizens without written notice, paying them just one dollar, and defying them to sue the commonwealth if they objected. This ruthless course forced many landowners to panic and settle for less than their property was worth. It gave new meaning to the term *highway robbery*. I heard stories of landowners who got eviction notices and within thirty days had to abandon their property to the state or find their furniture moved into the street. Many other states required such agencies to pay for land before taking it. Not Massachusetts. People who went to court to protect their right to adequate compensation still had to abruptly find a new home. Reforms were long overdue.

At the same time, I wanted to make sure that property owners did not profit undeservedly. My Fin Com work had taught me how often Boston had overpaid for land owned by the unscrupulous or well connected. I appointed my old *Boston University Law Review* associate, Jack Bottomly, to be chief of the Eminent Domain Division of the attorney general's office. I instructed the division to make sure that property owners were offered a fair price but not a penny more. I told Jack that I would not second-guess the decisions he and his colleagues made. For a few months, I had a stream of telephone calls from lawyers and prominent citizens asking me to adjust a settlement upwards. I told them all that I had absolute faith in Jack Bottomly and his staff. The phone calls stopped; the word was out. Jack and his staff handled thousands of cases and saved the taxpayers many millions of dollars. Keeping my campaign promise to western Massachusetts, I appointed Assistant Attorney General Frank H. Freedman (later chief judge of the U.S. District Court), a Boston University friend and *Law Review* colleague, to man our office in Springfield, handling eminent domain cases and others.

In 1961, the state legislature had created the Massachusetts Crime Commission. Governor John Volpe had appointed seven outstanding citizens to the commission, headed by Boston lawyer Alfred Gardner. It was given subpoena power and immediately began looking into corruption in state government. Some people foresaw tension between my office and Gardner's office, but that was not to be. Our office worked closely with the Crime Commission's attorneys and investigators. When the commission determined it had credible evidence to present to a grand jury, I would review the evidence with Chairman Gardner and either accept or reject its recommendations. If it was acceptable, my office would present the evidence to the grand jury.

As the lone Republican among Massachusetts's constitutional officers, I was often accused of undertaking a Republican witch hunt. "All Brooke is doing is indicting Democrats," my critics would say. I would reply, "There's nobody here but Democrats." I was fortunate to be working so closely with Al Gardner, a man of integrity who proved himself a vigorous crime fighter. If the legislature had known what his commission was going to do, it probably would not have created it. The grand jury indicted the chief of the State Waterways Division of the Department of Public Works. My office prosecuted, and he was convicted. The grand jury indicted a former Republican Speaker of the Massachusetts House. He was convicted. The grand jury indicted several members of the Governor's Council, and they were convicted. The grand jury indicted the Massachusetts public safety commissioner; he was acquitted. The grand jury indicted others for conflict of interest, conspiracy, bribery, and perjury.

These convictions were widely publicized. The newspapers hailed me as a crime buster. Whenever our office won a major conviction, my staff and I experienced a real sense of accomplishment. We felt we were turning the tide of corruption. Yet I frequently reminded them that when we obtained a conviction, there was to be no gloating. "Act somber," I told them. "Our real enemy is the system, not the man; the sin, not the sinner." We tried to be sensitive to the rights of the accused. We recognized our duty to protect public officials from unfounded allegations.

One of the most important cases our office tried involved the Under Common Garage scandal. The Boston Common, the nation's oldest public park, running along the base of Beacon Hill adjoining the historic Bulfinch State House, is a beautiful and historic space, beloved by the people of Boston. But parking around the Common and on Beacon Hill had been a mess for a long time. During the 1950s, civic leaders, journalists, and the public had begun to debate the idea of building a garage under the Common. In 1958, Governor Foster Furculo convinced our state legislature to create the Massachusetts Parking Authority and to give it the power to build, operate, and maintain a garage under the Boston Common. The authority got its operating funds from a revenue-bond issue, under a statutory grant that exempted it from state supervision. This was a crucial mistake; it meant that the authority was excused from mandated competitive bidding and that no state auditor examined its records. In Boston, that was a blueprint for disaster.

In 1959, George Brady, a flamboyant former editorial writer for the Boston *Record American*, was appointed chairman of the Massachusetts Parking Authority. He needed a bonding company to underwrite the garage's cost and a contractor to build it. Later testimony alleged that he told some local contractors that the contract would cost them several hundred thousand dollars cash. In the end, the Foundation Company of New York City was awarded the contract. Whether it paid a bribe for it I do not know. But there is no doubt that Brady and some conspirators siphoned off huge amounts of money for themselves. Richard Gordon, a special justice of the Ipswich District Court was also involved in the scheme, as was his former law partner Richard Simmers. Simmers and Gordon took $100,000 for legal work that they never performed. Francis Kiernan, a construction engineer, got $344,468 for doing almost nothing. In his trial it was proven he had visited the garage site under Boston Common thirteen times over a two-year period, often so briefly that he kept his cab waiting. Brady and his cronies falsified records and stole about $750,000 in all.

My predecessor, Attorney General Edward McCormack, had broken the scandal in May 1962, about six months before my election. Many people thought that I should ask the lawyers he had assigned to the case to continue working on it. I disagreed and even considered trying the case myself, but my administrative responsibilities and common sense killed that idea. Instead I chose Gael Mahony, who had served so ably as counsel to the Boston Finance Commission, to handle this vital case, together with another first-rate attorney, William Dockser, and highly professional public accountant Seth Armen. As a pro bono gesture, Gael's law firm, Hill & Barlow, not the taxpayers, paid his salary. I stayed as involved as my duties would permit with Gael reporting to me on a regular basis.

There were two trials. The first came in April 1963 and examined the roles of Judge Richard Gordon, Richard Simmers, and Francis Kiernan. All three men were convicted of larceny and conspiracy, and received prison terms of five to five-and-a-half years each. In the second trial, in June and July of that year, three officials were charged with conspiracy and larceny. Two were found guilty and got the same sentences given out in the first trial: five to five-and-a-half years in prison. One was found not guilty. George Brady was committed to a mental health center in August 1963 and was afterward declared mentally incompetent to stand trial. He later vanished.

I considered our successful prosecution of the Under Common Garage offenders critical in the fight against corruption in Massachusetts state government. It was a big, important case, and it played a major role in keeping my promise to restore public confidence in government. As I saw it, we had brought the sinners to justice, but we still had to deal with the sin. Therefore, in October 1963, I proposed to the legislature that state law require all public authorities to hold their meetings in public, to open their records to the public, and to make their annual reports public. I also urged that we criminalize the falsifying of records of a public authority and open all public authority contracts over one thousand dollars to competitive bidding. All our proposals were accepted.

―――――――

We faced another controversy over the issue of religion in public schools. A Massachusetts statute required daily Bible reading in the schools. Then in 1963, the United States Supreme Court ruled unconstitutional a Pennsylvania statute almost identical to ours. Suddenly, everything had changed. Not only were our public schools no longer compelled to conduct Bible readings, they were prohibited from doing so. I issued a formal opinion paralleling the Supreme Court decision. I stressed that the principle at issue was not the merit of school prayer, but the need for every American to comply with Supreme Court decisions. There was no objection to students gathering on their own initiative to read the Bible before or after school and no objection to prayer at graduation exercises. But, when a school made devotional Bible verses part of its regular curriculum, it was disobeying the law of the land.

My opinion inspired a few irate citizens to burn me in effigy on the State House lawn, but the response was generally favorable. The Massachusetts commissioner of education, Owen B. Kiernan, sent my opinion to every school committee in Massachusetts and (proud that ours was the first such ruling in the country) to every commissioner of education in the other forty-nine states. Soon, 350 of the commonwealth's 351 towns complied with the law. Only North Brookfield did not. It was proud of its tradition of daily Bible reading in its public schools, and it meant to continue, no matter what Ed Brooke or the Supreme Court had to say.

Commissioner Kiernan forwarded to me a letter he had received from the school superintendent in North Brookfield, declaring that they would not comply with the Supreme Court's decision. I responded in a ten-page letter to the North Brookfield School Committee, asking them to help my office set up a meeting to explore how we could bring their schools into compliance with the law, without offending the spirit of the prayer program. In reply, I received a letter from the local school superintendent informing me that North Brookfield would have no conference with me or anyone in my office. They had asked for a hearing in the state's superior court, and until that was resolved, North Brookfield intended to break the law. I filed for a writ of mandamus to order the school committee to comply with the law. The state's Supreme Judicial Court upheld my position.

I still hoped to win the support and understanding of the people of North Brookfield. I requested an open meeting with the citizens, to be hosted by the North Brookfield School Committee. The meeting was held in a local church. As I walked down the center aisle that night, I could feel the anger and hostility. Speaking at the front of the church, I explained that my oath of office, and my own conscience, compelled me to seek uniform compliance with the law. The audience listened politely, and I listened to them with equal care. When I left there were many warm and friendly comments. I am convinced that if we listen to people and treat them with respect, basic commonality can usually be achieved. In a nation of laws most individuals and groups will accept the law of the land, if they feel they have had their say. This proved to be true in the case of North Brookfield.

I could only accept a fraction of the speaking invitations I received. One that I did agree to took me to the University of Utah on November 22, 1963. The invitation came from the Reverend Lawrence P. Sweeney of the Newman Foundation, a Catholic organization with offices in Salt Lake City. Because Utah was at that time the only state outside of the South that did not have at least one civil rights law, I chose to speak on racial justice. I was giving my speech when a nun raced up to me and whispered that President Kennedy had been shot. My reaction, like that of millions of others, was shock and disbelief. As calmly as I could, I told the audience what the nun had told me. I expressed my deepest and heartfelt sympathy to them and left the platform. It was all the worse to break the news to an audience of students, nuns, and priests to whom John F. Kennedy was such a beloved hero.

The next week was an awful one for the entire nation and especially for Massachusetts. John F. Kennedy had traveled a long way from the young man I had met eleven years before. He had inspired the nation, won worldwide respect and affection, and made millions of Americans believe in their government again. I had seen him for the last time five months before when he had called me to the White House to attend a meeting with some leading attorneys to discuss civil rights legislation.

From Governor Peabody on down the line, no elected Democrat in Massachusetts could afford to miss the Kennedy funeral in Washington. It therefore made sense for me, as the state's only Republican constitutional office holder, to stay behind and mind the store. I was thus acting governor for one of the saddest days in the history of the commonwealth. In the aftermath of the Kennedy assassination, public officials realized more than ever how vulnerable they are to seriously disturbed persons. Some of my associates were concerned about my safety. It was true that I received more than my share of bizarre letters and death threats. If you get enough threats, you have to be concerned that one might be serious. Once or twice we added additional bodyguards for a few days after a particularly vivid threat. But mostly I ignored these intrusions. Leo Martin, the state police officer who had volunteered for my campaign, and my old friend Bill Jackson, were my bodyguards, and I trusted them. They and Nicholas "Nick" Nikitas, another valued staff assistant, occupied a small room at the entrance to our office on the second floor of the State House. Their job was to screen anyone who came to see me, including an array of eccentric individuals who would show up every month on the day of the full moon. I had never believed in this myth, but like many in law enforcement I came to agree that the full moon brings out many strange characters.

Given good protection, and a certain fatalism that came from my wartime experience, I never changed my routines. I walked the same route to my car, drove home the same route, walked into and out of my office usually at the same time, in the same way. I continued to walk in parades, make speeches, and attend conventions. You cannot be a politician and avoid people. My staff might worry, but I could not do my work living in fear. My experience in public life was that the serious threats did not come from unstable individuals but from more sinister forces that use more subtle means than a high-powered rifle to bring down their political foes. Soon after I had been sworn in as attorney general, some IRS agents arrived in my office and said they wanted to see me. I assumed they had come on a legal matter. Instead, they informed me I was being audited.

Since my days at the Boston Finance Committee, I had found little time to take care of personal financial matters. I left the payment of bills, keeping of records, and filing of tax returns to my secretary and accountants. I trusted them to handle these chores and leave me free to do my job. Before I got into politics, my friend Al Brothers and my secretary Oitzelle Epps kept my records and prepared my tax returns. Later, attorney Herb Tucker, who had worked for the IRS, prepared my returns. I signed them, but I rarely read them. It was not a smart thing to do, especially for a lawyer. But I did. I had faith in the people I authorized to act for me, and that faith was never misplaced.

To my astonishment the agents asked for all my financial records and my income tax returns for 1959, 1960, and 1961, and they asked some strikingly petty questions. I later found out that they had asked Howard University's Alumni Fund treasurer if I had indeed sent Howard University a check for five dollars. Officials of the Opera Company of Boston were asked to swear in an affidavit that they had received a donation of fifty dollars. They even asked a Cambridge clothing store to produce a record of a seventy-five-dollar payment I had made there. My tax lawyer, John F. Kendrick, reassured me that he had reviewed my records and "there is no basis for the audit. We will just let it run its course." So we did. After several months of investigation and the expenditure of thousands of dollars of taxpayers' money, the IRS concluded that I owed no additional tax.

Many of my friends thought I was being audited because I was a Republican attorney general who had vowed to crack down on corruption in a state run by Democrats. I never knew the truth about what motivated the audit, but I suspected that some people thought they could intimidate me. If they came up empty, they had still gotten my attention and wasted my time and money. If they found something, they could use it to undercut my anticorruption campaign. Whether the idea originated at the state or the federal level, I do not know. But history proves that they did not scare me. I had my supporters. James Doyle of the *Boston Globe* wrote a stirring defense, blasting the IRS investigation. Maybe I should have made more of an outcry. Some friends thought the scrutiny was racially motivated and that I should say so. But I never wanted to play the race card. I cooperated with the investigation and put it out of my mind. I was prepared for abuse. I did not like it, but it came with the territory.

One emotional issue I faced as attorney general came when Negro parents and opponents of school segregation proposed that Negro schoolchildren be kept home from school on February 26, 1964, to protest racial segregation in Boston public schools. In the first of many conflicts that would culminate in the 1970s with the Boston Schools Desegregation Case, the proposed boycott was an attempt to focus the state and the nation's attention on segregation.

Commissioner Kiernan, faced with a boycott and the prospect of thousands of children missing school, requested a ruling from the attorney general. He asked three questions: (1) if such a boycott was legal; (2) if it was not, then what the legal remedies were; and (3) whose responsibility it was to enforce the law. His request put this highly emotional issue in my hands. I was aware that in Massachusetts the opinions of the attorney general are usually followed until successfully challenged in court. By any measure, that is a lot of power. I thought busing, because of the systemic segregation-by-design that characterized Boston's public schools, was a necessary tactic to arrive at desegregation. But after researching Massachusetts's statutes, I concluded that the law clearly did not allow keeping children out of school for the purpose of protest. In an opinion issued sixteen days before the proposed boycott, I said that absence from school is unlawful if permission is not given, and that it was the responsibility of the local school committees to enforce attendance laws.

The black community was highly upset with my opinion. They felt I was supporting the antibusing faction in Boston and its outspoken leader, Louise Day Hicks. At one point I spoke to several hundred parents who crowded into Roxbury's Freedom House. The room was filled with angry parents, many of whom were my longtime friends. I told them that I understood their position and sympathized with their attempt to protest an injustice. But I also understood that keeping children out of school for the purpose of protest was in violation of Massachusetts law. It is true that my position was exploited by Hicks and her followers. They relished their legal victory even more because a black attorney general had rendered the opinion. My standing in the civil rights community suffered, and there was talk that I was selling out. In my view, I was simply doing my duty to uphold the law. To do otherwise, in my opinion, would truly be selling out and would do an injustice to blacks as well. When the day came, some parents sent their children to school and others kept them home, but we had done what we had to do to comply with the law.

The political event that caused me the most pain in 1964 was not a local issue but a national one. I had joined the Republican Party in part because I admired some of the moderates who were among its national leaders—men like Nelson Rockefeller, Dwight Eisenhower, and in my own state Henry Cabot Lodge and Leverett Saltonstall. But 1964 was not a year of moderation for the Republican Party. I was elected a Massachusetts delegate-at-large to the Republican National Convention in San Francisco, one of a handful of Negro delegates elected to participate. Our uncommitted slate had defeated a slate loyal to Senator Barry Goldwater of Arizona decisively in the presidential preference primary. Massachusetts Republicans gave almost seventy-one thousand votes to our favorite son, moderate Henry Cabot Lodge, and fewer than ten thousand to Goldwater, making it clear that we did not want the ultraconservative Goldwater as our nominee.

At the National Convention I favored New York Governor Nelson Rockefeller. When the Rockefeller movement failed, I backed another moderate, Governor William Scranton of Pennsylvania and gave a seconding speech for him. But we moderates were outgunned. We saw our party taken over by zealous right-wingers. To me, theirs was a pseudoconservatism, sharply at odds with our party's honored past. Their racial views would have appalled Abraham Lincoln. Their contempt for our environment would have disgusted Theodore Roosevelt. Their blind hatred of every federal program was a slap at every veteran who had used the GI Bill to go to college or buy a house.

In 1964, civil rights was an idea whose time had come. America had seen the sit-in movement and the Freedom Rides in the South (and the ugly, violent resistance to them); had heard the eloquence of Dr. Martin Luther King Jr.; and now, under the Democratic leadership of Lyndon Johnson, was witnessing important civil rights legislation about to move through Congress. The party of Lincoln should have led the way. Instead we missed a historic opportunity. The archconservatives who had rallied around Barry Goldwater did not believe that equal access to schools, hospitals, restaurants, and hotels were basic American rights. A tragic result of their ascendance was that the party of Lincoln did not back the Civil Rights Act of 1964. Of course, the ultraconservatives rarely admitted to racism or to opposing equal rights. They would say they were defending states' rights or were opposing the intrusion of the federal government into private matters. But the practical result of their position was to deny opportunity to black Americans at a time when the majority of Americans wanted progress and social justice.

Their obstructionism was painful to all moderate Republicans but particularly to me. I had braved a lot of hostility and ridicule to urge blacks to become Republicans. I told them we should not allow ourselves to be taken for granted by the Democrats. Rather, I believed that minority groups, limited in strength, should use shrewd alliances to make the most of their power. But after Barry Goldwater, the Republican nominee for president, rejected the Civil Rights Act of 1964, it was difficult, if not impossible, for a black Republican like myself to recruit other blacks into the Republican Party.

America is the only country in the world that classifies as Negro any person who has one drop of African blood in his or her veins. As a boy, when I first heard this, I thought, black blood must surely be powerful. How insecure white America must be to fear one drop of blood. But I also thought how ridiculous the whole issue of skin color is. People of all shades want basic freedoms. We all want good jobs, good housing, good education, respect, and a future for our children. The 1964 convention should have been a wonderful moment for me.

National conventions still meant something then. Important decisions were made. The television networks covered the assembly gavel
to gavel. I gave not one but three speeches. In addition to seconding
the Scranton nomination, I spoke on behalf of a civil rights plank for
our party platform and introduced former President Eisenhower to
the convention.

But the Goldwater forces set the tone of the convention. They
delayed Nelson Rockefeller's speech until near midnight (3 A.M. back
on the East Coast), and then the delegates greeted him with three
minutes of booing. Worse, they promoted an "Operation Dixie" campaign. It was a crude attempt to exploit white anger about the progress
of civil rights, especially in the South. Nor did the candidate help his
cause when he declared in his acceptance speech that "extremism in
the name of liberty is no vice." All this made inevitable Lyndon
Johnson's landslide victory in November. The black vote across the
country was the greatest rejection of a major party candidate by any
single racial or ethnic group in American history. But white voters
also deserted Goldwater. He carried his native Arizona and five states
in the Deep South, and lost everywhere else. The Operation Dixie
strategy cost our party millions of votes and hundreds of offices at
every level of government.

Despite the Goldwater fiasco, in my campaign for reelection as
attorney general in 1964, running against former State Senator
James W. Hennigan, I swept to victory with 1,543,900 votes, and a
plurality of almost 800,000 votes. It was the largest plurality of any
Republican in Massachusetts history and the largest plurality of any
Republican in the country that year. The commonwealth had 351
cities and towns. We carried 349 of them. We lost only two small
towns, Blackstone and Millville, deeply Democratic mill towns on
the Rhode Island border. It was a great victory but a bittersweet one,
when I surveyed the ruins of our state and national party that the
Goldwater candidacy had brought. Fortunately, John Volpe was elected
governor and Elliot Richardson was elected lieutenant governor.

After the nominating convention, the national Republican leadership expected me to paper over my differences with Goldwater and
campaign for him against Lyndon Johnson. It would have been the
expedient course, enhancing my position in the national party and

with conservative Republicans in Massachusetts, but it was a course I could not follow in good conscience. I refused to support Goldwater. During the fall, Goldwater held a huge rally at Fenway Park, and I was the only Republican candidate for statewide office who did not attend. He noted my absence by saying, "I am so sorry my good friend Ed Brooke is otherwise engaged and cannot be here with us this evening," a remark received with boos, laughter, and the anger of the party faithful, who long remembered my act of party disloyalty.

Although I did not support Goldwater, I never attacked him personally. He was a likeable man, and I understood that on issue after issue, he had voted his convictions. Without doubt, his principles came before his politics. So did mine. However, our convictions and principles were far apart. But many of his supporters, who loved him for his adherence to his principles, resented *my* adherence to *my* principles. Many party regulars saw my failure to endorse the ticket as an act of disloyalty. A few of my campaign workers resigned in protest. My stand against Goldwater haunted me for the rest of my political career. But I felt I was serving not only my conscience but the best interests of my country and the party.

After the election, Goldwater conceded that his rejection of the Civil Rights Act had helped seal his disastrous defeat. Yet, amazingly, he said, "Honestly, I would do it again." That lit a fire under me. Not only was his candidacy an utter failure, but he would not admit his mistakes. The Democrats geared their program to voters' daily needs, addressed the great social movements changing America, and offered solutions to voters' problems. Republican leaders seemed to deny the very existence of the problems. Not surprisingly, a strong majority voted Democratic. Politics of course is unpredictable. Four years later, after the escalation in Vietnam and assassinations and riots in America, Johnson's landslide victory of 1964 was forgotten, and he chose not to seek reelection, whereupon a much more agile Republican candidate than Goldwater, Richard Nixon, narrowly won the White House.

American politics needs two healthy political parties. After the 1964 election, I called for a national Republican conference to rebuild the party. On NBC's *Meet the Press*, I suggested we invite Goldwater and others of our party to try to hammer out an agreement on the future of the party. I hoped we could draft responsible Republican positions on Social Security and health care, and on bread-and-butter issues crucial to women, minorities, the young, the poor, the elderly, and the ill housed, the very groups that had rejected us in droves on Election Day.

My proposal drew little support in our still bitterly divided party, so instead I wrote a book, *The Challenge of Change: Crisis in Our Two-Party System* (Boston: Little, Brown, 1966). In it I tried to make the case for moderate Republicanism and urged that we find a better tool than racist appeals to bring white southerners into our party. In the book I chided the conservative wing of the Republican Party: "It is safe to say that millions of Americans do not take us seriously as a party that can be trusted to govern." I also said, "Our over-riding, overwhelming distrust of big government as the 'Great Evil of Our Time' must be abandoned. . . . Does anyone seriously believe that order, education, opportunity, racial justice and social betterment are going to produce themselves without participation of government?" My book attracted no attention and won me few friends among Republican leaders. The truth is, my party's leadership was never really comfortable with me or I with it.

Since joining the Republican Party, I have strongly advocated the merits of centrism. I believe it is right for the country. Historically we have rejected extremism on the left and the right. Centrism is the right course for America. John P. Avalon, a prolific and bold writer for the *New York Sun*, in his insightful book *Independent Nation*, writes, "Centrism is not only a winning political strategy, but an enlightened governing philosophy that best respects the will of the people by putting patriotism ahead of partisanship and the national interests ahead of special interests." Amen.

Politics aside, 1964 was a hard year for me. On January 9, my father died at the age of seventy-four. My high school and college classmate Dr. William H. Bullock did all he could, but my father could not be saved. He died of cirrhosis of the liver. He was a good man and a good father who contributed greatly to whatever success I achieved. I was consoled that he had lived to see me elected attorney general of Massachusetts. My mother always said he died a very proud father.

Late in 1964, we sold our four-decker home in Roxbury and purchased a single-family home in Newton. Remigia found a new split-level house on the corner of Beacon Street and Hammond Pond Parkway. I never liked the house. I thought the location was better suited for a gas station, but it became our home and to this day is occupied by my daughter Edwina and grandsons Vincent and Christophe.

As attorney general, it was not uncommon for me to work long days into the night and on weekends. I could shake hands for three hours, meet with my staff, go home, shower for ten minutes, lie down for ten more minutes and feel refreshed and ready for a dinner engagement. But those long hours exacted a toll, and my marriage was under ever mounting strain. In addition, the girls were growing up, perhaps too fast. Remi, at thirteen, and Edwina, at ten, had both learned how to manipulate their mother. Our home life often turned into a screaming match, with Remigia yelling at the girls and the girls at her. I decided that both girls would be better off in private schools, where they would have more consistent discipline and greater stability.

Remigia wanted the girls to attend schools close to home. But in this matter, unlike many others governing the girls, I prevailed. I enrolled Remi in Wyckham Rise, an academically challenging Episcopal boarding school with a beautiful campus in Washington, Connecticut. Both Remi and Edwina had attended Beaver Country Day School. When the time came for Edwina to begin high school I chose House-in-the-Pines, a progressive boarding school in Norton, Massachusetts, near Wheaton College.

But even with the girls away, the arguments continued.

Early in 1965, I flew to St. Thomas to visit my sister Helene and her husband Bun, who had just been diagnosed with a smoking-related cancer. Some time before, my sister Helene had retired from teaching and she and Bun had moved to Puerto Rico, where at first Bun had captained a ferryboat running from Puerto Rico to St. Thomas, a boat in which I had had a financial interest. Later they moved to St. Thomas, where Bun worked as a police training officer and where Helene worked with the Virgin Island Department of Tourism. Bun's illness was the latest tragedy to strike them since their three-year-old Patsy was killed by a car in 1945. Patsy's death had a corrosive effect on both Helene and Bun. He gave up on God and on himself. Helene also lost her faith and withdrew into a private world. For years, she asked why God had let her child die. She avoided her friends and sought consolation in food, which led to excessive weight and serious health problems. My beautiful and beloved older sister, a gifted and dedicated English teacher and a good mother, suffered terribly. It was horrible to watch.

I had gone to St. Thomas to spend some quiet and prayful time with them, but while I was there, tragedy struck back in Massachusetts. One freezing January night, Remi telephoned from her boarding school in Connecticut and said she was sick and wanted to come home. Remigia decided to drive to school to retrieve her. For some reason our family car was not running properly. Remigia took her mother and jumped in a state car parked in front of our garage and headed for Washington, Connecticut. It was not my official car, but an unregistered, uninsured state Dodge sedan meant to be used for state emergency purposes only. To Remigia, *this* was an emergency.

Remigia was driving with her mother in the seat beside her when they collided with another car in a blinding snowstorm on Route 47 in Connecticut. They were not going very fast, and Remigia's injuries were minor. But Teresa's back was injured. Firemen gave her a sedative and took her to Waterbury General Hospital, where her injuries were found to be more serious than first suspected. She was left a quadriplegic and spent most of the rest of her life in hospitals or nursing homes.

Massachusetts newspaper reports of the accident focused not on the devastating injury to my mother-in-law but on the fact that the state car was neither registered nor insured and was not being used for state business. In a grandstanding gesture, the Connecticut traffic commissioner quickly banned all Massachusetts state cars from Connecticut highways. Twenty-four hours later, Massachusetts had insured all of its state cars, and the ban was lifted.

With Teresa in need of long-term medical care, Remigia asked Jack Bottomly to pursue a tort claim for her. He found a Connecticut law firm to handle her case. The driver of the other vehicle, a rental car, had no license. Several years later, Teresa was awarded a $100,000 settlement by the insurer of the rental car. After attorney's fees, she received $68,000. Teresa and her three children, Remigia, Mina, and Pino, asked me to hold the settlement money and to make payments as she directed. I did not want to hold Teresa's money, but she insisted that she trusted me and knew I would look out for her best interests. Reluctantly, I did as she asked. I placed the money in my checking account and asked Caryle Connelly, a trusted assistant, to keep a record, to write checks for Teresa's doctors, ambulance services, or any other purpose Teresa, Remigia, and her siblings might direct.

My friend and tax preparer, Herb Tucker, later chief judge of the Dukes County District Court, had suggested that I set up a trust account. "Oh, Herb, let's keep it simple," I said. "One account will be easier for Caryle to handle. This is a family matter and not a large amount of money. I think this is the best way to do it." Thus, I placed the money in my account at Teresa's insistence, and with Remigia, Mina, and Pino's knowledge and approval. My decision on the "best way" to handle my mother-in-law's insurance money would come back to haunt me.

9

The Strange

Case of

the Boston

Strangler

These days murder in our cities is distressingly commonplace, but forty years ago, seemingly random killings were a unique phenomenon. The notorious killer who became known as the Boston Strangler first struck on June 14, 1962, when he strangled a fifty-six-year-old housewife with her own bathrobe sash. Every few weeks thereafter, continuing through January 4, 1964, another woman was strangled to death in her own home in or around Boston. Eventually, eleven murders were directly attributed to this elusive killer. Because there were no signs of forced entry, it was believed that either the killer knew the women or had talked his way into their homes. He strangled the women, often sexually violated them, and left their corpses in obscene poses. The initial victims were mostly older women of northern European ancestry, who led modest, respectable lives. The later victims were mostly younger. One was an African American. Most were assaulted from behind and strangled, often with their own stockings, which were left tied in a bow. The details suggested strongly that we were not dealing with a burglar surprised by the presence of victims but with a psychopath.

It was assumed that the killer was a solitary male, but that was not certain.

As Boston area police launched the most extensive criminal investigation in American history, the community was gripped with fear. Hardware stores ran out of door and window locks. Pet stores sold out of guard dogs. People barricaded themselves in their homes, refusing entrance to strangers on legitimate business. Women feared to walk the streets, took cabs to their destinations, and tipped the drivers extra to walk them to their doors. Older women hid their stockings before they retired for the night, lest they be strangled with them. Men were fearful for the safety of their mothers, wives, daughters, and girlfriends. Remigia and I took every possible precaution to safeguard Remi and Edwina.

By the time the brutal rape and murder of a nineteen-year-old girl named Mary Sullivan occurred on January 4, 1964, hundreds of people had called my office demanding that we catch the Strangler. Police had questioned more than a thousand suspects, including every known sexual deviant in the Greater Boston area, and turned up not a single tangible clue. Local police were handling the case, as was customary, but they were under fire in the media for their lack of success. It was increasingly clear that the investigation was crippled by the fact that the crimes had occurred in so many jurisdictions. Women had been strangled in three counties: Suffolk, Middlesex, and Essex; and in five different cities: Boston, Cambridge, Lynn, Lawrence, and Salem. Repeated efforts to achieve cooperation among the several jurisdictions had failed.

On January 17, 1964, I took the unprecedented action of assuming responsibility for the coordination of the investigation of these murders. I based my action on specific provisions of state law. On that day I called a meeting in my office and invited the district attorneys of the three counties, the commissioner of the Boston Police Department, the chief law enforcement officers of the communities involved, and the captain of the state police detectives. I stressed that I was not trying to usurp their powers. I said our joint purpose must be to find the Strangler and in the meantime to reassure the people of Massachusetts that everything possible was being done. There was some resentment and charges that I was exploiting a gruesome tragedy for political gain, but with Boston gripped by terror, the killer still at large, and the investigation going nowhere, I believed I had a duty to take action. (From a political point of view, the case was likely to do me more harm than good, at least if the killer was not found.)

Although police had attributed fifteen unsolved homicides to the Strangler, four of the cases did not fit the pattern, whereas the other eleven were so similar that they were probably the work of one person. We agreed to leave those four investigations to the local police, unless subsequent facts merited their inclusion. I announced the creation of a central Strangler Investigation Bureau in my office, to be headed by Assistant Attorney General John Bottomly, who had done such an outstanding job heading our Eminent Domain Division. There was some grumbling by law enforcement officers who questioned both the need for the bureau and Jack's qualifications. It was true that Jack had no background in criminology. He was neither a prosecutor nor a criminal lawyer. But I knew him to be a man with a passion for detail and a bold, creative administrator. I trusted him completely. Jack brought Julian Soshnick with him from the Eminent Domain Division. Julian proved invaluable in setting up our coordination process and evaluating the massive flow of information that came through our office. I had no desire to micromanage their daily work, but I did insist that I be briefed daily and make the final decisions.

I found a room near my own office in the State House and made it the headquarters of the Strangler Bureau, as it came to be called. I told everyone, "Anything that can solve these crimes is worth doing. No stone will remain unturned." Throughout the investigation, Jack and I kept asking what kind of sickness drives a man to strangle a series of women he does not know. We consulted medical doctors, pathologists, psychiatrists, psychologists, a medical anthropologist, sociologists, hypnoanalysts, chemists, and other experts. We set up a medical-psychiatric committee to profile the kind of individual who would commit these crimes. I added a top psychologist well versed in the criminal mind. Erle Stanley Gardner, author of the Perry Mason novels, came to discuss the case with us.

At first, I hoped the case would be solved in a matter of weeks.

Police assured me that there is no perfect crime. Even polished criminals make mistakes. Psychopaths are rarely polished criminals, and stranglers leave clues. Surely we would find one of those clues. But as the months passed, despite our massive investigation, none turned up. At my request, Governor Peabody posted a $5,000 reward for information leading to the arrest of anyone who had committed one or more of the murders. The amount seems paltry by today's standards, but in 1964, $5,000 was a significant sum. Two months later, I asked him to raise it to $10,000. Still no one collected. We urged the public to report all suspicious behavior to their local or state police or to contact our Strangler Bureau telephone hot line. By August, we had received more than 1,200 tips from all over the world. Many were plausible, and we checked them out one by one. Other tips came from cranks and crackpots. We had cards and letters saying the Boston Strangler was everyone from Chou En-Lai to Clare Boothe Luce to Robert Kennedy to Jimmy Hoffa.

Soon after I entered the case I had a phone call from my dear friend Kivie Kaplan, a Boston philanthropist whose tireless efforts on behalf of the NAACP had generated income without which the organization might not have survived its expensive legal battles of the 1950s and early 1960s. Kivie told me that the Strangler situation was awful. I agreed.

Then he said, "Don't laugh, but I'm going to make a recommendation."

"I don't laugh at any idea from Kivie Kaplan," I said.

"I want you to bring in a man named Peter Hurkos to help you find the Strangler," said Kivie somberly.

"Who in the world is Peter Hurkos?" I asked.

Kivie told me that Peter Hurkos was a Dutch clairvoyant who could talk to police, visit a crime scene, and use psychic evidence to create a detailed profile of the criminal. Hurkos, he said, had helped solve murders in many different countries. In those days, psychics were an anomaly, and I was far more skeptical of their value than I am today. So my first response was, "Come on, Kivie . . ."

But my friend insisted he was dead serious. I spun around in my chair and looked out over the Boston Common. Should I inject a psychic into a conventional police investigation? I knew what the police would say. And I was clairvoyant enough to foresee the newspaper headlines: "Brooke Hires Dutch Psychic with State Funds."

"Kivie, I can't ask the Commonwealth of Massachusetts to pay to bring in a psychic. Society has not yet accepted psychics as part of law enforcement."

"You don't have to ask the commonwealth," he said. "I'll cover Hurkos's fee and all of his expenses. But I want to do it anonymously."

The next day we talked again over lunch. He made clear that he and some other concerned citizens would pay for the psychic. I still held back. Then Kivie reminded me of my public pledge to leave no stone unturned in our search for the killer. If we were willing to check out hundreds of anonymous tips, how could I reject a man with an international reputation for finding murderers? I asked Jack Bottomly to try to verify the claims that my friend had made about Peter Hurkos. As it turned out, Jack was receptive to the idea. Once, at a party, he had met a Hungarian psychic who had startled him by telling Jack things about his life that he had forgotten himself. Jack's own mother was intrigued by psychic phenomena and had suggested to him the use of a psychic in the Strangler case.

Jack gave me a book by an author named Jess Stearn called *Door to the Future* that had a long chapter on Peter Hurkos. It described how Hurkos could visit a crime scene and receive messages from the "auras, emanations or lingering life force clinging to that scene." Hurkos had been a house painter in German-occupied Holland when he fell thirty-five feet from a ladder, fractured his skull, went into a coma, and awakened three days later with psychic powers. When he regained consciousness he reportedly looked at the doctor standing over him and said, "The Nazis think you're a Jew." The doctor paled and left the hospital never to return.

Jack called police in many cities where Hurkos had worked. The results were startling. Again and again, police officials who began as skeptics ended as believers. Jack urged me to bring him in as a consultant, and I decided to give it a try. Jack traced Hurkos to Beverly Hills, where he was meeting with the actor Glenn Ford, who was working with actress Doris Day to make a TV movie about the Dutchman's life. At first Hurkos wanted no part of the Boston Strangler case. But Glenn Ford and Doris Day persuaded him to take it on, for the sake of all the terrified people in Boston (and possibly to give a sensational end to their movie).

Hurkos insisted on one condition: no press scrutiny. He believed that onlookers impaired his psychometric gift. But despite our best efforts at secrecy, word got out that I was consulting a psychic. On Friday afternoon, January 24, I called in the press and confirmed that I had asked Peter Hurkos to help us find the Boston Strangler. I told them I would conduct press briefings as the investigation progressed, but that Hurkos needed privacy to do his work. Both local and national reporters were present, and I asked them all to join in a voluntary embargo of the Hurkos story. At first, the reporters were incredulous, but to their great credit, they cooperated, without exception. It was a remarkable act of collaboration in their highly competitive business. I encountered resistance from some of my allies in politics and law enforcement, and Boston Police Commissioner Edmund McNamara, a former FBI agent, believed that putting any faith in psychometry made a mockery of law enforcement. "Why don't you just fire all my detectives and hire a bunch of gypsies with crystal balls to solve crimes?" McNamara asked.

Hurkos and his bodyguard, Jim Crane, reached New England on January 29. To protect his privacy, we had them fly to Theodore Green Airport, in nearby Providence, Rhode Island. Jack Bottomly, Julian Soshnick, and Leo Martin drove there to meet them. Hurkos was described to me as a husky man in his forties, with curly black hair and quick, dark eyes, who spoke accented English. He had quite an ego, but he was also quite a psychic. Jack and Leo took Hurkos and Crane to the Battle Green Motel in Lexington, where we had reserved rooms under a fictitious name. On the way there, they stopped at a Howard Johnson's. In the restaurant, Hurkos stared at Leo Martin and abruptly said, "You think I'm a faker!" Leo was thinking exactly that, but to be polite he said, "Oh, no, oh, no . . . " Hurkos proceeded to ask Leo about his mother's troubled eye and if she had gotten the glasses she needed. Leo was astounded. Hurkos rattled off many details of Leo's family life. Only one thing did not check out. Hurkos told Leo that Leo's wife, Jennie, had fallen down a flight of stairs as a girl, leaving her spine slightly curved. When he finally arrived home at 3 A.M., Leo woke his wife to ask her if, as a girl, she had ever fallen down a flight of stairs. Surprised, she said yes she had, and that the injury had slightly curved her spine. She had never told him that before.

Leo rushed to my office the next morning. "Boss, this guy Hurkos is really something. He wants to meet you. You're one of his heroes." "Oh, no," I told him. "I don't want to meet him." I never did. I had already gone out on a limb to bring this man into the investigation. Instinct told me to keep my distance. When I released the media from the Hurkos embargo on February 6, one newspaper cartoon portrayed me as a witch doctor and another as a turbaned swami, which was quite a bit different from my image as a crime buster.

Hurkos stayed in the Boston area six days, working mostly from his Lexington motel room. He complained that he slept poorly, that he was troubled by flickering images of many of the people who had stayed in the suite before him. Shifts of police kept everyone out of the motel suite, even the maids. One evening, a Boston detective arrived late for his shift at the motel. He blamed a breakdown of his police car. Hurkos declared angrily, "You're not late because car broke down!" He went on to say loudly that the detective had been delayed by a raucous sexual interlude with a girlfriend. The detective tried to deny it, but as Hurkos described the encounter in graphic detail, he finally begged for mercy. Another time, investigators showed him crime scene photos but to test him, they included a few photos from an unrelated murder case. Hurkos rubbed the photos and picked out the false ones right away. "Phony baloney!" he cried. "Phony baloney!"

One day, Hurkos, Crane, and Soshnick were in Bottomly's office when Leo Martin rushed in and cried, "I've got something!" It was a letter from the dean of the Boston College nursing school. Without reading the letter, Hurkos said—accurately—that the letter contained a report that an odd little man had been accosting nursing students at Boston College, while claiming to be a shoe salesman. Hurkos demanded a map of Boston and pointed to what he insisted was the exact location of the shoe salesman's home. He already thought this might be the Strangler. All four men jumped in an unmarked state police car and drove to that address. On the way over, Hurkos said that the man they would find there slept directly on his bedsprings, without a mattress, and wore shoes when taking showers.

On arrival, Hurkos pointed to a building. The janitor there confirmed that a man who fit that description did live in the building. He directed them to the apartment, but the man was not at home. When investigators later found him at a nearby church, the man was most cooperative, but he was a very odd, shy, birdlike character, as our medical-psychiatric experts had predicted the Strangler would be. He also turned out to be a shoe salesman. His shower stall was scuffed with shoe marks. And he kept his mattress under his bed and slept on the bedsprings. His apartment contained photographs of women, cut from magazines, many in grotesque positions, some of them with knives drawn through them, and ligatures drawn around their necks. That could mean he was the Strangler, but it could also mean he was simply a fan of the Strangler. The man was deeply troubled. His brother had been trying to get professional help for him. We found a doctor who was willing to sign committal papers, and he was detained in a state mental hospital while detectives searched his apartment for clues. They found no direct evidence tying him to the killings. Hurkos was restless. He kept saying, "I want my baby!" He was making long phone calls to his girlfriend in Hollywood, the actress Sherree North, and was anxious to be with her. I decided that rather than have him return to California, it would be best to have her join him, so we flew Miss North to Boston. It did not help. In the end, convinced that the shoe salesman was the Strangler, Peter Hurkos left the investigation. He was a colorful and interesting character, but as far as we could see, he had not solved our case.

His employment was not the only unorthodox approach that we considered or used. Jack Bottomly wrote me a memo outlining the case for using drugs as an investigative tool. Psychiatrists frequently used substances such as sodium amytal and sodium pentothal as diagnostic and treatment aids. But Jack's memo recommended we go a step further and start using "truth serums" in our criminal investigation. Bottomly suggested we seek a court order for the administration of one of these drugs to three men being held in Bridgewater State Hospital, a facility for the criminally insane, who were suspected of complicity in one or more strangulation homicides. I was concerned about the legality of the use of drugs in interrogation and asked Assistant Attorney General Lee Kozol, then chief of our Civil Rights Division, for an opinion. He said that if our office utilized the drugs as an investigative tool, we would clearly be violating the right against self-incrimination. Our scruples might seem old-fashioned and self-limiting by today's circumstances, when numerous coercive methods are applied, contrary to our own Constitution and the rules of international law. But while we were, in fact, dealing with a "terrorist" in our community, I knew at the time—and I still strongly believe—that the rule of law is the strongest protection for all our citizens. I ruled out truth serums.

Another modern method was employed with great success, however; we were the first jurisdiction in the country to use computer technology to sort through clues and to help solve a crime. The case reports sent to us by all of the police departments and district attorneys offices filled thirty-seven thousand sheets of paper. To help us cope with this material, the Xerox Corporation volunteered not only the use of its equipment but the time and talent of its staff as well. These experts devoted more than eight hundred hours to compiling data on punch cards and feeding it into the big machine. This new technology was so helpful in correlating material and detecting similarities between crimes that I proposed legislation to the legislature for a study of the application of computer technology to law enforcement. Computers have, of course, come a long way since 1964.

After a long and fruitless investigation, the Boston Strangler case was finally cracked—like the murders of the Kansas family that Truman Capote chronicled in the book *In Cold Blood*—by a tip from a jail inmate who said he knew the killer. Early in March 1965, an ambitious young lawyer named F. Lee Bailey was talking to one of his clients in the prisoners' waiting room in the Superior Court in Salem. The client, a highly intelligent murderer named George Nassar, then an inmate of Bridgewater State Hospital, said that a fellow Bridgewater patient, Albert DeSalvo, claimed to be the Boston Strangler.

Bailey, still in his early thirties, was an extremely tough and able lawyer who had already enjoyed national publicity by winning the release of Dr. Sam Sheppard, the Cleveland osteopath who had been convicted of murdering his wife. The prospect of representing the Boston Strangler clearly appealed to him, and in the next two years he and I would play a complex, dual role of adversaries and collaborators as we attempted to find a satisfactory solution to this troubling case.

Albert DeSalvo was then thirty-three years old. He had served in the U.S. Army, married a German woman, and then returned to the Boston area. He worked as a press operator in a rubber factory and was liked by his coworkers. He and his wife had two children. However, as his wife later told police, after their first child was born with a birth defect, she had avoided sex, which created a problem because her husband was obsessed with sex. He also had a history of sex-related crimes. Around 1960, a man had gone to apartments in the Boston area and told women that he could get them work as models. To that end, he persuaded them to let him take their measurements with a tape measure. He would then leave, assuring them that the model agency would call. When no one called, several of the women complained to police, who called the glib intruder the Measuring Man. When DeSalvo was arrested in 1961 for breaking and entering, he confessed to being the Measuring Man. He told a sympathetic judge that he just "liked to put something over on educated people," and got off with eighteen months in jail. He was released in April 1962, just two months before the first murder attributed to the Strangler.

In November 1964, DeSalvo was again arrested. He had broken into an apartment, put a knife to a young woman's throat, tied her to the bed, and fondled and abused her before leaving. The victim got a good look at him and worked with a police sketch artist. Alert police realized that the sketch resembled that of the Measuring Man. DeSalvo was put in a line-up, and the woman identified him. He also resembled a criminal called the Green Man, for the green work pants he wore as he had tied a series of women to their beds in Connecticut and sexually abused them. DeSalvo confessed to being the Green Man and to literally hundreds of break-ins and sex offenses in four states, including some rapes. Some police thought DeSalvo was a braggart and that those figures were high, but it was clear that he was a one-man crime wave. He was sent to Bridgewater for mental examination but was not suspected of being the Strangler because DeSalvo, despite his record, was not considered a killer.

That was the situation when George Nassar told F. Lee Bailey that DeSalvo claimed to be the Boston Strangler. Bailey, seeing an opportunity to become involved in a sensational murder case, asked Nassar to arrange a meeting. But he was not DeSalvo's attorney, and he had no good reason to visit the man. He did not call DeSalvo's attorney of record, Jon Asgeirsson, to ask permission to see his client. Rather, on March 4, 1965, Bailey simply talked his way into a visit with DeSalvo. He became convinced that DeSalvo was the Strangler, and on a second meeting he taped DeSalvo's detailed confession. He then told police he might have found the Strangler and asked them for facts about the crimes that he could use to test DeSalvo's story. He taped a second confession and played it for police—without revealing DeSalvo's identity—and they were soon convinced that this was their man.

When I learned of this, I had a number of concerns. I urgently wanted to see the Strangler arrested and convicted, but I had to make sure we had the right man. I always feared that Bailey was largely motivated by publicity, and I became worried that DeSalvo had a similar motivation. It was clear to DeSalvo and everyone else that simply on the basis of the Green Man crimes, he was likely to spend the rest of his life in confinement. It was his clear preference to serve in a mental institution, and he also hoped that he could gain money from a book or movie on the Boston Strangler that would provide for his wife and children. I suspected that Bailey was already negotiating a book deal and the movie rights to the Strangler story, using the promise of money to win DeSalvo's trust. At the time there was no prohibition against criminals profiting from their crimes. But it was my job to make sure we had the right man and, if we did, to make sure his rights were protected so that any conviction would stand up on appeal.

Troubled by Bailey's aggressive moves, I called Jon Asgeirsson to my office and asked if he had given Bailey permission to approach his client. He told me he had not and was unaware that Bailey was holding himself out to be DeSalvo's lawyer. But he did not seem outraged by Bailey's efforts to hijack his client. From my perspective, Bailey was exploiting a mental patient in a state hospital, a patient whose rights I was charged with protecting. I thought his actions bordered on the unethical. I therefore asked the superintendent of Bridgewater State Hospital to prohibit Bailey from having further contact with DeSalvo. I also asked him to tell Bailey that if he continued to contact DeSalvo, I was prepared to take action against him.

At the same time, I thought Bailey was probably right and that DeSalvo was the Strangler. DeSalvo certainly knew an enormous amount about the stranglings. He could describe minor items in the victims' rooms. He identified the objects found inserted in the vaginas of some of the slain women. No one had revealed those details publicly. In almost every instance, DeSalvo's memory was phenomenal. The Boston *Record American* broke the story that the Boston Strangler was an inmate at Bridgewater and that F. Lee Bailey was his lawyer. I got a telephone call informing me that a television crew had arrived at Bridgewater and was trying to film the wing of the hospital where DeSalvo was kept. I strongly suspected that Bailey had tipped off the media, both to gain publicity for himself and so he could later claim that DeSalvo's rights to a fair trial had been infringed through pretrial publicity.

On March 10, I sought an injunction from the Supreme Judicial Court of Massachusetts forbidding anyone directly involved in the Strangler case from speaking to the press about it. When Bailey learned of my action, he called my office and demanded that Nancy Porter put me on the line. Instead, I passed him along to Walter Jay Skinner, chief of our criminal division (later a highly respected judge of the U.S. District Court), who arranged a meeting. The next afternoon an angry F. Lee Bailey came to my office. I had invited Asgeirsson and Skinner to sit in. I told Bailey I was disturbed by his move to take over a case where there was already counsel of record. He insisted he had every right to do what he had done. When I told him this was nonsense, he fired back that I was using the Strangler investigation as a stage from which to run for higher office. Bailey threatened me with legal action and stormed out of the office. Later, in court, I took the position that DeSalvo was incompetent to choose his own counsel and a court-appointed guardian should help him do so. A well-qualified guardian was appointed for DeSalvo, but in the end he still chose Bailey to be his lawyer.

Although Bailey and I often clashed, we eventually sought an agreement on DeSalvo. Bailey often tried to throw his antagonists off-balance, but he knew when to strike a deal. In the quiet of my office, we tried to reach an understanding that we both could live with. We both knew that DeSalvo's confession was not admissible in court and that, without it, he could not be convicted of the Strangler crimes because there was no physical evidence that tied him to them. We also knew that he was likely to spend the rest of his life in prison for the Green Man crimes. No one had been executed in Massachusetts in more than a decade, but as long as the state had the death penalty, Bailey would not let DeSalvo confess to the Strangler crimes. He insisted the state could try DeSalvo only by agreeing from the start that he would not be executed. Bailey offered me a deal: DeSalvo would plead guilty, but to only one of the Strangler murders. And even in that one case, Bailey intended to plead DeSalvo insane. I rejected that deal because of the risk that in a few years a psychiatrist might come along and declare, "Mr. DeSalvo is now sane." Then we could have Albert DeSalvo free, walking the streets again, and I could not in good conscience agree to that.

Bailey and I agreed that DeSalvo should be sent to a mental institution where medical and psychological tests could determine his sanity. Under an agreement with Bailey and DeSalvo's guardian, and with Bailey present, Jack Bottomly interviewed DeSalvo at length and obtained his taped confession. As part of the agreement, however, DeSalvo's statements could not be used against him in court. The confession, moreover, was taken from DeSalvo after he was declared mentally incompetent. The result was that there was never any admissible evidence that could be used to convict DeSalvo of any of the stranglings. In the end, Albert DeSalvo did not plead guilty to being the Boston Strangler. Nor was he ever indicted for any of the stranglings. In his taped confession, he revealed a good deal of knowledge of the Strangler crimes, but whether that meant he had committed them or had received the details from other sources remains to this day a point in dispute.

By the time 1966 began, I had announced my candidacy for the U.S. Senate. If DeSalvo was tried for the Green Man crimes while I was a candidate, it might cast doubt on my motives and even endanger any conviction we obtained. Bailey and I therefore agreed to delay the DeSalvo trial until January 1967, after the election. When that trial took place, the jury rejected Bailey's insanity defense and convicted DeSalvo on all counts of sex offenses, assaults, and armed robbery. He was sentenced to life in prison at Walpole State Prison.

Even with DeSalvo convicted and behind bars, his case kept its hold on the public imagination. Gerold Frank wrote a bestseller called *The Boston Strangler*, which was made into a movie starring Tony Curtis as DeSalvo and Henry Fonda as Jack Bottomly. I was offered $125,000 to play myself in the film. It was a staggering sum. Jack Bottomly, a consultant on the movie, urged me to accept the offer. He said the film could educate the public about mental illness and about the danger of admitting strangers to your home. I was dubious. I disapproved of linking the office of attorney general with a commercial enterprise. Bottomly and the studio asked me at least to review the script. I did and thought it was crude and often inaccurate. I was offended by the portrayal of me as drinking Scotch in my office and using profanity, two things totally out of character. The writer changed the hard liquor to the hot tea I often drank in my office and eliminated the offensive language, but I continued to have misgivings. For one thing, I feared that the film might jeopardize any future trial of DeSalvo, whose appeal was still pending in court. Later, I discussed the situation with Elliot Richardson, who had been elected to succeed me as attorney general, and who shared my concerns. In a letter dated December 27, 1967, Richardson denied the studio's request for assistance from the attorney general's office in making the film. I never regretted rejecting the lucrative film offer, even though it was my one and only chance at movie stardom.

On Sunday, November 25, 1973, Albert DeSalvo was stabbed to death by a fellow inmate in his cell at Walpole State Prison. I cannot swear that he was the Boston Strangler—there are still those who argue that he was not. But I know one thing for sure. Once DeSalvo was behind bars, the stranglings stopped.

10

Running for

the Senate

In elective politics, it's up or out. You go up the ladder, or you get out of the game. For me, as attorney general, up the ladder meant two possible positions, governor or United States senator. In 1964, the year I completed my first term as attorney general, the Republican nomination for governor was open. John Volpe had lost his bid for reelection in 1962, but he was expected to run again. Since I was the only Republican elected to a constitutional office in Massachusetts in 1962, some friends advised me to challenge Volpe in the Republican primary. I disagreed. My job as attorney general was by no means finished. We were still working with the Massachusetts Crime Commission, and the Under Common Garage case was ongoing. The Boston Strangler case was still unsolved. Moreover, I loved my job, both because we were doing important work and because of the esprit de corps in our office. So I followed my instincts, stood for reelection in 1964, and was elected for a second two-year term.

By 1966, when my second term would end, the political situation had changed and so had my thinking. During my two terms as attorney general we had made serious inroads into ridding the state of corruption. We had successfully completed our work with the Crime Commission, and the Under Common Garage case was over. The man I believed to be the Boston Strangler was in custody; the stranglings had stopped and people felt safe again. Corrupt public officials had been prosecuted and convicted, and people had begun to have more faith in their public officials and state government.

I felt I could honorably turn the attorney general's office over to a successor. I was restless, ambitious, anxious to take on a new challenge. Sitting in my swivel chair, gazing out over the Boston Common, I considered my options. The big question was whether Senator Leverett Saltonstall would run for reelection. If he did not, John Volpe, who had again been elected governor in 1964, might run for the Senate, and I could run for governor. If John Volpe ran for reelection, and Senator Saltonstall retired, I could run for the U.S. Senate. Finally, I could run for a third term as attorney general or return to the private practice of law.

A couple of other options had also come my way. Alfred Gwynn Vanderbilt had asked me to work as the director of a world veterans organization in Paris, and an intriguing offer was made to me in 1965 by Laurance Rockefeller, Nelson Rockefeller's younger brother. Laurance Rockefeller was concerned that the Caribbean islands might go Communist. Nelson, whom I had come to know, was aware of my interest in the Caribbean, and I assume he recommended me to his brother. Laurance invited me down to New York to talk. He believed that because the Caribbean islands were in such proximity to the United States, it was logical that a closer relationship be formed between the islands and our nation. He offered me $75,000 a year, plus a generous expense account, to take on this assignment. I was tempted, but I told him that if Senator Saltonstall did not run for reelection, I would most likely seek his Senate seat. I got the feeling that Rockefeller was not optimistic about my chances, but neither were a lot of other people.

Senator Saltonstall was a highly respected political figure with twenty-two years in the Senate. For years, as the ranking Republican on the Senate Armed Services Committee, and on the subcommittee for defense appropriations, he had brought military contracts to Massachusetts. There was endless speculation about whether he would run again. At seventy-three, the senator was still lean and energetic, but another term would have kept him in office until the eve of his eightieth birthday. His beloved wife, Alice, had not been well. He had said nothing directly about his plans, but we all noted that he had done little to prepare for a reelection campaign. In one discussion, when the subject of the senator's possible departure came up, John Volpe told me, "Ed, Leverett will never step down for the likes of an Ed Brooke or a John Volpe." He meant that an aristocratic WASP like Saltonstall would not open the door to a black or an Italian American candidate to the Senate. I told Volpe I disagreed, that Senator Saltonstall was not that kind of man. When he persisted, "I just don't think Lev would step down with you and me as potential candidates," I could only say that time would tell.

In the fall of 1965, with still no indication of the senator's intentions, my advisers and I began to prepare for any eventuality. I decided that I would hold a press conference right after the senator's announcement, no matter what his decision was. On December 28, Senator Saltonstall called a press conference for the following day. I announced my press conference for the day after the senator's, but we gave no hint as to my plans—because we did not know them yet. My organization was poised, awaiting the word. We had three strategies. If the senator announced he was running for another term, I would strongly support both his reelection bid and Governor Volpe's, and would announce that I was running for reelection as attorney general. If the senator did not run again, and Governor Volpe decided to enter the race, I would announce my candidacy for governor. Or, if Saltonstall did not run again, and Volpe decided to remain as governor, I would announce my candidacy for the Senate.

On December 29, at 2:00 P.M., Senator Saltonstall held his press conference. He read a brief statement, which, typically, he had written himself in longhand. It began, "After painstaking thought and consultation with my family and friends I have reached the decision that I will not be a candidate to the United States Senate in 1966." A magnificent political career had come to an end. Reporters asked him who he hoped would take his Senate seat. The senator diplomatically replied that John Volpe, Elliot Richardson, Edward Brooke, and several popular Massachusetts Republican Congressmen, Brad Morse, William Bates, Hastings Keith, and Silvio Conte, were all fit candidates. Someone from my campaign attended the press conference and called me immediately. I took in the news and then put our plan into action. I dialed Governor Volpe, then Lieutenant Governor Elliot

Richardson, and then Congressmen Conte, Keith, Morse, and Bates. Within a matter of hours I had spoken to all of my potential rivals as well as Republican Party officials and stalwarts. With the exception of Governor Volpe, I said pretty much the same thing to them all: "I'm sure you've heard, Senator Saltonstall has announced he will not be a candidate for reelection. I wanted you to know it's my intention to run for his seat. I will announce my candidacy for the Republican nomination for United States Senator tomorrow."

It was a big jump from state attorney general to the Senate. Still, it does happen. Jacob Javits in New York, Thomas Eagleton in Missouri, Walter Mondale in Minnesota, and Joseph Lieberman in Connecticut were all attorneys general in their home states. However, most politicians do not try for the Senate until they have been governor or at least, as in Javits's case, served in Congress. I thought I could make that big leap but not by being shy. The purpose of my phone calls was to preempt the field and avoid a costly and divisive Republican primary. But because Volpe was the head of our party in Massachusetts, and because he had hinted that he might want that Senate seat himself, I called him first.

Volpe heard me out, then said, "Well, I've given some thought to running for the Senate myself . . . " We talked at length. He complained that the senator had not told him his intentions privately before making them public. Volpe made clear that he loved being governor but that he was also intrigued by the prestige of being a senator. I got the impression he wanted both offices. I also thought that if he did not run for the Senate, he would prefer to have his close friend Brad Morse seek the office. And I expected that if John ran for the Senate, he would endorse Elliot Richardson to replace him as governor. He wanted me to stay right where I was. But I was too ambitious to accept that fate, and Volpe should have known it. I believed that 1966 was my year and it might not come again.

It was essential to my strategy that if Volpe or anyone else later challenged what I had done, that I could remind them that I had deferred to Governor Volpe, but there was a limit to how far I would defer. Our telephone conversation went back and forth until finally I said, "John, the bottom line is, if you decide to run for the Senate, I will support you, and I will run for governor. But if you decide you're

not going to run for the Senate, I will. Either way, I'm going to announce my intentions tomorrow. So I need to know now what you
are going to do." Politicians may build huge organizations, but politics sometimes comes down to a clash of wills between two individuals; this was one of those moments. After a moment of stunned
silence, Volpe asked,

"Ed, why the rush? Why are you in such a hurry?"

"John, I don't consider that I'm in a hurry. We've known for
almost two years that the senator might not run for reelection.
We've talked about it and had more than enough time to think
about it. Now that we know the senator is retiring, if you don't
go for it, I will. The road is long, and I've got to get started. I've
got to raise a lot of money, and if I wait, a lot of formidable
candidates could enter the race. I can't wait."

Volpe said, "It looks as though you have planned this. Well, I
think you're jumping the gun. I still think we need more time."

"John, I'd like to know your intentions now."

"What do you mean by 'now,' Ed?"

"Now, John. In this conversation."

"Well, I think you are moving too quickly. Other people are
involved, and they need time."

"John, I've considered all the pros and cons. We have got to
come to an understanding now."

"Can I call you back?"

I reluctantly agreed, but when he called me back shortly afterward, he still could not say whether he intended to run for the Senate. He never told me he would. He never told me he would not. He
never gave me his blessing. My next call was to Elliot Richardson.

"Elliot, Senator Saltonstall has spoken."

"Yes, I heard," said Elliot, being his usual cautious self. "Were
you shocked?"

I said I was not shocked and speculated that the senator's
decision was based on his desire to spend more time with his
wife. Then I came to the point.

"Elliot, I'm going to announce tomorrow."

His reaction was much like Volpe's. "My goodness. Isn't that pretty quick?"

"Yes," I said. I spoke of my need to raise money and to establish myself as a candidate early in the process. "I can't waste a day."

"Well, I've been thinking of running myself," said Richardson. "Ed, I think you should wait. Time will clear this up."

"Time is of the essence, Elliot. I can't wait."

I called Brad Morse and told him the same thing. I thought Brad would be a more formidable rival than all the others. Brad was a good, smart congressman who had worked for Senator Saltonstall, as had Elliot, and might seem to some a more logical successor to the senator than I. He said he was considering running himself and that he thought my jumping into the race now would be a hasty decision. I disagreed. Next, I called Silvio Conte, who said he was almost certainly going to run and that he was almost ready to announce.

I told him and all of them, "If you want to run against me, that's fine. But I am going to make my announcement tomorrow." I was amazed that they all seemed so shocked by my plans. Why had they not positioned themselves to move quickly if Senator Saltonstall did not run? Politics is not a tea party. When it is time to act, you have to move fast and decisively. In military terms, I was making a preemptive first strike. The threat was real and imminent.

I called other major players in state Republican politics to inform them of my intentions, including the state committee chairman, Buck Domaine; the national committeewoman, Mary Bancroft Wheeler; and national committeeman, Bruce Crane. After all the pleas to slow down I received from potential opponents, the response of the party leaders was a wonderful tonic. They expressed delight that I was willing to run. They saw me as a strong candidate, perhaps the strongest the party had to offer to hold on to the Senate seat. I had a solid record as attorney general, and in my last campaign I had won by eight hundred thousand votes, the largest plurality in the history of Massachusetts. I was organized and ready to run. The national media would clearly be covering me. As I had hoped, all these factors dimmed the hopes of other would-be candidates. No major Republican challenged me for the nomination.

On December 30, 1965, just twenty-four hours after the senator's announcement, I held my press conference in the Copley Plaza Hotel and announced that I would seek the Republican nomination for the Senate. More than five hundred of my supporters greeted my announcement with raucous cheers. The national press and the television networks were there, drawn by the novelty of an African American running for the Senate. I was trying to do something that had never been done before. The first elected black attorney general was trying to become the first black senator elected by popular vote. I launched my campaign in the context of a harsh reality: in America in 1966, 103 years after the Emancipation Proclamation, no American of African descent had ever been elected to the United States Senate by popular vote, nor had any ever been nominated by a major political party. With the civil rights movement at high pitch and race on everyone's mind, my nomination was national news.

My campaign was important in another way. The actions of Presidents Johnson and Kennedy had convinced many Americans that only the Democratic Party cared about civil rights. My break with the party in 1964 over the Goldwater nomination made my candidacy all the more interesting to the media. Despite Goldwater, I still believed the Republican Party could and should reach out to black Americans. All in all, I was quite an oddity: an African American, a civil rights advocate, and a Republican Party rebel, who had a fighting chance to be elected to the Senate from a New England state that had become a Democratic Party stronghold. The press would follow my campaign closely, not just because it was historic, but because reporters love a good story and, win or lose, I was a good story. As the new year arrived, I thought my fast announcement, and the coverage of it, had gotten us off to an excellent start.

I launched my campaign in Millville and Blackstone, the only two communities in the commonwealth that I had lost in 1964. Touring those towns, I would joke, "Whatever happened down here the last time?" I promised to forgive them if they voted "right" this time. Their reaction was good-natured and friendly. No one on the streets of Millville or Blackstone asked me about the burden of being an

African American running for the Senate, but reporters must have asked me in a thousand tiresome ways if race would hurt my chances. It made me better understand what Jack Kennedy had faced as a Catholic running for president. I told the press that I was proud of my heritage and that my being African American had not hurt me in my previous campaigns, so I did not see why it should hurt me now. That, I thought, was the real story—not that my race would hurt me but that it would not. The endless questions about my race sometimes annoyed me, but I could not complain. The media gave us the kind of coverage that we could never have bought.

I intended to run an issue-oriented campaign, and I had to broaden my knowledge on some issues. Because the Senate so often focuses on foreign affairs, I had to think in global terms. I needed briefings and position papers. I soon called on Boston University, Harvard, Wellesley, Boston College, and Massachusetts Institute of Technology faculty members for assistance. I asked a young MIT professor named Jack Saloma to be my director of research. Jack was a leader in the Ripon Society, a progressive Republican group. Unfortunately, Jack went skiing before joining the campaign and severely broke a leg. Then Jack's friend Alton Frye agreed to come aboard in his place. Alton was a bright young Yale-trained Tennessean who had worked for the Rand Corporation. We had immediate rapport, and he became a close and trusted adviser, friend, and confidant.

My Senate campaign, like my earlier campaigns, attracted some remarkable volunteers. Cam Newberry was one. He walked in off the street one day and offered to help. Nobody knew him. Sally Saltonstall asked him what he thought he could do, and he said he could open the mail and draft responses. I told Sally to put him to work "before he changes his mind." After several weeks, the campaign received a check for one thousand dollars from a Cammann Newberry. The campaign treasurer called this to my attention. I called Cam in to thank him and was surprised to learn that he had served for six years as the administrative assistant to Henry Cabot Lodge in the Senate and was an heir to the J. J. Newberry five-and-dime stores. Another walk-in was Marilyn Dexheimer, a Democrat and a doctoral candidate in political science at Boston University whose planned summer trip to Europe was cancelled by an airline strike.

Looking for something interesting to do, she was headed for the campaign office of my opponent, Governor Peabody, when she happened upon my office first and dropped in out of curiosity. She stayed, and her first assignment was doing opposition research—on Peabody!

In June we had our state preprimary convention. It was not such an ordeal as my battle with Elliot Richardson four years earlier, but many conservatives were angry with me. One, J. Alan McKay, ran against me. McKay, vice-president of the pro-Goldwater Young Americans for Freedom, bridled at much that I had written in *The Challenge of Change: Crisis in Our Two-Party System*. I was content for him to have his say. When the roll was called, the totals were McKay, 215 and Brooke, 1,485.

We watched closely the Democratic primary contest between the top two contenders, former Governor Endicott "Chub" Peabody and Boston Mayor John Collins, and developed a strategy for competing against whoever was victorious. I thought that Mayor Collins would be the more formidable foe, but Peabody won comfortably. He was a cherubic, balding man with a dazzling smile. He was also a first-rate campaigner and a liberal pro–civil rights Democrat from Cambridge. His seventy-four-year-old mother, whom I admired, had recently received national attention after being arrested at a civil rights demonstration in Florida. The resulting press coverage helped her son's standing with pro–civil rights voters in Massachusetts. The Peabody family embodied some of the state's finest traditions. Chub Peabody had been one of Harvard's last All-American football players. Both his father and grandfather had been Episcopal bishops. His grandfather and namesake had been, for fifty-four years, the headmaster of the Groton School.

Peabody's critics thought him a likable fellow who was coasting on his family name and his gridiron fame, but I took his campaign seriously. In 1962, he had defeated incumbent John Volpe in the governor's race, and beating John at anything took some doing. He was also close to the Kennedy family and had their powerful organization behind him. President Johnson, late in the campaign, appeared with him at a rally in Boston. My response was that I was always pleased to have the president visit Massachusetts but not for this particular purpose.

I campaigned hard, rising early to shake hands at factory gates at 5 A.M. I never needed an alarm clock to wake me; since my days in the army, my alarm clock has always been in my head. I went to the meat market district in the north end of Boston, put on a meat cutter's uniform, and talked to anyone who would listen. I talked about the importance of having a vital two-party system. I talked about what I had achieved as attorney general and what I wanted to achieve in the Senate. No matter how long the day or how tired I was, face-to-face contact with voters always left me energized, ready to shake one more hand, listen to one more problem, or see a smile on one more face. I could hardly wait to visit another picturesque Massachusetts town, speak at another rally, or encourage another citizen to vote, preferably for me. In East Boston, I would talk to elderly Italian ladies in their own language. I worked the crowd. And it *is* work. But I was driven by the importance of the office I was seeking and thrived on the energy of the crowds.

I loved parades. I would race from one side of the street to the other to shake hands and sometimes dash up the steps to front porches to greet people. In an East Boston parade that year, when I was hurrying from voter to voter, Chub Peabody suddenly came riding down the street on a big white horse. We presented quite a contrast and I did not think it hurt me any. I thought the dramatic difference between my background and his worked in my favor. There is a saying in journalism that it is not news if a dog bites a man, but it is news if a man bites a dog. In political terms, if the grandson of slaves could defeat the grandson of the headmaster of Groton, that was a man-bites-dog story, a big story.

Television was beginning to play a larger role in political campaigning, and I was never entirely comfortable with it. To me, the people-to-people contact was what politics was all about. The cold eye of the camera unnerved me. My staff often would gather a live audience when I was to appear on camera. I would talk to them, look into their eyes, and if the camera wanted to observe us, that was fine.

An element of fun was essential to our campaign. Sally Saltonstall found the Town and Country Singers who wound up playing at many of our rallies. Their specialty was a sing-along to the tune of Woody Guthrie's "This Land Is Your Land":

This man is your man—this man is my man
From the Berkshire Mountains to Nantucket Island
From the piers in Gloucester to the Newton Highlands
Ed Brooke's the man for you and me.

I never tired of hearing that song.

Insofar as race was an issue, it was largely unspoken. Because our state's African American population was so small, perhaps 2 percent of the voters, I shook mostly white hands, looked into mostly white faces, and with very few exceptions, saw no anger in their eyes. But the press kept writing about white backlash. I must have said a thousand times, "Judge me on my qualifications. The racial issue has been beaten, beaten, beaten. Take me for what I am and what I stand for."

The war in Vietnam was the most important issue in my campaign. The *Boston Globe* urged its readers to make their decision based on the candidates' positions on Vietnam. Peabody backed President Johnson's Vietnam policy without reservation. I stressed that mine would be an independent judgment. I opposed further escalation of the war and favored flexible negotiation strategies. I wanted to push for peace.

When Peabody and I debated face-to-face at Assumption College, in Worcester, and the student moderator asked each of us to detail our background in foreign affairs, Chub drew some laughs by replying in all seriousness that he had traveled widely as a tourist in western Europe. I gave the audience a more complete outline of my policy positions. "The prolonged ordeal in South Vietnam has become a source of grief and despair to all men of conscience and consciousness," I began. "As a concerned American and a candidate . . . I have sought to define in my own mind what is a reasonable, effective, and just policy for our nation." In reviewing America's strategy in Vietnam, I expressed conviction that President Johnson was doing what was "in his judgment proper and in the best interests of the Vietnamese people and the United States" but reserved the right to reassess the national commitment, expressing my distress at "what appears to be a growing imbalance between our military objectives and our political goals in South Vietnam." My comments on foreign affairs reflected my briefings with Alton Frye, Jeremy Stone, and Morton Halperin, all of the Harvard Center for International Affairs; with Jack Saloma of MIT; with the distinguished economist Otto Eckstein; Wellesley economics professor and Soviet expert Marshall Goldman; and a little-known Harvard professor named Henry Kissinger.

There were those who questioned how much of my time in the Senate would be spent on racial issues. It was true that as attorney general I had often acted in support of civil rights. I had attacked the use of literacy tests to exclude African American voters. I had led the effort to uphold the constitutionality of the 1965 Voting Rights Act and had appointed former U.S. Solicitor General Archibald Cox as a special assistant attorney general to present our argument before the United States Supreme Court. Massachusetts was not one of the states targeted by the law designed to prevent states from excluding African Americans and other minorities from voting, but I felt so strongly about the issue that I thought Massachusetts should play an important role. In this effort I had the strong support of the chief of my civil rights division, Levin H. Campbell, who later became a distinguished chief judge of the U.S. First Circuit Court of Appeals. I sought and received the support of fifteen state attorneys general in a "friend of the court" brief. The U.S. Supreme Court came down on our side, in *South Carolina v. Katzenbach*, in declaring the constitutionality of the Voting Rights Act. I took pride in our leadership in the fight for this crucial civil rights law. The power of white southerners to deny the vote to black people had been the bulwark of southern segregation, and we could not run the risk of any state finding new ways to disenfranchise black voters.

But none of this meant that if elected I would limit myself to civil rights issues. I wanted to prove that an African American in the U.S. Senate could impartially represent people of all races, as I had done as attorney general. That was the message I wanted to send to African American candidates across the country and to young African Americans who aspired to elective office. I never doubted that the vast majority of Massachusetts voters, black and white, were proud of my role in championing civil rights.

Still, we had to be concerned about the civil and racial strife across the country. In April 1965 violence in the Los Angeles community of

Watts had erupted, leaving thirty-four people dead and the neighborhood in ashes. During the summer of 1966, at the height of our campaign, violence broke out in Baltimore, Chicago, Cleveland, and other cities across the country. Racial tensions were as bad as they had ever been. It was an uneasy time for an African American to be running for such a visible office. I had never felt any backlash against me, but it was possible that some sudden event, like a race riot, could unexpectedly cost me votes or even the election.

Our polls showed me ahead, but Massachusetts's political history is replete with last-minute turnarounds. In many campaigns the trailing candidate had landed a one-punch haymaker. The question in my mind was: could Chub Peabody land a powerful blow—an "October surprise," as it is called? Election Day was Tuesday, November 8. On Thursday, November 3, five days before voters would go to the polls, the haymaker came: our October surprise was a few days late. To my astonishment, it did not arrive in the form of an allegation against me by the Peabody camp, but in an unexpected charge made by Elliot Richardson against his own opponent. Elliot, having decided not to challenge me for the Senate nomination, was instead running to replace me as attorney general.

Elliot sent me a telegram accusing his Democratic opponent, Francis X. Bellotti, of improperly taking money from national insurance companies while serving as lieutenant governor. This bombshell was soon all over the news. Elliot's charges impeached the ethics of a man seeking to be the commonwealth's chief law enforcer. If Elliot was right, it was a serious blow to Bellotti's credibility; if not, Elliot's own credibility was in doubt. He was asking me, as attorney general, to take action. The problem was that there was no clear evidence of abuse of the public trust. Bellotti did not deny that he had represented the insurance companies, nor was it illegal for him to represent them. The question was whether he had done special pleading for these firms before the state Department of Insurance in an illegal fashion? Or had he merely taken a standard retainer for routine representation? Elliot insisted that Bellotti had acted in an illegal fashion. I asked him to produce evidence, but he offered none. Since there was no plausible reason for Elliot to withhold such evidence, I had to conclude that he had none. I was willing to do what I could, but with only four days remaining until the election, a thorough investigation was impossible.

Election eve allegations are always suspect. They are considered dirty pool. The idea is to make an allegation too late for your opponent to rebut—so the voters will enter the polling booths with your accusations in mind. The Richardson-Bellotti campaign, always a clash of competing political cultures, now became a grudge match. Bellotti counterattacked. In a televised debate the next day, Friday, he strongly denied Elliot's charges and declared that Elliot himself had violated the conflict of interest laws while lieutenant governor. Bellotti, like Elliot, asked me to make an immediate investigation.

Thus, the whole mess landed on my desk. I knew there was not sufficient evidence to resolve the charges. The election was only four days away, and two of them were Saturday and Sunday. Early Sunday morning, I paced up and down my office, asking myself, "What is the truth?" and "How will these charges impact my own campaign?" The danger was that I would lose votes from both Elliot's supporters and Bellotti's for not endorsing their man's charges. Had I come this far in my own political career only to lose it at the last minute because of probably bogus charges between two candidates over whom I had no control? The irony was that the polls had showed Elliot comfortably ahead of Bellotti. I could not understand why he would make such explosive charges without evidence to back them up. Had he not foreseen that Bellotti would counterattack? The charges could backfire and hurt Elliot more than they helped him. The same was true of Bellotti.

Elliot won the election, and nothing ever came of either man's charges. If either was corrupt, it did not harm his future. Bellotti went on to be elected attorney general for three terms, from 1975 to 1987. Elliot, after serving as our state's attorney general, later served as ambassador to Great Britain; secretary of commerce; secretary of health, education, and welfare; secretary of defense; and United States attorney general.

Both men would criticize me for not prosecuting the other in those hectic days just before the 1966 election. But neither gave me any evidence upon which I could make a judgment, much less base a prosecution. I have no doubt that some Democrats and Italian

American voters who had been inclined to vote for me changed their minds, thinking I was part of a Republican conspiracy to defeat Bellotti.

On Election Day, we had volunteers calling in results from across the state. When we got tallies from Boston as well as from Chicopee and Holyoke, two communities that voted by machine, we knew we were close. By 9 P.M., we had a fair sampling of the whole state, and all of the figures showed that we were going to win by several hundred thousand votes. By 9:15, the news media began to declare me the winner. I decided that I would not claim victory until Peabody had made his concession speech. That came at about 11 P.M. In the end, I received 1,213,473 votes, a plurality of over 400,000 votes, winning 61 percent of the total.

When my family and I entered the ballroom of the Copley Plaza Hotel, it was packed with hundreds of supporters, friends, and members of the media. The band was playing, and hundreds of blue and white balloons filled the air. People were waving and shouting at the top of their voices. Volunteers and campaign workers were hugging and kissing and shedding tears of joy. Everyone sensed that history was being made and was proud to be part of it. I had no prepared speech. I just spoke from the heart. With Remigia and my daughters by my side, and my mother and sister close by, I vowed to go to Washington to bring people together, to work for peace and to bring an end to the war.

Congratulations poured in from all over the country. The one that moved me the most was a telegram from my friend and pastor, Dr. Theodore Parker Ferris, the rector of Boston's Trinity Church. It was one word: "Hallelujah!" I keep the yellowed telegram in my copy of *Selected Sermons*, a collection of his teachings and a book I still read for inspiration and spiritual comfort.

I would be attorney general until January 18, 1967, when my term expired. But I resigned effective at the close of business on January 2, because Leverett Saltonstall's Senate term expired at noon the next day. I had already begun a friendly transition with Elliot Richardson as he prepared to take my place. Despite all the excitement of being elected to the Senate, I felt regrets about leaving my adopted Massachusetts to live in the city of my birth. Massachusetts was where I had learned the political trade and where I had been greatly honored by the voters. I loved the state and its people, and although I never lost the hint of the South in my accent, I considered Massachusetts my home. With a sharp sense of personal regret, I sent my letter of resignation to Governor Volpe.

11

Back to

Washington

My excitement upon entering the Senate was dampened by the death on December 30, 1966, of Christian Herter, a cherished mentor and friend. He had planned a Washington dinner party in my honor, before my swearing-in. The former governor of Massachusetts and secretary of state under President Eisenhower had invited several members of the Senate and hoped thereby to assist my smooth entry into "the world's most exclusive club."

The Herter funeral service was held at St. John's, an Episcopal church across Lafayette Park from the White House, known as "the President's Church." After the service I stood in line, with scores of others, to express my sympathy to his widow, Mary Herter. To my surprise, when it came my turn, Mrs. Herter told me she was looking forward to the dinner scheduled for January 8, less than a week away. I protested that at this difficult time she would want to cancel the dinner. She replied, "Ed, Chris wanted to do this. I am sure he would want us to go forward and we will." A few days later Mrs. Herter welcomed Remigia and me to Washington's elegant Cosmos Club, where the guests included Vice President Hubert Humphrey; Secretary of State Dean Rusk; columnist Walter Lippmann; Democratic leaders Mike Mansfield of Montana, John Stennis of Mississippi, Russell Long of Louisiana, Claiborne Pell of Rhode Island, and John Sparkman of Alabama; as well as Republicans Margaret Chase Smith of Maine, George Aiken of Vermont, Barry Goldwater of Arizona, Jacob Javits of New York, and Roman Hruska of Nebraska. Remigia, aglow in a simple blue brocade suit with a powder blue princess coat, thoroughly enjoyed our Washington debut, as did I.

The next day, Ted and Joan Kennedy had Remigia and me to lunch at their home in Georgetown. It was an informal occasion for just the four of us. Joan had filled the living room with roses and chrysanthemums, and Ted had a fire in the fireplace. We dined on quiche lorraine, green salad, and fresh strawberries and cream. I knew and liked Joan, as did Remigia. Ted and I discussed life in Washington, the next day's swearing-in ceremony, and what might await me in the Senate. When we left, newspaper photographers captured a smiling Remigia and me leaving, with Joan and Ted in the background.

Finally the big day arrived. Congress convened on January 10. Ted Kennedy, thirteen years my junior but now our state's senior senator, escorted me down the center aisle of the Senate chamber. As is the custom, the Senate gave me a standing ovation. Vice President Humphrey swore me in. As I stood in the well of the U.S. Senate, taking the oath of office, I looked up at my mother and Remigia, my two daughters, Remi and Edwina, my sister, Helene, and other members of my family seated in the gallery. Tears filled my eyes. I thought of my father and how proud he would have been had he lived to see this day. I felt his presence as I joined the world's greatest deliberative body. I was the first African American ever elected to the U.S. Senate by popular vote, and the first African American to be sworn into the Senate since Hiram Rhodes Revels and Blanche Kelso Bruce were chosen by a "carpetbag" Mississippi legislature during Reconstruction.

As I took the oath, aware of the historical importance of the moment, I could not help asking myself questions. Would I be worthy of this challenge? Would I measure up to expectations? Would I let my race down and prove the bigots right? But I thought I was prepared for the challenge, and I knew I could only do my best.

I was allotted only enough seats in the gallery for the swearing-in to accommodate my family, but many others deserved to share in this day. My office was too small for everyone, so we reserved a large reception room in the Russell Building. Thousands of friends and supporters filled the room, overflowed into the corridors, down the stairs, and out into the street. For the rest of the day, politicians and diplomats, farmers and parki... campaign workers, high school a... ington, and fellow law school studen... offer their congratulations.

Ironically, the day I was being sworn in, H... representative, the Reverend Adam Clayton Powell, w... mired since I was a boy, was leaving Congress. One of only ... of African American Congressmen, he had fought tirelessly for ... rights and had been reelected eleven times. He was the Jackie Robinson of American politics, paving the way for those of us who followed. But now he had been barred from taking his seat. The House already had removed him as chairman of the Education and Labor Committee, the most powerful committee assignment ever held by an African American. He was accused of misusing public funds, a charge that was never proven.

As Powell made a dramatic exit down the steps of the Capitol, hundreds of his supporters, who had come from Harlem by bus, were there to cheer him. Less than two months later, on March 1, the House formally excluded him by a vote of 307 to 116, a decision he successfully challenged in the Supreme Court. He held the seat until 1970, when he was defeated for reelection by 150 votes. The end of his illustrious and turbulent career was painful to witness. Whatever his faults, he had fought for black Americans at a time when precious few other politicians did. At a speech I gave later at the National Press Club, I said that one thing I had learned already was, "You get more attention going out than coming in."

My reception in 1967 was vastly different from what Adam Clayton Powell received when he first took his congressional seat in 1945. Powell had been denied the use of the congressional barbershop and steam bath and had encountered the same discrimination that all African Americans then experienced in the nation's capital. The shameful treatment of blacks in Congress went back to the Reconstruction era. The first African American to be sent to the House of Representatives had been denied his seat. John Willis Menard, the great-grandfather of Edith Menard, one of my Dunbar High School classmates, was elected to Congress from Louisiana in 1868. When he arrived, Congress refused to seat him. James A. Garfield, later the

Back to Washington

...handful
...I had pa-
...whom I had pa-
Harlem's flamboyant
...filed in to
...from Wash-
...from Boston all
...college classmates,
...former staff members
...lot attendants,

...rly to admit
...ction of being
...of the House of
...e. Despite refus-
...n his full congres-
...ey were committing

...y time. In late Novem-
...covers, along with five
...d, Charles Percy, Nelson
...d Reagan. Although I was
...ayed by the labeling that was
...e form trapped in amber, I was
forev... ...When I served as Massachusetts's
attorney g... ...of my membership in the Episcopal Church, my p... ...and tennis, my love of art, and my
home on Martha's Vine... ...en my preference for tea over coffee
was seen by one writer as a mimicking of "white" tastes. Yet I had
been an Episcopalian since childhood, grew up listening to opera,
played tennis since my high school days, and had never drunk a cup
of coffee in my life. I was amused when *Time* called me a "NASP,"
their play on the term for the WASP elite.

Amid many distractions, Remigia and I had decisions to make.
We talked about relocating the family to Washington, but Remigia
chose to stay in Massachusetts with the girls, her mother, and other
family members and friends. I did not try to change her mind. In
many ways, I was relieved. Our marriage had continued to deterio-
rate, and I believe we both welcomed the separation. It was understood that I would come home whenever I could to be with Remi and
Edwina. For years we had put up a brave front for the public. We
went where we had to go and did what we had to do. The Herter
dinner and lunch with the Kennedys were examples of this. But otherwise our only conversations were about the girls or household and
financial matters.

Washington had changed a great deal since I left it twenty years
before. The segregation I had grown up with was largely gone. I rented
an apartment in the new Tiber Island complex in Washington SW,

overlooking the Potomac River. My mother sold our family home and moved there too. In 1972, I purchased a duplex apartment at the Watergate East, just before it achieved political fame. I paid $67,500 for it and of course took out a mortgage. Soon my mother purchased an apartment two floors above mine, where she lived until her death. Senators were paid only $30,000 a year when I arrived. Later that rose to $57,500. Many members of the Senate were millionaires and did not need their government paychecks, but I did. I welcomed the additional money I earned by speaking around the country. At that time there was no limit on the speaking honoraria a senator could receive. One year my fees were among the highest in the Senate, around $21,000.

The reception I received in the Senate was friendly and warm. The Senate was then composed of ninety-nine men and one woman, Margaret Chase Smith of Maine. As a freshman senator, I sat in one of the chamber's back rows, called "the outfield," or "Boy's Town." I was delighted to claim a desk next to incoming Senator Mark Hatfield, with whom I had become friendly when he was governor of Oregon and I was attorney general of Massachusetts. When I came to the Senate I did not intend to thrust myself on anyone, but I certainly intended to use all of the services provided to all of the members. I planned to treat my colleagues with respect, and I expected to be treated with respect in return. And I was. I was never patronized, which I would have considered the worst insult of all.

One day, shortly after my arrival, I went to use the swimming pool in the "Senators Only" gym in the Russell Building. John Stennis of Mississippi, John McClellan of Arkansas, and Strom Thurmond of South Carolina were swimming laps. They invited me to join them and urged me to use the pool as often as I could. There was no hesitation or ill will that I could see. Yet these were men who consistently voted against legislation that would have provided equal opportunity to others of my race. I felt that if a senator truly believed in racial separatism I could live with that, but it was increasingly evident that some members of the Senate played on bigotry purely for political gain. They appealed to ignorance and prejudice to entrench themselves in office.

At first I attended the weekly Senate prayer breakfasts, which provided an opportunity for spiritual discourse. But I stopped going because I felt uncomfortable hearing pious words from men whose words and votes on the Senate floor were at odds with their professed religious beliefs of love and charity. I have little stomach for hypocrisy. Their duality of word and deed was incompatible with my understanding of Christianity.

The Senate is a place of small intimacies. Our names were imprinted in gold leaf on our own individual shaving bowls. When I got my first haircut, I integrated the Senate barbershop, becoming the first African American to sit in the barber's chair and not stand behind it. I used the massage rooms, the showers, and the gym. In all my years in the Senate, I never encountered an overt act of hostility. A few members were cool; most were warm. I made friends easily on both sides of the aisle. They called me "Senator" on the first day; many were soon calling me "Ed."

Barry Goldwater could have made things awkward for me, as I had declined to endorse him in 1964. Instead, he could not have been more gracious. As we served together in the Senate, I got to know him better, and I think that with age he became a more thoughtful man. He seemed to learn the difference between authentic conservatism and shoot-from-the-hip negativism. I was pleased to see him come around later in his life to at least support a woman's right to choose. Barry's last years were characterized by his cheerful common sense.

The United States Senate is modeled on the Roman Senate. Like that ancient body, it has always been dominated by its senior members. Power flows not from wisdom, achievement, or eloquence—they are optional—but from seniority. Unfortunately, for much of the twentieth century, southern segregationists used seniority to block racial progress. In the Senate's elaborate committee system, tradition dictates that the senator from the majority party who has served longest automatically becomes a committee's chairman; the longest-serving senator from the minority party becomes the "ranking member" of the committee. Few exceptions have been made. Freshman senators seldom get the committee assignments they desire, and I was no exception.

My first choice was the Foreign Relations Committee. In my first conversation with J. William Fulbright, the Arkansas Democrat who chaired it, he encouraged me, saying he thought I could make a real contribution. But a seat on Foreign Relations was not available. So I sought and was assigned a seat on the Banking and Currency Committee. That made sense, because banking is a key component of the Massachusetts economy. It would also allow me to influence federal housing policy for the poor, a special concern of mine.

My other assignment was the Aeronautical and Space Sciences Committee, chaired by Clinton P. Anderson of New Mexico, a tough, shrewd old-timer. Liberal on most issues, he had a maverick streak and a rich vein of country humor. I liked him but was less than thrilled with the appointment. I knew little about the space program. However, Anderson saw me as an expert on the space industry. After all, I came from Massachusetts, an aeronautics hotbed that was the home of MIT, Harvard, and the emerging Route 128 technology corridor. I began to read everything I could about space.

I was soon tested. On January 27, 1967, astronauts Virgil I. "Gus" Grissom, Edward H. White, and Roger B. Chaffee were trapped in a fire on the launching pad when an electrical spark ignited a fire in the command module. They died within minutes. The nation was stunned by this disaster, NASA's worst up until then, and our committee quickly held hearings. Senator Anderson, knowing I was a lawyer, would often turn to me and say, "You do the interrogation." I vigorously questioned James Webb, the head of NASA. Our investigation revealed many examples of poor wiring and plumbing that allowed combustible by-products into the cabin. The design problems were made worse by haphazard documentation of spacecraft modifications. On the basis of recommendations by our committee, NASA made changes that enabled the space program to move forward and meet President Kennedy's 1961 challenge to put a man on the moon, a triumphant achievement which took place in 1969.

My first Senate office was a three-room suite in the Russell Building, part of a series of offices vacated by the recently defeated Democrat, Paul Douglas of Illinois. Our staff marshaled every inch of available space, trying to fulfill their duties amid the din of jangling telephones and the clatter of typewriters. I brought several members of my attorney general staff with me to Washington. Nancy Porter became my executive assistant. Bill Cowin and Roger Woodworth came aboard as legislative assistants. Jerry Sadow continued as my press secretary. My old friend Clarence Elam, with his wealth of experience with inner-city problems, came too, as did Marilyn Dexheimer, whose expertise on African affairs was invaluable. No one was hired without a personal interview with me. When you joined our staff, you joined a family. Often working six days a week, late into the night, we needed people who were compatible, who shared a sense of commitment, and who really cared about our government.

My staff and I used to joke that our Massachusetts constituents never stayed at home. It was a relatively short trip from Massachusetts to Washington, and when commonwealth people came they wanted to see their senator, which meant me as well as Ted Kennedy. We scheduled many handshaking sessions, which we called "meet and greets." Massachusetts's industry and labor representatives often came to town and invited senators to evening receptions that featured an abundance of food and drink. Senator Saltonstall gave me valuable parting advice: "Ed, attend those events only when it is absolutely necessary. Never eat or drink anything, and stay only a few minutes, telling your hosts that you have a prior engagement. If you don't, you'll end up overweight, alcoholic, or worse. As for the prior engagement, I always had a standing commitment to have dinner with my wife."

The sheer volume of people who wanted to see me was staggering. But when a union representative or business executive asked for some time, I found it. The member of Congress who forgets his constituents' needs usually serves only one term. When Massachusetts cranberry bogs were threatened with disease, I jumped into action. When reports of a "red tide" jeopardized the state's clam diggers, I sampled the state's prized delicacies in full view of the cameras to reassure consumers.

Ever since my postwar work with the AMVETS, I had been sensitive to the needs of veterans, and much of our casework was military-related. We handled everything from young men seeking alternatives to service in Vietnam to veterans seeking help with their health benefits. Every letter had to be answered. My military caseworker, Linda Bunce, became a friend to thousands of families in her six years on my staff. Although I knew that congressmen and senators were allotted appointments to the nation's military academies, I was surprised at the large number of young men and, eventually, women who sought those few highly coveted appointments. Cam Newberry, my first administrative assistant, handled all applicants. He would narrow the list to ten, and I would interview those finalists personally. Many of these young men and women went on to distinguished records in and out of the military, and many have kept in touch with me over the years, which has given me much pleasure.

Like Margaret Chase Smith, I stood out in the Senate—I was one of a kind. My office was flooded with mail from around the country and hundreds of speaking invitations. On the floor of the Senate, I felt the eyes of visitors in the gallery. People would look to see if I was there much as they would Bobby and Ted Kennedy, who were then both serving in the Senate. In airports and on city streets people recognized me and reached for my hand. Although I was elected from Massachusetts, I understood that as the only African American senator, I was also viewed by millions of black Americans, in every state, as "their" senator. Out of the one hundred of us, I was often the one to whom African Americans, Hispanics, and members of other minorities turned to for help. I was determined to serve all the people, black, brown, and white. I intended to tackle racism and other national priorities as well. By addressing other issues, from housing to China policy to nuclear disarmament, I thought I could help shatter stereotypes that had lived on since slavery.

A black politician representing exclusively black interests would have been no better than a white politician representing exclusively white interests. The trip from Boston to Washington was 460 miles, but it was also far more than that. It was a dramatic reminder that I lived in two worlds, that I had two heritages, that my life had a closely interwoven pattern that combined black and white. My work was cut out for me. As I stood on the threshold of my Senate career, I had no idea how challenging, exciting, fulfilling, and ultimately heartbreaking those years would be.

12

Vietnam

I had not been in the Senate long when I decided I should go to Vietnam. America was deeply and bitterly divided over the war. The Johnson administration, and many fellow senators, seemed confident of victory there. Yet I knew how many people in Massachusetts, and in the rest of the country as well, considered the war a tragic mistake and were in despair over it. Without question, the war had been the biggest issue in my Senate campaign, and my promise to work for peace won me many votes over an opponent who seemed tied to President Johnson's military escalation. Every day I saw how the deaths of our soldiers in Vietnam caused pain that spread from their families and friends to millions of other Americans. I was also saddened by the untold number of Vietnamese being killed. People came to my office who could barely contain their rage and frustration. Based on my own wartime experiences, I was concerned about the morale of our troops as they fought a war that many Americans did not support.

In addition I was deeply troubled by the vast sums of money that were being diverted to Vietnam: about $2 billion a month by 1966. Every dollar spent on the war was a dollar we needed to spend on pressing problems at home. Inflation was on the rise, and that pernicious development, affecting every American, arose primarily from our increased spending in Vietnam. To me, spending so heavily on a foreign war that so many Americans opposed, when there was so much domestic distress in America, raised serious moral questions.

From the time I decided to run for the Senate, I had consulted with Southeast Asia experts, who were easily found in the academic community around Boston. I issued my first Vietnam policy statement in March 1966. It said the war in Vietnam was chiefly about Vietnamese issues. South Vietnam needed a civilian government more inclusive than the one it had. I warned that if democratic factions in South Vietnam failed to build a strong political and economic foundation, we might win the war militarily, but lose the peace. In August, with my campaign in full swing, I issued a second position paper. By this time, our government seemed bent on a policy of mindless escalation. I declared that neither escalation nor withdrawal addressed the realities in Southeast Asia; nor were these policies in our own best interests. I emphasized the need to create a climate for negotiation, by strengthening Vietnam's own political and economic structures and by keeping our military actions consistent with our interests and objectives.

Soon after I arrived in Washington in January 1967, Secretary of State Dean Rusk invited new Republican Senators Mark Hatfield, Charles Percy, Howard Baker, and me to have lunch with him and his under secretary, Nicholas Katzenbach, in his private dining room at the State Department. The stated purpose of the luncheon was to brief us on Vietnam, but I knew it would be aimed at winning our support for the administration's policy. Before we began, Secretary Rusk offered us drinks. Hatfield, a rock-ribbed Baptist, refused; Percy, a devout Christian Scientist, refused; Baker was not a drinker, and he refused. I declined as well. Secretary Rusk and Katzenbach looked at us in surprise and the secretary said, "Well, I can see you all are freshmen—wait until you've been here a few months." We all laughed, and while we sipped our iced teas, he and Katzenbach proceeded to drink double martinis. Nonetheless, they gave us a sober, informed, and articulate briefing on Vietnam. Still, when I questioned them about the bombing of North Vietnam and the rationale for sending more ground troops, they could not give me what I considered an acceptable response.

By then I knew that I should go see the war for myself. I recalled my father's aphorism: "The quality of a man's judgment is no better than the quality of his information." I wanted to see Vietnam firsthand, and I wanted to study the political, economic, and military status of Vietnam's neighbors: Japan, Taiwan, Cambodia, Hong Kong, Thailand, and, if possible, North Vietnam and China.

I arranged my trip in close consultation with the State Department, although the diplomats there were dismayed that I was going to Cambodia and even more alarmed that I was hoping to visit North Vietnam. Despite my reassurances, they feared I might upset U.S. negotiations with the North. I saw the purpose of my trip as twofold: to evaluate U.S. economic assistance programs, parts of which the Senate Banking and Currency Committee oversaw, and to examine our conduct of the war. I intended to report back to the Senate and the country with a speech on the Senate floor.

I chose Bill Cowin of my staff to join me on the trip. Bill was a skeptic on Vietnam, physically fit, well trained in the law, and had a knack for cutting to the heart of an issue. On March 4, less than two months after I entered the Senate, Bill and I boarded a commercial flight from Dulles Airport. We flew first to Japan, the grand postwar success story in Asia, and then to Taiwan, where we inspected factories and met with Taiwanese political and business leaders. Even though I had spoken frequently on the need to open up communications with mainland China, I was welcomed warmly by the Taiwanese.

After a stop in the bustling economic center of Hong Kong, we flew to Saigon, where my old friend Henry Cabot Lodge, now our ambassador, met us at the airport. As we shook hands, he whispered in my ear, "Ed, don't let them work you too hard while you're here." Lodge, though always effective in his long public service career, never believed in excessive work. When he was the vice presidential candidate with Richard Nixon in 1960, it was reported he never campaigned after 6 o'clock. Reporters saw him whisper to me and assumed it was something important. When I reached them, the reporters cried, "What did Ambassador Lodge tell you, Senator?" With a smile, I gave my stock response: "I'm not at liberty to say."

Lodge and his wife, Emily, invited Bill and me to stay at their residence in Saigon. Once there, the ambassador gave us a briefing and scheduled other briefings and meetings for us. I knew that Lodge had private doubts about the war, but he was a team player, and as long as he was our ambassador and our policy was to fight this war, he would support it.

The U.S. Army gave us more of a hard sell. They provided me

with military fatigues with "Brooke" printed on the breast pocket, and told me confidently, "we are going to win this damn war." I had a lengthy meeting with General William C. Westmoreland, the force-ful four-star general in charge of our forces, who emphasized that the United States had not lost a major battle in the war and did not in-tend to do so.

Ambassador Lodge escorted me to a meeting with South Vietnam's Prime Minister Nguyen Cao Ky, and Foreign Minister Tran Van Do. Ky had a military bearing and a swashbuckling manner. Through a translator, I tried to impress on him the need to permit the Constituent Assembly to draft the electoral laws and to bring about broader public support for the coming elections. Ky assured me that Vietnam was moving away from military control and to-ward constitutional government. I also spoke with foreign journal-ists in Saigon and with a range of citizens, from farmers to politicians. I visited refugee resettlement projects and spoke to intellectuals. I asked questions and tried to test the official line I was given in brief-ings against the reality of what I could see and learn in Vietnam.

It was often said that the military guided visiting politicians around the war zones and screened the GIs they spoke with. I never felt that. I moved about freely to new places and spoke to soldiers I sought out. I urged them to speak freely and was impressed that not one of them expressed doubts about the war. As far as I could see, the divisions back home had not harmed the morale of the troops. To me this was the key to our long-term presence in Vietnam—not what the generals thought, but how the soldiers on the ground felt about the war. Almost all of the men I saw said they could keep up the fight for as long as it would take; I remembered the same sentiment among our troops in World War II, though I realized it was a very different war. I visited hospitals and talked to the wounded, saddened to see so many young men injured so badly. I was struck by their determination. The troops' courage and high spirits weighed heavily in my thinking about the war.

The most dramatic transformation in the military since my days in uniform was the fact that black and white soldiers fought side by side in Vietnam. Even though President Truman had desegregated the military by executive order in 1948, segregation had persisted until the Korean War. In the early days of the Korean War, desperate commanders, in need of immediate replacement units in the face of heavy casualties, utilized any troops available, black or white. By the time of the Vietnam War, segregated units were military history.

In my travels around the country I found a South Vietnam that was tragically ravaged. The Vietnamese were a physically beautiful people, who carried themselves with simple dignity. Even in the middle of a war, they had a courtesy, a warmth and lightness about them that was quite affecting. Yet most were desperately poor. Many, who had once enjoyed a comfortable standard of living, became prostitutes and petty thieves just to survive. I had seen the same tragic consequences in Italy.

The army provided a helicopter to take us to the Mekong Delta and other areas outside of Saigon. It was a good-sized chopper, under the command of a seasoned pilot, who told us right away not to worry; he had logged hundreds of flight-hours. Still, this was a war zone. The doors to the chopper were disconcertingly open all the time, with mounted machine guns at the ready. We flew low enough to be in the range of small arms fire. Others who went up in choppers in Vietnam had talked about how lush the country looked from above, with its winding rivers, rice fields, and rubber plantations. What struck me was how dense the country was, so much of it jungle.

Over the roar of the chopper blades, we got a shouted briefing about the terrain, the movement of the troops, the supply routes. "Look down here: that's a hamlet we've just liberated from the Viet Cong." "Look over there: there's where our troops are." "And over there—there's where the Viet Cong are." I would look down and then I would ask, "Where?" Then the response was, "You have to look quickly to see them, Senator." That was a metaphor for the entire war. The whole time the United States was in Vietnam, we were never sure who or where the enemy was. The enemy had friends and family who were our allies, and our allies had friends and family who were the enemy. Physically, the Viet Cong and our Vietnamese allies looked alike. They were the same people. They spoke the same language. No one could ever be quite sure who was who. This was a jungle war, pure and simple. It was nearly impossible to identify or find the enemy, much less destroy him. It was hard to see how we could win the war in the conventional way. The fact is, we could not.

I came to South Vietnam prepared for anti-American displays, but I saw almost none. Most of the Vietnamese knew that without the U.S. military, their country would have already fallen to the communists. They knew we had helped their country make political, social, and economic progress. They welcomed our help. At the same time, talking to poor farmers in Vietnam reminded me that most people in every country just want to be left alone. To the farmers, *communism* and *democracy* were just words. We talked about "resisting the spread of communism." They cared about rice.

On my last day in Saigon, Bill and I lunched with Ambassador and Mrs. Lodge. After lunch Mrs. Lodge excused herself, and Lodge seated Bill and me in another room. Taking some handwritten notes from his pocket, he said that because I was his old friend, he was going to tell me what was really going on. Bill Cowin got his hopes up, thinking the ambassador was about to admit that the war could not be won. I knew him better. True to form, he simply walked us through the administration's party line and made the case for staying the course. I doubt Lodge expected to persuade me, but he had a job to do. Bill was disappointed. I was not. We caught the next plane to Cambodia.

Cambodia had cut diplomatic ties with the United States. No American official had been allowed to enter for several years. But Mike Mansfield, the Democratic majority leader in the Senate, was friendly with Prince Norodom Sihanouk, the head of the Cambodian government. Mike Mansfield was a wonderful man—introverted, devoutly Catholic, and deeply knowledgeable about Asian policy. Because the United States did not have diplomatic relations with Cambodia, it was he who arranged my visit through the Cambodian representative to the United Nations. We arrived in the capital of Phnom Penh, where we were met by the Australian ambassador, a charming, old-fashioned bachelor named Noel St. Clair DesChamps. He took us to his residence and gave us a sumptuous lunch, served up with some of his own tart criticism of U.S. policy. Later he briefed us thoroughly on Cambodia's internal problems and its anger over U.S. military incursions across its borders. Ambassador DesChamps also gave us in-depth background on Prince Sihanouk and told us that the next morning, in Sangkum, the prince would inaugurate the opening of an important bridge. He had arranged for us to attend the ceremony as guests of the prince.

Early the next morning, a limousine drove us to Sangkum. Prince Sihanouk had been in France for some months and felt it was time to make a statement about Cambodia's foreign policy. The prince was nominally neutral in the Cold War, but he had befriended Communist China and North Vietnam. He denied most vehemently that the Viet Cong were hiding from U.S. attacks in sanctuaries in Cambodia. It was a steaming hot day as we gathered on an uncovered wooden platform with ambassadors and military officers from several countries. Thousands of people were assembled, including hundreds of uniformed schoolchildren. The prince gave me a place of honor on the platform on his right. Nearby were Ambassador DesChamps and envoys from both China and North Vietnam. As I listened, he began his lengthy speech in Cambodian. I enjoyed watching a charismatic orator, even if I could not understand him. But when the prince had finished, he repeated his speech in French. I gathered that Prince Sihanouk was saying that he greatly admired the American people, and that Ho Chi Minh did, too. He noted his fondness for Senator Mansfield, for whom an avenue in Phnom Penh had been named. Then he got to the real issue: Cambodia had no wish to join the ideological struggle between East and West and wanted only to be left in peace to develop in its own way.

Switching to English, the prince called the war in Vietnam a civil conflict. In scathing tones, he said it would never have threatened world peace had the United States not intervened so massively. He angrily blamed the United States for both escalating and prolonging the conflict. I thought of walking off the platform in response to his harsh rhetoric. But I decided that to do so would be poor manners and might undermine America's interests. So I continued to sit, sweat, and stew.

After the speech, the prince and I walked across the new bridge together, and then, to prove that the United States was violating Cambodian borders, he took me by car on a ten-mile trip and showed me a downed U.S. airplane that he said had flown over his country in disregard for his nation's sovereignty. He strongly criticized the incursion of U.S. troops on Cambodian soil. At the same time he insisted that he hoped to resume diplomatic relations with the United States. His was an interesting and impressive performance, but I cannot say that much was changed by our encounter.

I hoped to meet with Ho Chi Minh or another North Vietnamese leader during my trip. I wanted to explore any possibility of settling the war through negotiation. While I was in South Vietnam, I asked journalist Peter Arnett to help arrange a meeting through his contacts in North Vietnam. He made several attempts, but nothing came of them. I continued this effort in Cambodia. I tried through newspaper reporters and the Australian Embassy to make contact with Ho Chi Minh or other leaders in Hanoi. While in Cambodia, I talked at length with Wilfred Burchett, an Australian journalist well connected in Hanoi, and he too, tried to set up a meeting for me with Ho Chi Minh. I made and received a series of inconclusive, frustrating phone calls, but without results. It was increasingly clear that Ho Chi Minh, well aware of the division in America over the war, intended to keep fighting until we lost patience and withdrew. Probably my flurry of calls never had much chance of success. A North Vietnamese official finally told me that further attempts would serve no purpose. My hope for a meeting was always a long shot. Perhaps I was naive. But I was a United States senator, and a person of color, who was independent of the Johnson administration and urgently wanted peace in Vietnam. I felt an obligation to reach out in the hope that perhaps I could do some good. But the other side was not yet ready for such contact.

Our final stop was Thailand. The Thai were our allies, and the officials who met us were very supportive of U.S. policy. They were pleased to have the United States use their country as a launching site for bombing raids on North Vietnam. The Thai ambassador to the United States told me that his country, and indeed all of Asia, needed our help resisting communism. He said pointedly, "The time to put out a fire is when the fire is a small one." On the long flight home, those words kept ringing in my ears.

On March 22, I shared my impressions of my trip with Vice President Humphrey and Secretary of State Rusk. Shortly after noon the next day, with my mother in the gallery, I reported on my trip to my Senate colleagues in my first formal speech on the floor of the Senate. I criticized the incessant harping on whether or not we ought to have sent troops to Vietnam in the first place. Policymakers lack the luxury of hindsight. The inescapable fact was that we were in Vietnam in a massive way. The loss of life, both American and Vietnamese, had already been staggering. The challenge was to find the best way to end it.

It seemed to me that three inescapable facts shaped U.S. policy. First, the South Vietnamese government wanted us in Vietnam. Second, Hanoi had not given the slightest indication it was willing to enter into peace talks. Finally, and most important, the trip had convinced me that Ho Chi Minh was taking heart as the war divided the American people. I strongly believed we should give him no such solace. Ho Chi Minh had everything to gain in refusing to engage in peace talks. I thought peace could best be achieved if we presented a united front at home, or as near to one as possible. I believed that the more U.S. opinion was divided, the more Ho Chi Minh would accelerate the war. I thought we had to signal Ho Chi Minh not to put his faith in our division at home and to see instead that a negotiated peace was his best option. "Don't underestimate the will of the American people," I warned, "When the chips are down, we'll be there." I also said that we should not escalate the war. I said we should not mine Haiphong harbor, or send planes into mainland China, or bomb air bases near China, and or do anything that might provoke the Chinese into entering the war. But I did not want to see our country cut and run or be defeated as the French had been.

After my speech, much of the media reported I had gone to Vietnam a dove and returned a hawk. I was never a hawk, and my point, as I tried to make clear, was that Ho Chi Minh was taking comfort from the divisiveness in our country. The day after my speech, the *New York Times* reported, "President Johnson won a prize convert today in the Congressional debate on the Vietnam War. Senator Brooke, who had advocated a reduction of the American military effort, said he had changed his mind after touring Southeast Asia." I was stung by that article. I was one senator groping for a balanced policy, not a "prize convert." My admonition to Ho Chi Minh not to underestimate American resolve should not have been equated with my belief in the justification of the war. I still favored a reduction of the American military effort. Yet, the nation's most respected newspaper portrayed me that way, and other media followed, describing my speech in similar terms. Obviously, I had not made myself clear. In retrospect, I see that the unity I called for, however desirable, was unobtainable. The vast division between those who supported the war and those who opposed it was not going to go away. The war at home would go on as long as the war did.

Seeking to clarify my position, I expanded on my speech at a news conference on March 24, and again two days later in an interview on *Face the Nation*. Under questioning by commentators Martin Agronsky, Alex Kendrick, and Robert Novak, I described my differences with President Johnson on the war. I said that we should use tear gas in Vietnam not napalm, as napalm was often fatal and tear gas was not. I said I had seen no evidence that Cambodia was harboring communists, but I had seen evidence that our forces were violating the Cambodian border. I said that we needed to persevere with firmness and means "proportionate" to the important stakes we had at risk in the conflict.

Moments after my *Face the Nation* interview, President Johnson, ignoring my expressed reservations, telephoned to thank me. He was effusive in his praise. He assured me that I had done "a great service to the country and to the American people" and invited me to the White House. Soon I was in the Oval Office, watching the president pound his desk and talk for an hour. I did not get a chance to say much. With a bitterness and insecurity quite striking in the most powerful man on earth, he talked mostly about how the eastern establishment would never accept him. At one point in the tirade, he said, "Senator, they'll accept you," an obvious reference to my race, "but they won't accept me as their president."

In retrospect, I believe my speech was probably overly influenced by the dedication I found among our fighting men and women in Vietnam. There was no doubt about their courage and willingness to sacrifice. But ultimately that was not the question. The question was whether we had any business in Vietnam, trying to determine the fate of that distant land about which we knew so little. Today it is clear that the answer is no, but it was not so clear in 1967. We had hundreds of thousands of troops on the ground, and few if any responsible leaders were saying we should just withdraw them. The only exception I recall was Vermont's wise and affable Senator George Aiken, who said we should simply declare victory and get out. Our leaders were stubborn men who thought our military could prevail. The North Vietnamese leaders were stubborn men who thought they could outlast us. In the end, they were right. It was a tragic miscalculation on our part, from which we can only pray we have learned lessons for the future.

As early as April 1966, Martin Luther King had come out strongly and publicly against the war. On *Face the Nation* in May of that year, he urged a halt to the bombing of North Vietnam. He pointed out that in proportion to our population, twice as many African American soldiers as whites were fighting in Vietnam. In April 1967, when Dr. King went so far as to advise young African Americans to resist the draft by opting for conscientious objector status, many people were offended. They might have grudging respect for Dr. King as a civil rights leader, but they were angry when he moved beyond civil rights and took on the Vietnam War.

I wanted to talk to Martin about Vietnam, and he sent word he wanted to talk to me, too. Our meeting occurred in May 1967, when we were both in Geneva attending Pacem in Terris II, the second international conference on the requirements for world peace following the famous papal encyclical. I had great admiration for Martin, and I asked him bluntly if he thought it might be a mistake to advise young African American men to disobey the draft laws. Offering no explanation or apology, he simply said, "No." I continued, "Martin, no one really knows what the outcome of this tragic war will be, but do you think, as some fear, that taking a leadership role against the war might impair your effectiveness as our foremost civil rights leader?" He looked me straight in the eye and with a soft but determined voice said, "Ed, I was a preacher of the Word of God long before I was a civil rights leader."

I found his words and his moral strength moving, and we went on to have a lengthy discussion about the civil rights movement, its goals, its progress, and its future. He and I agreed that the first steps, winning the right to sit in the front of a bus or to sit at a lunch counter, were easy, compared with what lay ahead. The right to economic justice and economic equality would come much harder. Although he was an advocate of "people power," he understood the need for political power as well.

The Tet offensive of January 1968 marked the turning point in the Vietnam War and in American public opinion. To this day, the military will argue that Tet was a military victory, because it broke the backbone of the Viet Cong. But the televised pictures of American military installations being overrun by Asian forces and the U.S. Embassy itself being attacked was also the final straw that broke the resolve of any remaining American support for the war. Within weeks, the war had become so overwhelmingly unpopular that President Lyndon Johnson announced that he would not seek reelection.

With the election of Richard Nixon in November 1968, there was great hope that a new president would bring the war to a swift and honorable conclusion. But the war continued almost unabated. Peace negotiations led nowhere. In May 1970, much to my dismay, U.S. troops invaded Cambodia. A million marchers gathered on the Mall in Washington, my twenty-one-year-old daughter, Remi, among them, and the Congress was up in arms. Almost immediately, several senators including Frank Church, Democrat of Idaho; George McGovern, Democrat of South Dakota; John Sherman Cooper, Republican of Kentucky; and Mark Hatfield, Republican of Oregon, began introducing amendments to end the war. At first these took the form of limited measures to cut off funds for ground troops in Cambodia or to call for general withdrawal of U.S. forces. But when that failed to achieve any results, tougher amendments were introduced that employed the Congress's power of the purse. These amendments, usually to an appropriations bill, would cut off funds for certain activities, such as bombing North Vietnam, or maintaining U.S. troops in Vietnam, after a certain date. As time went on, these amendments garnered more and more support, including my own.

After my reelection in 1972, my priority continued to be Vietnam. On March 27, 1973, I returned to Southeast Asia. This time, I went as a member of the Foreign Operations Subcommittee of the Appropriations Committee, and my focus was on the rehabilitation and reconstruction of all of Indochina: Vietnam, Laos, and Cambodia. Though war continued, it was time for a serious examination of the impact of the war on the people of Indochina, and a projection of what could be done to restore economic and political stability. What I found was not promising. Civil war now raged in all three countries. The refugee situation was out of hand. Economies and infrastructures had been destroyed. It was clear that massive infusions of American aid would be required if civilian control were to be maintained in any of the three countries.

In the end, the war only stopped when Richard Nixon was forced out of office and his successor, Gerald Ford, withdrew American troops. At that point, almost no one objected. The war ended with the humiliating fall of Saigon in late April 1975. The long nightmare was finally over. After Vietnam fell to communism, no dominoes fell, as had been predicted by Presidents Johnson and Nixon and their experts; no other nations in Southeast Asia went communist. We underestimated the determination of our opponents, and we put too much faith in what proved to be a weak, unpopular government in South Vietnam. Our presence in Vietnam was rife with folly, hubris, and human tragedy. But the nation will always owe a great debt of gratitude to the patriotism of the American men and women who made the supreme sacrifice there, no matter how misguided or ill-advised our government's policy may have been.

In March 1969, two years after my first trip to Vietnam, I received a letter from Vietnam veteran Ronald Ridenour alleging that he had learned from other veterans of a massacre of more than three hundred Vietnamese women, children, and old men in a tiny village called My Lai. He said this massacre had been part of a search-and-destroy mission in an area regarded as a haven for Viet Cong. I was shocked by the charges and looked into them. I found that Ridenour had sent at least thirty letters to members of Congress, the Pentagon, and President Nixon. His own Arizona representatives, Congressman Mo Udall and Senator Barry Goldwater, and I were the only ones to respond to his call for an investigation of the events at My Lai.

I forwarded the letter to Secretary of Defense Melvin Laird, saying that if the charges were accurate, I expected the Department of the Army to take action. In time, I was briefed by a delegation of senior army officers, who told me that the killing of civilians had indeed taken place and that Lieutenant William Calley would be brought to trial. His trial of course led to great controversy. Calley had many defenders. They argued that Calley had simply done his duty, and that the death of civilians was inevitable in a guerrilla war. Having helped bring Ridenour's charges to light, I felt an obligation to defend the army's pursuit of justice. I therefore wrote an op-ed article for the *Washington Post* in October 1969 rebutting those who said that Calley should not be brought to trial. Only a scrupulous proceeding could determine the facts, clear the innocent, and punish the guilty, I said. I believed that then, and I still believe it now.

As I write this in 2006, American troops are engaged in combat in Iraq, and there have been charges of the needless deaths of Iraqi civilians, not unlike those that emerged in Vietnam. Perhaps I can add a contemporary postscript to my public comments on Vietnam. During that war, as a senator, I could at least try to influence events. Today, I watch our occupation of Iraq only as a concerned citizen. As events unfold there, I fear that those who gave us today's war did not learn the lesson of yesterday's.

Clearly, the terrorist attacks of September 11, 2001, demanded a military response. The retaliation against Al Qaeda and its Taliban protectors in Afghanistan was well conceived and well executed. Yet the proposition that the 9/11 attacks justified the subsequent assault on Iraq is highly dubious. The lack of evidence for Iraq's involvement in the 9/11 catastrophes, together with failure to discover Saddam Hussein's reputed weapons of mass destruction, has profoundly undermined the U.S. rationale for the war.

Ours is the greatest, most powerful, most advanced civilization the world has ever known. We like to think of our democracy as a beacon to all the people of the world. Yet the fact remains that much of the world hates us, and it is only prudent to examine why this should be. We must recognize that our decisions to circumvent the international rule of law, to bypass the United Nations, or to engage in preventive rather than preemptive war are fraught with danger. They may bring short-term satisfaction, but are likely in the long run to create more fear and hatred of us. We must ask ourselves if we want to pursue policies that spawn terrorism and cause us to live in fear in our own country, in our own homes. Do we want to "stay the course" when the course is legally and morally wrong? Or do we want to reconsider the policies that have so isolated us not only from the Islamic world but also from our own traditional democratic allies?

What if we engaged in war only as a last resort when diplomacy has clearly failed? What if the tens of billions of dollars that are being spent on military action in Iraq were being spent to reduce poverty, illiteracy, and illness around the world? Would that not greatly increase our world standing and our national security, far more than military adventures?

No one can turn a blind eye to the suicide bombings and terrorist attacks directed against Israelis. Nor can one ignore the ineptitude and corruption that has made the Palestinian leadership a poor, sometimes impotent diplomatic partner. But a powerful, democratic Israel, like a powerful, democratic America, must also recognize that military force, ungoverned by far-sighted diplomacy, will often compound the dangers it seeks to meet.

One should be able to question Israeli policies without being called anti-Semitic. One should be able to question the policies of Arab countries without being called anti-Muslim/Islamic. And, one should be able to question the policies of the United States without being called unpatriotic. Peace and justice in the Middle East can only be achieved with visionary, bold, and courageous Israeli, Arab, and American political leadership.

13

Member of

the Club

During my first years in the Senate I spent a lot of time on airplanes. In April 1967, only a month after my return from Southeast Asia, I flew to Israel to lay the cornerstone of the aeronautical wing of the Amal Comprehensive Trade School, in the city of Beersheba, not far from the Sea of Galilee. The Boston Committee of Histadrut, the Israeli Federation of Labor Committee, had honored me in the fall of 1966 with the organization's Brotherhood Award for my support of technical education in Israel, and this wing of the school had been named for me.

During this, my first trip to Israel, Remigia and I visited the Tomb of David and the room of the Last Supper. We walked through the streets of Nazareth where Christ had walked. I was moved by the holy places and impressed by what the Israelis had done to transform a desert into a land of plenty. Being so close to the site of Palestinian-Israeli conflict gave me a new perspective on the East-West arms race and the influence of the superpower rivalry on international conflicts. After meeting with Israeli President Zalman Shazer and Prime Minister Levi Eshkol, I boarded a plane for a brief visit to Greece and was the first American official to visit there since the military coup.

My globetrotting soon inspired derision. Critics said I was trying to be a one-man State Department. The *Boston Herald* warned that I was "playing a dangerous game." Cartoonist Paul Szep depicted me in Bermuda shorts and a flowered shirt talking to a reporter in front of an airplane. My suitcase bore travel stickers from Vietnam, Thailand, Cambodia, Hong Kong, Japan, Greece, Israel, and the Virgin Islands. The caption was, "I Also Have High Hopes of Visiting Washington One of These Days." I was amused but not deterred.

In January 1968, I made my first trip to Africa. I felt that continent deserved more U.S. economic and political support, and I had been a critic of our government for not having a coherent policy toward this emerging continent as well as Asia, Latin America, and the Caribbean. Today, more than ever, I think of the words spoken by Winston Churchill more than a century ago: "Do not let us do anything which makes us the champion of only one race and consequently deprives us forever of the confidence of the other."

My legislative assistant, Marilyn Dexheimer, and Clarence Elam went with me. Marilyn prepared a voluminous briefing book that included everything from economic facts and biographies of key leaders to an analysis of the political dynamics of each of the countries we were to visit. We went to Senegal, Guinea, Liberia, Ivory Coast, Ghana, Nigeria, Congo (Kinshasa), Zambia, Botswana, Tanzania, Uganda, and Kenya: twelve countries in twenty-six days. Most of these nations were just emerging from colonialism, and we encountered some leftist ideologies. But we also met Africans who revered American democracy. They had surging pride in their hard-won freedom and stubborn confidence in their future.

I was struck by the vastness and beauty of sub-Saharan Africa, the variety of its cultures, and the tremendous obstacles ahead for its future. The purpose of my trip was to study economic development and political conditions, but I was also interested in the U.S. aid program, the Peace Corps, and the role of American private investment. I wanted to see how these former colonies were making the transition to independence. I was able to meet with many of the legendary founders of African independence: the poet-philosopher Leopold Sédar-Senghor in Senegal, the revolutionary Sekou Touré in Guinea, the bureaucratic William V. S. Tubman in Liberia, the embattled General Yakubu Gowon in Nigeria, the dignified Sir Seretse Khama in Botswana, and the visionary Julius Nyerere in Tanzania. Each leader brought his own perspective, but the problems they faced were strikingly similar: an uneducated populace, deplorable health conditions, ethnic tensions, and lack of investment and economic development.

Only two American reporters joined the first trip of an African American senator to Africa. One was Howard Knowles, the highly regarded reporter from the *Worcester Gazette*, who covered the trip from a local political angle. The other was Anne Chamberlin from *Cosmopolitan*, a magazine better known for discussing sex than politics. She was a delightful woman who took great pleasure in chronicling my dancing with villagers and my zest for native cuisine. Her article, "Senator Brooke, I Presume? Or: How the Only Negro in the U.S. Senate Keeps His Cool in Hottest Africa," is an account that I treasure to this day.

Back in the Senate, I told my colleagues of the tremendous opportunities in Africa. The people of Africa were looking to the United States as a model and as a source of aid. My speech was as much a plea as it was a report: "It is no small accomplishment to be an ally in the struggle for freedom and welfare of over 250 million people," I said. "As model and midwife, the United States can help speed the birth of democracy and prosperity in that mighty continent." Sadly, I was a voice in the wilderness. Despite all the emphasis being placed on civil rights, America's political leaders were not yet concerned about the continent that was the ancestral home to so many Americans.

My trip to Africa crystallized my thinking on the insidious institution of apartheid. A month later, I made another speech before the Senate, this time calling on the Johnson administration to end all trade with South Africa unless it lifted its policy of oppressing blacks. I proposed isolation of all the white regimes of southern Africa (South Africa, Angola, Mozambique, and Rhodesia) that subjugated black majorities. I said, "The record of what we have not done speaks more clearly than the verbal condemnations and token sanctions against the white regimes. We have done nothing to discourage American private investment in South Africa. The time has come to wrench ourselves from this pattern of implied complicity with the Southern African regimes." Slowly, opposition to apartheid did grow in this country, and a long two decades later the system collapsed.

Civil war was raging in Nigeria. Televised images of skeletal Biafran children with bloated bellies brought the misery into our nation's living rooms. The people needed food and medicines but, above all, they needed a negotiated peace. After Richard Nixon took office in 1969, there was considerable pressure on the United States to back the Biafran rebels. National Security Adviser Henry Kissinger was an advocate for Biafra: there were many Biafrans at Harvard, and some had close ties to Kissinger. As a result, Nixon was being nudged toward intervention. It was my public and private advice to the president that he not take sides in the brutal civil war but focus on humanitarian assistance. I advised him to stay out of it, and he did. This was one of the few times Nixon agreed with me, or perhaps anyone, against Kissinger.

Mine was an unpopular position. But I had seen the face of war, and I knew that ultimately the best hope for the people of Nigeria, of Biafra, and indeed of all of Africa, was to end the struggle and to bring the sides together. Africa was entirely too divided along ethnic and tribal lines; support for one breakaway effort would only encourage a dozen more. I was able to persuade my Senate colleagues of the correctness of this position and in turn to help hold our policy in support of existing states.

In 1967, racial tensions at home reached an all-time high. That summer a wave of destructive violence swept through seventy-five American cities and towns. As the rioting raged on, I told a national convention of the NAACP, "Riots and violence are the mortal enemies, not the servants, of the civil rights movement." I added, "To stand still is to regress. The word 'wait' engenders hate. If Congress, out of fear or anger continues to choose the path of inaction, racial violence in the United States will not only continue, it will recur with ever-increasing intensity."

On July 28, after two weeks of rioting in Newark and Detroit, President Johnson asked me to serve as one of eleven members of the President's National Advisory Commission on Civil Disorders, chaired by Illinois Governor Otto Kerner. The Kerner Commission, as it became known, was initiated with great fanfare and charged with finding out what happened, why it happened, and what could be done to prevent such riots from happening again. We undertook our task with an open mind. Governor Kerner had asked us "to probe into the soul of America," and we tried to meet that challenge. With the help of a ninety-member staff, headed by David Ginsburg, the commission completed its 250,000-word report four months ahead of schedule.

On February 29, 1968, we reported that America was "moving toward two societies, one black, one white, separate and unequal." We concluded that "white racism is essentially responsible" for the explosive violence that engulfed many cities and declared that "race prejudice has shaped our history decisively; it now threatens to affect our future." We pointed out that Negro frustration grew out of underrepresentation in the political system, the police, the media, and all aspects of American life. We urged massive new investments in jobs, schools, and housing. We declared that segregation and poverty had created in the racial ghetto a destructive environment totally unknown to most white Americans, and we avowed that white America had created and maintained the ghetto and that white society condoned it. These were strong words, but we believed that the truth needed telling.

I thought President Johnson would applaud our painstaking analysis and support our recommendations. But the president who had done so much for civil rights distanced himself from our findings. He did not invite us to the White House for the report's release, nor did he embrace its recommendations. Members of the commission were shocked and disappointed. I faulted the president for not using the bully pulpit of the White House to support our frank statement. Because of his silence, precious little official attention was paid to the report. Had Johnson seized the moment, our country might be further along on the road of improved race relations today.

In retrospect, however, I can see that our report was too strong for him to take. It suggested that all his great achievements—his civil rights legislation, his antipoverty program, Head Start, housing legislation, and all the rest of it—had been only a beginning. It asked him, in an election year, to endorse the idea that white America bore much of the responsibility for black rioting and rebellion. However true that might be, the message was politically too hot to handle. So the Kerner Commission Report gathered dust while America's racial problems grew worse.

In 1978, I wrote an op-ed piece for the *Washington Post* that commented on the Kerner report ten years later. I said that, despite some progress, America's problems with racism and poverty were even worse than they had been in 1968. One point I made was that the "two Americas" we had warned of were becoming "three Americas" as Hispanics emerged as a growing underclass that was distinct from the African American poor. That was true in 1978, but since then Hispanics have made remarkable progress toward entering the political mainstream, both as officeholders and as voters. At the start of the twenty-first century, the Kerner Commission's 1968 prediction of "two societies, one black, one white, separate and unequal," remains all too accurate.

During the worst of the 1967 rioting, I met with H. Rap Brown, the militant leader of the Black Power movement, and some of his followers in a shabby basement apartment on 7th Avenue in Harlem. Brown had become active in the Student Nonviolent Coordinating Committee while a student in the early 1960s. As the national director of SNCC, Brown dropped "Nonviolent" from the organization's name and turned away from integration in favor of Black Nationalism and separatism. He advocated an alliance with the Black Panther Party, which promoted armed self-defense of black communities. He coined the phrase "Burn, Baby, Burn" and often said that "violence is as American as cherry pie."

Brown extended the invitation and, against the wishes of my closest advisers, I accepted. As he insisted, I went alone. He seated me in a wooden chair facing him and a dozen supporters. I was in my blue suit, white shirt, and blue and white tie before an assembly of angry revolutionaries in blue jeans and Afros. I listened attentively to bitter, profane criticism of me and the American system of government as a whole. "You're not black," Brown told me. "You are not one of us. In the Senate you are part of the white establishment. You are what's wrong with America."

"I am what I think is right for America and for all of us," I responded. "I think what we need is to be part of the system and change it for the betterment of our people. What's wrong with being in the U.S. Senate? That's where the power is. That's where we can get housing, jobs, education, and protection. That's where we can end police brutality. We need more of us there." I insisted that existing political mechanisms were part of the answer to the racial problem. I told them that I had experienced bigotry in America, but most Americans are decent, hardworking people, and we had to reach out to them, not alienate them. They wanted to hear none of that. But I continued. To their demands for "black power," I responded, "What is power but the ability to change the basic conditions of life? Intemperance and intolerance serve no one, and hatred guarantees failure. It seems to me that your advocacy and vying for black power is self-defeating."

No women were present; when Brown spoke of "black power," he was talking about power for black males. What he had to say about the role of women in his movement was remarkably crude. He and his friends made clear their disapproval of me, but they were not really rude, although they sometimes muttered their disagreement. The meeting lasted the better part of two hours, then Brown and some others escorted me to my car. No one shook my hand or thanked me, nor did I expect it. They went their way and I went mine.

To me, the Fair Housing Act of 1968 was the most vital issue before the Senate that year. I had always believed that the insidious cluster of ghetto problems, including poor schools and a lack of jobs and opportunity, could be eased by an end to discrimination in housing. I thought that open housing could help break education and employment barriers and show that the ghetto was not an immutable institution in America. How could black people improve their lives as long as white people could refuse to sell or rent property to them on the basis of race? To me, the issue of open housing went beyond politics and asked white America to cast off prejudice, avarice, and fear, and to embrace equal justice for all.

The act, which I cosponsored with Democratic Senator Walter Mondale of Minnesota, was a strong federal law against housing discrimination. At first, no one thought the bill could pass. It faced a filibuster by southern senators. President Johnson supported a more limited ban on discrimination in the sale and renting of housing. As the former Senate majority leader, Johnson was an expert on the racial insensitivities of southern senators, and he believed that our broader bill would fail. Fritz Mondale, and I, both members of the Banking and Currency Committee, brought our Mondale-Brooke Fair Housing bill to the floor over the objections of the president. Opponents filibustered, and we got no help from the White House in breaking the filibuster. Although I thought he privately favored our measure, Johnson was never a man to waste political capital on what he believed to be a lost cause.

In one speech, I said in support of the legislation, "Fair housing does not promise an end to the ghetto; it promises only to demonstrate that the ghetto is not an immutable institution in America. It will scarcely lead to a mass dispersal of the ghetto population to the suburbs, but it will make possible for those who have the resources to escape the stranglehold now suffocating the inner cities of America."

In 1968, any senator could filibuster for any length of time, until two-thirds of all senators present and voting adopted a parliamentary motion of "cloture." Cloture ends debate on a bill and forces a direct vote on it. But unless that happens, the filibuster can continue until the bill is withdrawn. Eventually, in 1975, the Senate adopted a compromise rule, which allows cloture with a vote of three-fifths of the Senate, or sixty votes. This reform did much to weaken the long-time power of southern conservatives to block progressive legislation via a filibuster.

Rarely do a bill's sponsors get more than two attempts to reach cloture. We lost three cloture votes—by narrow margins, but we still lost. At that point, negotiations led to the drafting of a modified version of the bill, which became known as the Dirksen substitute, after Minority Leader Everett Dirksen. With the minority leader now engaged, the Democratic leadership, which favored the bill, agreed to one more cloture vote, an unheard-of fourth try. Victory was not certain. I targeted Republican Jack Miller of Iowa as the key man in getting the cloture votes we needed. Jack was a pillar of the Senate's conservative wing and a decent man. Some members called him "Typewriter Jack" because he liked to type up his own amendments in the Senate cloakroom. Jack and I were always friendly though far apart on many issues.

Jack had his own amendment forbidding discrimination in housing against Armed Forces veterans. In return for his promise to vote for cloture, I agreed to support his amendment and to question him about it on the Senate floor so he could build a legislative record in

Brooke's mother, Helen Seldon Brooke, in a photograph taken before her marriage. *From Edward W. Brooke's private collection.*

Photograph of Brooke's father, Edward William Brooke Jr., who worked as a government lawyer in Washington, D.C. *From Edward W. Brooke's private collection.*

Edward W. Brooke III, at the age of three, standing next to sister Helene in their LeDroit Park neighborhood in Washington, D.C., in 1922. Brooke's parents raised their children in the protective cocoon of the capital's middle-class African American community. *From Edward W. Brooke's private collection.*

Following his graduation from Howard University in 1941, where he was a member of the ROTC program, Brooke was assigned to the all-black 366th Combat Infantry Regiment and sent to Fort Devens in Massachusetts. The 366th would eventually see combat in Italy in 1944–1945. It was during his time in Italy that Brooke met Remigia Ferrari-Scacco, whom he would marry in 1947. *From Edward W. Brooke's private collection.*

After graduating from the Boston University School of Law's accelerated program following the war, Brooke started a law practice in Roxbury and became involved in Massachusetts Republican politics. Edwina, Edward, Remigia, and Remi Brooke are shown here in a
1962 photo on the night of his election to the office of attorney general. Brooke became
the first African American to be elected a state's attorney general in the United States.
From Edward W. Brooke's private collection.

In his role as the commonwealth's chief law enforcement officer, Brooke vigorously fought
corruption and stepped in to coordinate the fragmented police investigation of the Boston Strangler, whose string of sexual assaults and murders of women terrorized the greater
metropolitan Boston area. *From Edward W. Brooke's personal collection on loan to the Howard
Gotlieb Archival Research Center at Boston University.*

Elliot Richardson, shown here with Dr. Martin Luther King Jr. and Brooke at the Massachusetts State House in 1962, was a chief rival within the Massachusetts Republican Party. The two would forge an amicable alliance in the years that followed as their paths crossed during state and national service. Brooke and fellow Alpha Phi Alpha member Martin Luther King would meet again privately in May 1967 to discuss King's fervent opposition to the war in Vietnam. Dr. King was assassinated less than a year later in Memphis, Tennessee. *From Edward W. Brooke's personal collection on loan to the Howard Gotlieb Archival Research Center at Boston University.*

Newly elected junior senator from Massachusetts, Edward W. Brooke, and the senior senator, Edward M. Kennedy, on the steps of the U.S. Capitol. Brooke became the first African American to be popularly elected to the United States Senate. Only two African Americans have been elected to the U.S. Senate since. *From Edward W. Brooke's personal collection on loan to the Howard Gotlieb Archival Research Center at Boston University.*

Brooke was featured on the cover of the November 18, 1966, issue of *Time* magazine as part of its coverage of the "Republican Resurgence" in that pivotal election. Also appearing on the cover were newly elected Republicans Ronald Reagan, governor of California; George Romney, governor of Michigan; Charles Percy, senator from Illinois; Mark Hatfield, senator from Oregon; and Nelson Rockefeller, governor of New York. *TIME magazine © 1966 Time, Inc. Reprinted by permission.*

Brooke once again appeared on the cover of *Time* magazine one month after taking his Senate seat. At the height of the civil rights movement, the election of a black man (a Republican from one of the nation's most liberal states, no less) to the United States Senate was big news. Brooke's image also graced the cover of *Newsweek* and appeared in newspapers across the country and around the world. *TIME magazine © 1967 Time, Inc. Reprinted by permission.*

When violent race riots broke out, putting many American cities in flames, Brooke was one of eleven individuals tapped by President Lyndon B. Johnson to investigate inequities that could lead to such violence. The landmark Kerner Commission completed its report in record time, concluding that America was "moving toward two societies, one black, one white, separate and unequal." Brooke criticized President Johnson's failure to seize their findings and recommend sweeping changes that would have improved race relations in the United States. *From Edward W. Brooke's personal collection on loan to the Howard Gotlieb Archival Research Center at Boston University.*

Brooke enjoyed an uneasy relationship with fellow Republican Richard Nixon, who as president was mystified by Brooke's ability to be elected as a black Republican Episcopalian from a predominantly white, Democratic, and Catholic state. Nixon was responsive to Brooke's early agitation for greater recognition by the United States of mainland China but was unresponsive to Brooke's consistent efforts to persuade him to abandon his "southern strategy." Brooke became the first Republican senator to call for President Nixon's resignation in the wake of the Watergate break-in and cover-up. *Photo by Stan Forman, Boston* Record American, *1968. From Edward W. Brooke's personal collection on loan to the Howard Gotlieb Archival Research Center at Boston University.*

Following a devastating 1978 reelection defeat in a bid for a third term in the Senate—a race influenced by negative headlines surrounding his divorce from Remigia and estrangement from his two adult daughters—Brooke retreated from public life. In time, he resumed the practice of law and married Anne Fleming, from the island of St. Martin in the Caribbean, shown here on their wedding day in Washington, D.C. *From Edward W. Brooke's private collection.*

Fatherhood the second time around was a new experience for Brooke, whose only son was born in 1981. He and Anne bought a farm in the Virginia countryside where Edward W. Brooke IV, shown here at their St. Martin home as a toddler, was raised. *From Edward W. Brooke's private collection.*

To Sen. & Mrs. Ed Brooke — With every good wish & Warm Regard — Ronald Reagan

Republican President Ronald Reagan invited former Senator Brooke and Anne to the White House for an informal dinner in 1982. President Reagan tapped Brooke, who had championed fair housing legislation during his tenure in the Senate, to serve on the President's Commission on Housing. *From Edward W. Brooke's private collection.*

On June 29, 2004, during ceremonies at the White House, President George W. Bush presented former Senator Edward W. Brooke with the Presidential Medal of Freedom, the nation's highest civilian award. *White House photo by Paul Morse, used with permission.*

support of it. In our exchange, he had to admit that his amendment would protect me, a veteran, against discrimination but would not cover my children, my mother, or other minorities who were nonveterans. I kept my word and voted for his amendment, but its defects were apparent, and it failed. The bargain was an uncomfortable one for me, but my discomfort was trivial in comparison with the historic goal we were pursuing. Jack Miller's vote for cloture was decisive in paving the way for passage of the Fair Housing Act of 1968. With the filibuster defeated, the Dirksen compromise bill came to a vote on March 11 and passed, 71–20.

In the House of Representatives, the bill stalled in the Rules Committee. But Republican Congressman John Anderson of Illinois, with whom I worked closely, rescued it. The House passed the bill on April 10, and President Johnson signed the legislation into law on April 11, one week after Dr. King's assassination. The powerful emotions stirred by the assassination helped us achieve final passage in the House. It was an important achievement, yet the housing bill was far from perfect. Senator Dirksen, who was given to theatrics, had often proclaimed the need to protect "Mrs. Murphy's Rooming House" from federal regulation, and in fact the final compromise bill exempted small apartment houses from coverage. The Dirksen bill covered 80 percent of the nation's housing, as opposed to 91 percent in the Mondale-Brooke bill. Worse, the bill's enforcement powers were weak, and the battle to put teeth in them went on for years.

The next year, 1969, I was able to gain passage of the Brooke Amendment, another housing measure, which provided that tenants of federally financed public housing could not be required to spend more than 25 percent of their income on rent. I took pride in this rule, which was simple, practical, and fair, and might ease many people's lives each month when the rent came due. In later years, however, conservatives chipped away at the law until it was possible for housing-project tenants to pay up to 40 percent of their income on rent.

Fair and affordable housing remained a priority of mine throughout my time in the Senate. After Richard Nixon became president, I fought an annual battle to get some mention of housing in his State of the Union Message. It was such a basic issue that it tended to be ignored. At one point I tried to get passed the Young Families Housing Act, which would have made it easier for young couples to buy their first home, but I was defeated. Even after I left the Senate, I continued to battle for better housing for poor people in the face of cutbacks by the Reagan administration. One of the points that has been ignored in recent political debate is that if you fail to build affordable housing, if you refuse to raise the minimum wage, if inflation keeps raising rents, and if the population continues to grow, the inevitable result is rising homelessness—which, tragically, our nation has come to accept in recent years.

Despair hung heavy in the air in 1968. By the summer, assassins' bullets would fell two of our nation's great leaders. Martin Luther King Jr. was the first to die, on April 4, and then on June 5, Senator Robert F. Kennedy. I knew Bobby Kennedy only briefly. For a short time we had offices next to each other in the Dirksen Building. I would remember the loyalty and devotion of his staff, his quick smile, his abbreviated "high five," and the big shaggy dog he brought to the office with him.

Dr. King's assassination sent waves of shock and anger through Washington and through our country. Upon word of his death, the Senate adjourned. I went to my apartment in Tiber Island and prayed for him and his family as I would just two months later for Bobby and his family. Soon billowing smoke filled the air from hundreds of fires that consumed stores, homes, and whole blocks of the city where I had grown up. Three days of rioting in Washington left 14th Street NW, 7th Street NW, and H Street NE, in ruins and resulted in the deaths of 12 people, injury to 1,200 others, and staggering property losses.

Following the assassination, Congressman John Conyers introduced a bill to honor Martin Luther King by making his birthday, January 15, a national holiday. It became clear that his bill was not going to pass, so I offered an alternative that would have made Dr. King's birthday a "day of commemoration" but not an actual national holiday that gave workers the day off. Not even my more modest proposal could overcome the combined opposition of some southern senators and that of the business community, who saw even my bill as a first step toward a holiday that would force them to shut down for a day. It was another fifteen years before the King national holiday bill was approved and signed into law by President Ronald Reagan.

In the aftermath of Dr. King's assassination, the high ideals of the civil rights movement were challenged. Many of its younger, newer members called for black separatism. I warned that excluding whites from the civil rights movement would be a grave mistake. I opposed black separatism, militancy, and violence as strongly as I had opposed white discrimination, segregation, and violence. The civil rights movement needed allies, not enemies. But soon the peace and brotherhood Dr. King sought for all Americans was even more elusive than it had appeared in the darkest days of Montgomery, Selma, and Birmingham.

In the 1960s and well into the 1970s, the Senate was still a civil, collegial place where bipartisanship was not only possible but common, and where moderate-to-liberal Republicans were a large and influential force. There were sharp disagreements, to be sure, and some members were easier to deal with than others, but most of our dealings were pleasant or at least proper. Today's bitter adversary could be tomorrow's valued ally, so it was always desirable to maintain good relations. You can accomplish little or nothing in the Senate without the help of others. So we made flowery references on the Senate floor to this or that "distinguished colleague." You probably did not mean it, you might hold that colleague in what was jokingly called "minimum high regard," but it was the civil way to do business.

When I arrived in the Senate, the moderate, so-called Rockefeller Republicans held the balance of power. The Democrats were in the majority, but their southern members usually opposed civil rights and other progressive legislation. Often only by forging alliances with Republicans could the Democrats pass their progressive agenda. I was entirely comfortable reaching across the Senate aisle to work with Democrats. I considered myself one of the least partisan senators. I was proud to be a Republican, but my ultimate loyalty was to certain goals and ideals, not to party.

As I became comfortable in my role as senator, I sought ways to increase my effectiveness. To that end, I became one of the founders of the Wednesday Club, a group of moderate Republicans who met every Wednesday for lunch. We took turns as host. Over informal lunches we sometimes reached a consensus on legislation and then voted as a bloc. The core of the Wednesday Club included Jacob Javits of New York, Clifford Case of New Jersey, John Sherman Cooper of Kentucky, Lowell Weicker of Connecticut, Charles Percy of Illinois, Mark Hatfield (and later Bob Packwood) of Oregon, and Charles "Mac" Mathias of Maryland. Other senators who sometimes voted with us included Hugh Scott and Richard Schweiker of Pennsylvania, Robert Griffin of Michigan, James Pearson of Kansas, and Margaret Chase Smith of Maine. Theirs were often swing votes on important issues, and they were my frequent allies in the progress we were able to achieve in civil rights, housing, education, and women's rights during my years in the Senate.

My colleagues in the Senate were a decidedly mixed bag. Some were brilliant, others not. Some were ambitious, their eye always on the White House, and others were content just to be where they were. Some spoke eloquently on major issues of the day; others sounded off when they felt like it, whether or not they had anything of significance to say. As a moderate Republican, I was rarely befriended by the conservative Republicans, or by the conservative southern Democrats. My closest friends were the other moderate Republicans in our Wednesday Club, and a few liberal Democrats like Birch Bayh, Thomas Eagleton, Phil Hart, Hubert Humphrey, and Floyd Haskell.

The Senate is called "the world's most exclusive club," but it is less a club than an assembly of one hundred mostly self-centered, ambitious individuals, each of whom has his or her own agenda, own little fiefdom, and own problems and priorities, all of which does not leave much time for congeniality. There are lines all about you. Each party sits on its own side of the center aisle in the Senate chamber, and each has its own dining room and own caucus meetings. Each is endlessly scheming to gain the advantage both on specific issues and on control of the Senate and all the powers and privileges that accompany majority status.

For all the ritual and the flowery rhetoric, there is a harsh undercurrent to the Senate and to all of politics. Power, money, and reputations hang in the balance as issues are debated. I remember once seeing a Republican senator cast a vote that outraged our minority leader, Everett Dirksen. Dirksen was known to the public as a semicomic figure, who liked to ham it up for reporters (the Wizard of Ooze, he was called), but he also liked to exercise power. Dirksen pointed his finger at the offending Republican and said, "You must be out of your ——— mind! You get your ——— up there and change that vote." The erring senator, his tail between his legs, scampered up to do as he was told. Other times, I've seen powerful senators or party leaders coldly remind another senator, "I elected you." In truth, many of my colleagues did arrive politically and financially beholden to this or that individual or group. I took pride in the fact that I came to office beholden to no one except the voters of Massachusetts; no party leader or special interest group ever presumed to tell me how to cast my votes.

By the 1980s, the increasingly fierce partisanship embodied by people like Senator Jesse Helms and Congressman Newt Gingrich had contributed to the defeat or retirement of many moderate Republicans and to the bitter divisiveness that dominates Congress today. The polarization of Congress; the decline of civility; and the rise of attack politics in the 1980s, the 1990s, and the early years of the new century are a blot on our political system and a disservice to the American people. I do not see any signs of a return to civility, and I can only look back on my time in the Senate as a golden era that I pray will come again.

During my Senate years, I spoke at many high school and college commencements, but the one that received the most attention was at Wellesley College on May 31, 1969. I felt close to Wellesley; many of its students had worked in my campaigns. It was a beautiful spring day when I arrived on its lovely campus, but the atmosphere on college campuses that tumultuous year was anything but beautiful. There were widespread student demonstrations against the Vietnam War, and often commencement speakers had been booed or even prevented from finishing their remarks.

In this climate of protest, I chose to speak about student dissent in a free society. I attempted to make a distinction between productive dissent and disruption. I told the graduates, their families, and friends that as long as a society retains a capacity for nonviolent political change, violent political action is unacceptable. I ended my remarks by citing some tangible progress that the country had made against its social ills. I mentioned that the poverty rate of 22 percent in 1959 had fallen to 13.3 percent in 1967. This decline, I suggested, reflected a society that was concerned about all its people. But I said we must do much more, and I encouraged the graduates to devote their energies to meeting the profound social problems facing our nation. This was a time for pitching in, not opting out, I concluded.

The next speaker was the student government president and the first student ever to speak at a Wellesley commencement. She was blonde, slight in her academic robe, and wore the round oversize glasses that were popular then. What she had to say took me and most of the audience by surprise. The young woman was not rude, but her tone was strident. In an obvious departure from her prepared text, she challenged my comments as if we were in a debate. "What does it mean that 13.3 percent of Americans are poor?" she demanded. "How about talking about the humans, not the statistics?" When she finished, she was given a standing ovation by her classmates. She was featured prominently in the next day's *Boston Globe* and *Boston Herald*, and the following week *Life* magazine included her photograph in an article on the class of '69 and reprinted excerpts of her speech. She was even invited to appear on Johnny Carson's *Tonight Show* but had to decline because she was on her way to Alaska to spend the summer working in a fish cannery.

Wellesley's President Ruth Adams and several members of the faculty and graduating class complimented me on my speech and apologized for the stridency of the young woman's speech, which could only be taken as an affront to me. I was a little stunned by her anger and wondered how my rather mild remarks could have generated such fury. Still, the incident faded from memory until years later when the young woman rose to prominence as the wife of a governor of Arkansas who was headed to the White House.

Biographers of Hillary Rodham Clinton have cited "The Speech" as a watershed moment in her political development. I think that no matter who the commencement speaker had been that day, or what he or she had said, Hillary Rodham planned to use the situation to her own advantage. She certainly had no reason to criticize me or my record in the Senate; she had been a volunteer in my 1966 Senate campaign. But I was there representing authority, and she was representing the frustrations of her own generation, which she did most effectively. I recall the future senator from New York as a supremely confident young woman who knew where she wanted to go and how she wanted to get there. Nothing she has done or said since has changed my first impression.

Campus unrest continued into the 1970s as more and more Americans challenged the war in Southeast Asia. On May 4, 1970, four white students were shot and killed by Ohio National Guardsmen during an antiwar protest at Kent State University. Nine days later, in an event that won far less attention, two black students were shot to death and nine were wounded by police during a protest at Jackson State College, in Jackson, Mississippi. Unlike Kent State, the protest at Jackson State was not against the Vietnam War; it was against racism. And while many remember the shooting of four white students at Kent State University, few Americans recall the equally senseless killing of two black students at a black college in Mississippi.

Racial tensions between black students at Jackson State and white residents of Jackson had simmered for years. Lynch Street, a busy thoroughfare that runs through the campus had frequently been the scene of confrontations. Racial slurs and rock throwing had punctuated the ugly encounters. In the spring of 1970, a popular black female student was injured by a white motorist while crossing Lynch Street. Tensions rose and on May 13, Jackson State students gathered on the campus under the watchful eye of the Mississippi Highway Patrol. The school's president met with the students. Then a rumor circulated that Charles Evers, brother of slain civil rights activist Medgar Evers and mayor of Fayette, Mississippi, a town eighty miles southeast of Jackson, had been killed. The students began to riot. The Reserve Officers Training Corps building was set on fire. Police cordoned off a thirty-block area. Reports of gunfire prompted a call for the National Guard.

Firefighters battling a blaze on campus called for police backup. Seventy-five Mississippi State Police officers and Jackson City Police, led by a tank and armed with carbines, shotguns, service revolvers, and other weapons, marched down Lynch Street toward a woman's dormitory and confronted nearly one hundred students. Students were reported to have shouted obscenities and thrown bricks at the policemen. It was also reported that the sound of a crashing bottle breaking on the pavement caused police to open fire. Police claimed to have seen gunfire from a dormitory window. After thirty seconds of gunfire just after midnight on May 15, two students were dead.

Some students, racing for safety, were trampled. Others fell to buckshot pellets and bullets fired by the officers. Near the west entrance of the dormitory lay the body of Phillip Lafayette Gibbs, a twenty-one-year-old prelaw student and father. He had suffered four gunshots, two in his head, one under his left eye and another in his left armpit. James Earl Green, only seventeen, lay dead behind police lines, in front of the campus dining hall. He was a high school student on his way home from his job at a nearby grocery store. A single gunshot ended his life. Nine other students were wounded. FBI investigators estimated that 460 rounds of ammunition had been fired into the building, with 160 bullet holes on the outside stairwell alone.

Mayor Charles Evers, fearful of even more violence, asked me to come to Jackson. I was in Brookline, Massachusetts, attending a funeral when aides reached me with his request. When questioned by reporters, I told them, "I don't want to see an explosion in Mississippi. I don't want to see any more bloodshed and violence and senseless killings. Mayor Evers has asked me to come, and I am going." Senator John Stennis, chairman of the Armed Services Committee, arranged to have me flown to Jackson on an Air Force jet. I was met by Mayor Evers and given a police escort to the campus.

What I saw was deeply distressing. Shattered glass from the five-story dormitory was everywhere. A basket of flowers sat on the entrance steps. Dried blood on the first-floor landing had not been washed away. You could feel the outrage and the anger. I met with students, trying to help them make sense of what made no sense at all. "A lot of you wonder why the world isn't shocked when black kids get shot," I told them. "So do I." I called for an investigation and prosecution, and I urged the students to seek political power and not resort to violent protest. Working with Evers and local leaders, I tried to help keep the peace. The most difficult part of my trip came during private meetings with the mother of the seventeen-year-old high school student and with the family of the slain prelaw student. It was difficult to give words of consolation. The young people had been senselessly shot down by white police officers who had no good reason to use the firepower they used. I angrily called these deaths "heartbreaking examples of disproportionate force, recklessly applied." As at Kent State, the authorities had shot down the students with impunity. What could be a more tragic blot on our nation or on the rule of law?

Less than two months later, on July 11, yet another black youth lay dead. In New Bedford, Massachusetts, seventeen-year-old Lester Lima was shot to death, and three others were wounded by three white men in a random attack. The shootings touched off five days of rioting in which two dozen people were injured. Fires were set, and firefighters and police officers were the target of rocks and bullets. Twenty-one rioters, some of them members of the Black Panther Party, were jailed.

On July 13, I left the Senate and flew to New Bedford, a once prosperous whaling town and textile center that had fallen upon hard times. Accompanied by Bill Jackson, who had ties with the Portuguese community, I visited the angry black neighborhoods of the West End, which had been the scene of terrible violence and death. The city was besieged by police officers, many called in from neighboring towns, and was under curfew. I went on local radio and television and pleaded for calm and understanding.

While walking near the corner of Kempton and Cedar Streets, I was stopped by a group of two hundred residents, shouting their grievances. I offered to meet with some of the leaders and ended up in the basement of a house with about twenty young men armed with knives and shotguns. One young man rushed me with a knife, just to see if I would flinch. I was unaware that a short distance away, police detectives were undertaking a search for weapons. The officers found no weapons, but some young men bitterly accused me of collaborating with the police by distracting them during the search. It was a tense time.

Later I met with nearly a thousand residents, most of them blacks, Puerto Ricans, and Cape Verdeans, descendants of immigrants from the Atlantic islands off the coast of West Africa who found work in

Massachusetts textile mills in the 1800s. For more than three hours I listened to complaints of police brutality, unwarranted detention, excessive court fees, and unfair jury selection and to demands for an investigation into how federal money allocated to New Bedford was being spent. I knew that the investigation would take time, but many of the demands, such as requests for improved street lighting, regular garbage pickup, and police protection, were reasonable and could be met in short order. I called the mayor and persuaded him to meet with me and representatives of the black and Portuguese communities. He had previously refused to see the community activists. But after a six-hour meeting, the mayor had to agree that their demands were reasonable. By the time I left New Bedford, communication had been established and progress was being made.

As with most riots, the ostensible cause was symptomatic of deeper issues. The violence in New Bedford exposed a long-standing pattern of discrimination and wretched living conditions that confined so many to an endless cycle of dependency and despair. In the months that followed the rioting, I was able to get an in-depth investigation of federal programs in the city and to marshal federal and state agencies to improve conditions. The problems of cities like New Bedford were very much on my mind when, months later, I introduced legislation calling for the federal government to treat high unemployment areas as the disaster areas they are, breeding the economic hardship that invites violence.

When I was elected in 1966 I did not know the enormity of the duties and responsibilities of a United States senator. I did not imagine that I would be called on to move around the country, from one tragedy to another, trying to keep the peace. The job was as big as you wanted to make it. I found tremendous satisfaction in being a force for constructive change in those deeply troubled times.

14

The President

Nixon

I Knew

The year 1968 found the country as deeply divided as it had ever been since the dark days of the Civil War. Lyndon Johnson's surprise announcement on March 31 that he would not be a candidate for president left the field wide open. What is more, the polarizing issues of Vietnam and civil rights had left the Democratic Party itself deeply divided. The nation was ready for change—any change—and the Republicans had a chance to provide it. Throughout most of 1967, Governor George Romney of Michigan had been the Republican frontrunner. He was an impressive figure. He had been the dynamic head of the American Motors Corporation, then a rival to Ford, Chrysler, and General Motors, and had wrested control of Michigan politics away from the Democratic Party. During our respective campaigns in 1966, Romney and I had "exchanged pulpits." He came to Massachusetts to campaign for me for the Senate, and I went to Michigan to campaign for him for governor. I enjoyed knowing Romney, but I was nonetheless surprised in the spring of 1967 when red, white, and blue bumper stickers appeared in Massachusetts and Michigan reading, "The New Look—Romney and Brooke '68." It was a flattering notion, but it looked like a long shot to me, which it was.

Richard Nixon, by contrast, had not won an election on his own for eighteen years. But he was campaigning tirelessly and closing on Romney. The two of them presented a dramatic contrast: the bright new face and the shrewd old pro. Romney had the support of many other Republican moderates, including then New York Governor Nelson Rockefeller. But Romney's strong support of civil rights, along with his doubts about the Vietnam War, made him unacceptable to many conservative Republicans.

On August 31, 1967, just back from Vietnam, Romney held a press conference at which he said, "I just had the greatest brainwashing that anyone can get when you go over to Vietnam. Not only by the generals, but also by the diplomatic corps over there, and they do a very thorough job." I understood what he meant. Any American political leader, visiting the war zone, was likely to be influenced by all that the generals, the diplomats, and the soldiers themselves told him. But the media—and his political opponents—used Romney's "brainwashing" remark to ridicule him and destroy his campaign. He struggled on until two weeks before the New Hampshire primary when, trailing hopelessly, he withdrew from the race. It was a vivid example of how one slip of the tongue can be used to bring a candidate down in modern American politics.

While Romney's hopes faded, Nelson Rockefeller had been positioning himself to run. Rockefeller was a great campaigner and had been an outstanding governor of New York. But even Nelson's admirers questioned whether anything in his very privileged life had prepared him for a brutal campaign for the nomination and the presidency. Rockefeller called a meeting at his Fifth Avenue apartment to which I was invited. Other attendees included Jock Whitney, the multimillionaire "sportsman" and head of the media empire that included the *New York Herald-Tribune*; Governor Spiro Agnew of Maryland, then considered a moderate; Senator Jacob Javits of New York; and Mayor John Lindsay of New York. Rockefeller's huge apartment was filled with his collection of magnificent paintings and sculpture. But we were not there for the art. He wanted to use us as a sounding board. He questioned whether a man of his wealth could be a viable candidate for president. Each of us was asked to say if he should run. The responses were all positive. I said, "Nelson, look at history. Many of our presidents have been wealthy, including Franklin

Roosevelt and John Kennedy. Your wealth is not a negative, it's a positive. Go for it!" Rockefeller ended the meeting by assuring all of us that he would call us with his decision in a week or so.

But days passed, and he did not call. Instead, on March 21, 1968, Nelson held a press conference and stunned us all by announcing he would not be a candidate. I believed this was a strategic move. Nelson stood little chance of winning in the primaries. His only hope was to appeal to party leaders as a compromise candidate if Nixon should falter. Later we learned that Rockefeller's staff had advised him not to call any of us, for fear that we would persuade him to change his mind. The irony was that Rockefeller did change his mind.

On April 30, he reversed course again. At his invitation I stood with him in Albany, when he announced that he was, indeed, making the run for president. The announcement coincided with the date of the preferential primary in Massachusetts, where I had headed a Rockefeller write-in campaign. Rockefeller won, defeating Governor Volpe. Volpe had hoped to go to the Republican convention as a favorite son, pledged to Richard Nixon. It was said that Nixon had dangled the vice presidency before Volpe. There was also talk that either Rockefeller or Nixon might tap me as his running mate. Polls showed that my name on the ticket drew African American and moderate votes in major battleground states. When reporters asked if I had "ruled myself out" for the second spot on the ticket, I said no, but I never expected to be asked.

At the Republican convention, I delivered a speech seconding the Rockefeller nomination, but neither my rhetoric nor Rockefeller's wealth could win him the prize he sought. Nixon won the nomination on the first ballot. The final count was Nixon, 692; Rockefeller, 277; and Ronald Reagan, 182. Nixon chose Governor Agnew as his running mate. Agnew had reached the convention still smarting from Rockefeller's failure to keep him informed of his plans and had switched his allegiance to Nixon with a vengeance. Moderate Republicans were appalled. The Ripon Society mounted a futile "Dump Agnew" campaign and named me as their vice presidential candidate. That did not get far. During the campaign, Agnew was used to appeal to racist voters in the southern and border states. Some reporters dubbed him "Nixon's Nixon" during that campaign, and he continued to play a negative role throughout his unhappy time in office.

The outcome of the convention disturbed me. I hardly knew Nixon, and what little I did know, about his nasty, red-baiting campaigns in California, distressed me. In addition, I had learned that he had told southern delegations that he opposed busing and that his administration would not "ram anything down your throats." He had also expressed his opposition to federal involvement in local school board matters and vowed to appoint "strict constructionists" to the Supreme Court. That seemed to be Nixon's code word for judges who would oppose or slow desegregation. I was disappointed, but I accepted the will of the convention and hoped for the best.

I got to know him as I campaigned with him that fall. Even with his many negative attributes, Nixon had impressive strengths. He was intelligent, resourceful, and not afraid to make decisions. He was also one of the oddest, most complex, and paradoxical men I have ever met. Nixon was stiff and uncomfortable when mingling with the public. But in private he projected a real sense of what being president meant and had complete confidence in his ability to use presidential powers. He could be quite persuasive in private, and he had a focused intelligence that he could turn on and off like a switch. Most important, I saw him as a strong leader, which I believed was what the country needed.

My Senate career was destined to span four presidencies, but Nixon was the president I served under longest and knew best. I do not claim to have understood this complex man, but I think I was around him enough to gain at least some insights into his endlessly fascinating political personality. As we got to know one another during the 1968 campaign, he often praised me as a symbol of African American aspiration and of ability rewarded without regard to race. But on a deeper level, I believe I was a phenomenon he could not understand. I think he simply could not grasp how a Protestant African American Republican had been elected in a predominantly white, Democratic, Catholic state like Massachusetts. It defied political logic, and he was a logical man.

Nixon had much more interest in foreign policy than domestic policy. He was a tireless student of world problems and an enlightened internationalist. I hoped he would move in the direction of officially recognizing China and include the Chinese in future nuclear arms control talks. In early September, as we campaigned together, I raised the question of an overture to China. I was delighted when he promised a fresh approach to China if elected. He believed, as I did, that not only America's interest but world stability and peace required bringing China out of its isolation. This was remarkable at a time when horror stories from the Cultural Revolution were emerging, as if to confirm the worst American fears about Chinese Communists.

It was also during this trip that Nixon first indicated to me that he was serious about nuclear arms limitation, which gave me hope that his White House would provide leadership on this urgent issue. I always spoke frankly with him. When I thought him wrong on certain matters, such as his visceral distaste for protesters that kept him from grasping the social and economic conditions that produced them, I told him so.

I kept hearing reports of Nixon's "southern strategy," in which he and others used code words to appeal to white racists, especially in the South. I bluntly accused him and his campaign of this, but he strongly denied it. I told him that his vow to keep "law and order" evoked the age-old police abuse of African Americans. Nixon did recast the phrase as "order and justice," but I was still troubled by his lack of racial sensitivity. On Election Day 1968, Nixon narrowly defeated Vice President Humphrey. With hope more than conviction, I took Nixon at his word that he would try to "bring us together" and resolved to work with him as best I could.

It was exciting when Nixon was inaugurated in January 1969 and a Republican was back in the White House. It was an honor for Massachusetts that several of our leading citizens were named to important positions: John Volpe became secretary of transportation; Elliot Richardson was under secretary of state; and Henry Cabot Lodge was named ambassador to head the U.S. team to the Paris peace talks on Vietnam. For weeks I was racing from one committee hearing to another, introducing these nominees and helping smooth the way for their confirmations. I held a reception at the Federal City Club to welcome my Massachusetts colleagues to Washington—we expected 300 guests and 1,500 showed up.

With a Republican in the White House, many Massachusetts Republicans thought they were in line for government jobs, contracts, small business loans, and other assistance, and they looked to me for help. To help cope with the new workload, I created the position of commerce assistant in my Washington office and assigned the job to Hardy Nathan, a successful businessman from western Massachusetts who had played a key role in my campaign. I also hired new caseworkers for our Boston and Springfield offices.

Although my staff was growing, we kept a family spirit. In truth, my staff was my family. My forty or so staff members were young; we worked hard but we also found time for fun. One summer, Clarence Elam chartered a boat and took the entire staff on a dinner cruise on the Potomac. Another time, Nancy Porter rented a bus, stocked it with food and drink, and took us all on a nighttime tour of Washington and its monuments. Other times we drove to Baltimore to cheer our Red Sox against the Orioles. Our softball team, the Brooke Bloopers, competed against other Senate teams at Hains Point or on the Mall on summer evenings. I loved the warmth and spontaneity of these events. I contributed my annual staff party at our home on Martha's Vineyard, where Remigia and our daughters would entertain staff members and their spouses and children in a weekend of tennis, swimming, cookouts, and general fun.

Our moments of frivolity lightened the heavy workload, and many a long Senate session was enlivened with high spirits and harmless high jinx. Roger Woodworth was known to dance across the desk in his stocking feet. Bill Cowin and I engaged more than once in yo-yo spinning contests. A birthday, an engagement, vacation plans, or even a finished project furnished sufficient reason for impromptu office parties. While some of my colleagues suffered continuous staff turnover, my staff stayed for years, and many, to this day, form part of my extended family.

After Nixon won the election, black militants requested a meeting with the president-elect but were rebuffed. Aaron Henry, the Mississippi civil rights leader, wrote to me of the frustration and hostility that many African Americans felt for Nixon. He asked me to act as a conduit through which African American leaders could reach him. I tried to do so but with limited success. I arranged a meeting of President-elect Nixon with a number of African American leaders in New York, including Ralph Abernathy, Martin Luther King's successor as leader of the Southern Christian Leadership Conference, and Reverend Leon Sullivan, the dynamic founder and president of the Opportunities Industrialization Center (OIC). The group told the president-elect how they saw the nation's problems and what blacks expected of a new administration. Nixon listened but made no promises.

In our talks, Nixon had discounted his "southern strategy." He even intimated that, after the election, he would quietly drop the whole thing. Inaugurations are a time of hope, promise, and regeneration. I thought once Nixon had finally achieved his dream of the presidency, he would abandon the unsavory tactics that had helped elect him. But it soon became clear that his "southern strategy" was far from dead, and our relationship began to sour.

That spring, with Nixon in office only a few months, his administration began delaying the implementation of federal guidelines for school desegregation. In June, Republican Senators Clifford Case, Charles Goodell, Jacob Javits, Hugh Scott, Richard Schweiker, and I sent a telegram to the president expressing our alarm at foot-dragging by his Department of Health, Education, and Welfare. We noted that Secretary Robert Finch had several times stated the department's determination to eliminate unconstitutional discrimination in federally assisted programs, but news accounts "indicate a policy is being seriously considered which would require school districts only to submit a plan for desegregation—not actually to desegregate—by September 1970. This would be a serious setback for efforts to assure an equal educational opportunity for children in this country. We urge that there be no relaxation of the current schedule for school desegregation." Our position was vindicated in October when the Supreme Court ruled, in *Alexander v. Holmes County Board of Education*, that schools must desegregate "at once" and operate integrated schools "now and forever."

The foot-dragging on desegregation did not at first draw much attention. The real revelations about Nixon's southern strategy came when he made his first two nominations to the Supreme Court. In May 1969, Justice Abe Fortas resigned, and Nixon had his first chance to make an appointment. He had promised during the campaign that any Supreme Court justice he appointed would be a "strict constructionist," the term of art for a judicial conservative that he popularized during his campaign. On August 18, Nixon nominated a South Carolina federal judge named Clement F. Haynsworth Jr. He was a Harvard Law School graduate and the chief judge of the U.S. Fourth Circuit Court of Appeals. I assigned staff to research the nominee's record in depth.

Presidential appointments to the highest court in the land are usually confirmed by the Senate, but rejection is not unknown. Until 1969, the Senate had rejected about one-fifth of all Supreme Court nominees but none since 1930. Nonetheless, after reviewing Judge Haynsworth's record and reading his opinions, I was convinced that his nomination should be rejected. Haynsworth had shown small regard for the rights of African Americans. He had voted against court-ordered desegregation in Prince Edward County, Virginia. It looked as if Haynsworth had been chosen because of, not despite, this sorry record and that he was indeed part of a southern strategy.

Moreover, his record was full of conflict of interest problems and ethical lapses. He had ruled in favor of a corporation in a labor case while owning stock in a company that did business with the corporation. He had bought stock in a corporation after voting in its favor, but before the decision was announced. He ruled on a case even though he was a member of the board of directors of the company involved. Such lapses were unacceptable.

At first, I made no public comment on the nominee, believing that the Senate Judiciary Committee would reject him on his record. But after the committee approved the nomination on a vote of 10–7, I was compelled to speak out. On October 1, 1969, I wrote President Nixon a personal letter, outlining why I opposed the nomination. The White House advised Senate Minority Leader Hugh Scott the very next day that confirmation of Haynsworth was their top priority. In November, I again urged Nixon in a private conversation to withdraw the nomination. He listened with apparent sympathy but with no understanding. He said he regretted that I had publicly opposed his nomination, because he had the votes to get Haynsworth confirmed. "You're going to lose on this one, Ed," he told me. "No,

Mr. President," I replied. "One thing I've learned since I have been here is how to count."

On November 17, I spoke against the nomination from the Senate floor and followed up with personal telephone calls to some of my fellow moderate Republicans and borderline conservatives, who I feared would be under severe pressure from the White House. I urged them not to yield and in good conscience and for the good of the court and our country, to reject the Haynsworth nomination. On November 21, the Senate rejected the nomination 55–45. Seventeen Republicans joined in voting against Haynsworth, including the Senate's three top Republicans: Minority Leader Hugh Scott, Assistant Minority Leader Robert Griffin, and the Chairman of the Republican Conference Margaret Chase Smith. Nixon was furious. He blamed organized labor, the liberal media, and most of all the Republican senators who had "betrayed him." The Haynsworth rejection should have persuaded him to nominate a judge of superior qualifications to fill the still vacant seat. Instead, on January 19, 1970, the president nominated an even less qualified judge named G. Harrold Carswell. A native of Georgia, Carswell had been a U.S. District Court judge in northern Florida. In June 1969, he had been appointed to the Fifth Circuit Court of Appeals.

Nixon's staff claimed that they had searched Carswell's record and found nothing that would concern a patriotic American. But it took only two days for the news media to discover that in 1948, during a failed candidacy for the Georgia legislature, Carswell had told the American Legion, "I am a Southerner by ancestry, birth, training, inclination, belief and practice. I believe that segregation of the races is proper and the only practical and correct way of life in our states. I have always so believed, and I shall always so act."

Reaction to press reports of this speech was highly negative. His nomination in peril, Carswell went on television and repudiated his 1948 address, calling its ideas "obnoxious and abhorrent to my personal philosophy." This self-serving conversion left me skeptical, to say the least. Most of the labor unions and civil rights groups that had opposed the Haynsworth nomination lined up against Carswell as well. Determined to be fair, I dug deeper into the judge's extensive record, but I found no sign that his thinking had changed. His claim

now to find his racial separatism creed of 1948 "obnoxious and abhorrent" was simply not credible.

Nixon had looked the nation in the eye and claimed that G.
Harrold Carswell was the best judge he could find for our highest
court. It was a sorry spectacle. In 1953, Carswell had been a charter
member of a whites-only club in Tallahassee. In 1956, he had been
instrumental in converting Tallahassee's only public golf course into
a private club, a well-known tactic for excluding nonwhites. As a
judge, he had delayed implementation of the *Brown v. Board of Education* decision, which called for integration of public schools, post-
poning its effect in parts of Florida into the mid-1970s. So clearly
second-rate was Carswell that even his defenders were at a loss. Republican Senator Roman Hruska offered the bizarre defense that yes,
the judge might be mediocre, but America was full of mediocre citizens, and they, too, deserved representation on the Court. The press
and the American people ridiculed that remark, and it helped our
cause. Ridicule is a powerful tool in politics.

I felt strongly about the Senate's duty to examine judicial nominations, much more strongly, for example, than I did about cabinet
nominees. Cabinet members were extensions of the president, who
came and went with him, but Supreme Court justices wield vast
power and once approved are there for life. On February 25, I delivered a lengthy speech to the Senate, speaking without notes, in which
I made the strongest case I could against Carswell. I said in part:

> I think it is regrettable that there has been sent to the Senate for
> confirmation to the highest court in the land the nomination of
> a man who, by his own public pronouncements, demonstrated
> that he harbored racist views. I think it is even more regrettable
> that at no time during his relatively long public career has he
> showed any indication of having changed. I looked, as I have
> said, to find this change in his mind and in his heart, but I found
> no evidence of change which would enable me in good conscience
> to vote for confirmation of his nomination.

Following my detailed and carefully reasoned speech opposing
Carswell's confirmation, my colleague Senator Kennedy took to the

floor in lengthy commendation of my position. "I think the Senator has shown great courage," he said, "and has provided for the membership a very clear, precise and studious presentation." In response, I praised him for his "incisive questions to the nominee when he appeared before the Judiciary Committee" and for the "fairness of his interrogation."

Washington Star columnist Mary McGrory wrote the next day, "Few Republicans wanted to hear the Senate's only black member eloquently laying out the case against Carswell and removing, one by one, the props they are leaning on to justify a vote for a Southern judge whose partisans have admitted is mediocre." Soon after the speech, in a meeting with the president on other matters, I told him, "I want you to know that I am working night and day to defeat your nomination of Judge Carswell to the Supreme Court." Nixon smiled but did not respond.

Nixon had been incredibly cynical throughout this process. It was not just that his nominees' positions on racial issues offended advocates of civil rights. Their general mediocrity was an insult to every lawyer in America who believes that the Supreme Court should be a showcase for the finest legal minds our nation can produce. He was doubly cynical in the second nomination, because he clearly thought that the Senate would not have the will to twice reject his choice. It was not an easy thing to do. Senators tend to give the president the benefit of the doubt. We did not like being put in the position of seeming to have a vendetta against Nixon. Many senators, having rejected Nixon's first nominee, truly wanted to support his second one.

My anger at the president's failure of leadership led me to say in March, "Mr. Nixon said that he wanted to bring us together. I think that with few exceptions everything that has been done so far is designed to push us further apart." I was working feverishly with Democratic Senator Birch Bayh of Indiana to round up votes against Carswell. Margaret Chase Smith was a crucial vote. She was third in the Republican leadership behind Hugh Scott and Robert Griffin. I feared that both of them would vote to confirm Carswell, especially after voting against Haynsworth. The votes were so close that it became paramount that we win Smith's support.

Senator Smith was a classic Mainer, honest and unadorned, blessed with a steely intelligence, and famous for her rock-ribbed aversion to all personal lobbying before a Senate vote. On April 8, a few hours before the vote, she told me she had still not made up her mind. But a White House source assured Senator Bayh that she would vote for Carswell, and Birch passed the word to me. Cautiously, I approached Senator Smith in the Senate Dining Room, where she was eating lunch. As always, she was wearing the single fresh red rose that was her trademark.

I apologized for the intrusion, then sat down and asked if the rumor being circulated by the White House was true, that the president had her vote. Outraged, she telephoned Nixon aide Bryce Harlow in the White House, demanding to know if he had told other senators how she would vote on Carswell. Harlow, an experienced political operative, should have known better than to give a waffling answer to Margaret Chase Smith. She accused him of impugning her independence and slammed down the phone. A few hours later she voted against Carswell. Several other "undecided" senators joined her, including Republicans Marlow Cook of Kentucky and Winston Prouty of Vermont. In all, thirteen Republicans voted against Carswell, and the Senate defeated the nomination by a vote of 51–45.

When the vote ended, the Senate echoed with cheers from the gallery. Vice President Agnew, who was presiding over the proceedings and hoping for a tie vote he could break in the president's favor, angrily pounded his gavel, called for order, and finally ordered the sergeant-at-arms to clear the galleries. The crowd hurried down the stairs and gathered outside the Senate chamber. I will never forget walking out into that throng to cheers and shouts of "Bravo!" They felt, as I did, that it was a great day for America.

The next day, President Nixon bitterly blamed the defeat on "vicious assaults" and "malicious character assassination." He hinted darkly that by its actions, the Senate was threatening the very constitutional balance between the president and the Senate. He stated categorically that " . . . with the Senate presently constituted, I cannot successfully nominate to the Supreme Court any federal appellate judge from the South who believes as I do in the strict construction of the Constitution." I responded publicly that it was "incredible . . .

that the president would make such a mistaken and unfortunate statement." I asked him to let his anger cool and to reconsider his remarks, for the sake of all qualified southern nominees.

Not long thereafter, Chuck Colson, the White House Special Counsel, dropped by my office. I knew Chuck from Massachusetts and was aware that the White House considered him its emissary to me. Chuck asked me, if offered, would I accept a nomination to the Court. "Do you mean the Supreme Court?" I asked. "Yes," said Chuck with a grin. I gave him my standard response: "I am too young to sit and rock, Chuck. I wouldn't give up my Senate seat for the world." I never knew whether he was on a scouting expedition from the White House or was just playing games, but I was always happy to put to rest speculation that I was interested in any job other than the Senate.

It was not until I read John Dean's book, *The Rehnquist Choice* (New York: Free Press, 2001), which accessed newly available White House tapes, that I found out that President Nixon actually had considered me for an appointment to fill Justice Thurgood Marshall's slot if and when he retired. In a conversation with Attorney General John Mitchell, Nixon said,

> "I don't know whether he'd do it, but really the only man for the black seat [Marshall's seat] is, you got to offer it to Brooke. He's the best man, but who the hell [knows], let's be thinking of that black seat though, in case it comes up, because that's going to be one that you got to go to a black."
>
> "There are some others around," said Mitchell. "But I think we ought to offer it to Brooke."
>
> "He'd never take it," Nixon said.
>
> "I don't believe he would," Mitchell agreed.
>
> "Why the hell, he's a bigger man in the Senate. He wouldn't take the Court, it would be like being demoted."
>
> "He may. Ed's work was so good, as the Attorney General," Mitchell suggested.
>
> "Oh, yes. He is a very good man, John," said Nixon. "He's basically a liberal, he has to be. But in terms of, you talk [unintelligible], he's one of the few blacks who really talks in an intelligent way."

Nixon's last unfortunate comment aside, it was true that I was happy in the Senate, where I thought I could make a difference.

Nixon's next nominee, Harry Blackmun, easily won Senate approval later in 1970. Blackmun, a conservative and lifelong Republican, proceeded to surprise a lot of people three years later when he wrote the historic *Roe v. Wade* decision. In the fall of 1971, Nixon had yet another opening to fill on the Supreme Court. He called and asked me to meet his candidate, a conservative assistant attorney general by the name of William Rehnquist. Even though I was not a member of the Judiciary Committee, I had been such a thorn in his side on the Haynsworth and Carswell nominations that Nixon must have thought an advance meeting was prudent. I found Rehnquist candid and forthright, but I was not satisfied with his responses to my questions on civil rights.

Knowing it would be extremely difficult for the Senate to reject another nominee, I found out everything I could about Rehnquist. Nothing in his record eased my concerns about his views on social issues and toward criminal defendants. I was particularly troubled by a memo that Rehnquist had written to Justice Robert Jackson when he was a young law clerk to Jackson in 1952. In it, he had recommended that Jackson, of all people, go back to the discredited "separate but equal" reasoning of the court's 1896 *Plessy v. Ferguson* decision. The thinking reflected in that memo deeply disturbed me, as it did others when it became public. I was the first Republican to come out in opposition to the Rehnquist nomination, and on December 10, I was one of the "nays" in the 68–26 vote that put him on the Supreme Court, where he served as chief justice until his death on September 3, 2005.

Nixon and I also disagreed on the emotional question of school busing. The White House pledged support for "local control of local schools" and blasted the evils of "busing for the purpose of racial balance." On busing and civil rights in general, Nixon said he wanted to do "what was right," but he thought integration worked best when it came slowly, if at all.

Other signs of friction became apparent when I tried to restore cease-and-desist powers to the Equal Employment Opportunity Commission and when I pushed for full funding of the commission. I also protested Nixon's major cutback on the Job Corps; fought his assault on Legal Services, Inc., which provided legal services for the poor; and criticized his Justice Department for dragging its feet in enforcing court desegregation orders. In each instance, Nixon's policies were designed to reduce the ability of poor people and minorities to improve their lives, whether through education, employment, or the courts.

Nixon took another major step backward by deciding not to pursue a simple extension of the Voting Rights Act of 1965. I thought his refusal to take a stand for the basic American right to vote was morally wrong. It was one of the most important, if not the most important, pieces of civil rights legislation that had been enacted in the 1960s, and it was one that, as attorney general of Massachusetts, I had fought for in every way I could. In mid-March 1970, on the radio program *Capital Cloakroom*, I broke with the president over his "southern strategy." I said that Nixon, who had run for president vowing to unify our country, was now playing off black against white, North against South, class against class, the kind of cynically divisive politics I loathed. Nixon had made a calculated decision to stir up white resentment of blacks in the South and in the suburbs. I believe he knew those policies were immoral, but he was compulsively political, and he thought they would help him win reelection in 1972.

In September 1971, Senator Edward Muskie, then the leading Democratic candidate for president, said that if nominated he would not choose a black running mate because doing so would guarantee the defeat of the ticket. Muskie's unfortunate remark again started a flurry of talk about me as a Republican vice presidential nominee. I did not believe Muskie was correct in suggesting that a black candidate would doom a national ticket. I felt that we will never know until we try. Columnists Evans and Novak ran a poll showing a Nixon-Brooke ticket in 1972 topped either a Nixon-Agnew or a Nixon–John Connally ticket. But I did not take it seriously. It was difficult to see how I would square with a southern strategy.

My differences with Nixon were not only on domestic issues. Over the next four years, I broke with him on a range of foreign policy matters. Yet in some areas I had the deepest respect for Nixon's foresight and skill. United States policy toward Communist China was an example of Nixon at his best. As a candidate and as senator, I had spoken out for a better working relationship with China. We could not continue to pretend that the country did not exist. President Nixon and Henry Kissinger had begun secret negotiations with the Chinese. One day in 1971, Nixon summoned me to the Oval Office. Henry Kissinger was with him. After initial pleasantries, Nixon said,

> "Ed, I want you to know that your words up there in the Senate on China have not fallen on deaf ears. Henry and I know what you have been saying. We agree with you and we are going to do something with China. We're going to take a first step. But this is for your ears only."
>
> The president's words excited me. I wondered what kind of "first step" he meant. This could be an historic moment.
>
> "We're going to send a ping-pong team to China," Nixon said.
>
> Ping-pong? I couldn't believe my ears.
>
> "Mr. President," I heard myself say. "That's not exactly what I had in mind."
>
> The Chinese had invited the American ping-pong team that was competing in World Championship games in Japan to visit mainland China. Nixon had approved the visit.
>
> "Don't underestimate that!" said the President, seeing my look of disbelief. "We're a sports-loving nation, and China loves its ping-pong. This is the beginning of something very important."

In fact, it was. Two weeks after receiving the surprise invitation from the Chinese government, the United States sent fifteen ping-pong players and their spouses to China. These were more than the total number of Americans who had been in China on officially approved visits since 1950. The ping-pong competition gave a light and personal touch to America's serious talks with China. It was a positive, even a brilliant first step.

In foreign policy, in many instances, Nixon's instincts were healthy and his timing was good. The quiet nature of his approach muted the boldness of his course. The mosaic of his foreign policy, laid piece by piece, was pragmatic in style but prophetic in substance. For twenty years, China had been cut off from the United States. Throughout the Cold War, "Who lost China?" had been a Republican taunt to Democrats. It is hard now to imagine how much hostility there was against the Chinese Communists, especially among Republicans. Zhou En-lai and Mao Zedong were targets of hatred and ridicule. Alabama's segregationist Governor George Wallace used to speculate on how "Mousey Tongue" would have justified busing schoolchildren.

By 1969, the Chinese seemed close to war with the Soviet Union. When the Russians put almost fifty military divisions on the frontier, the Chinese knew that they had to do something. They took the initiative and played their "American card." Nixon responded with his boldest move as president. I doubt that Hubert Humphrey, as president, could have done the same, because as a liberal he would have faced a firestorm of criticism. Nixon had the credentials to get away with it. And he did.

Early in 1972, Nixon became the first American head of state to visit China. The nearly weeklong trip was the longest state visit any president had made to a foreign nation. Richard Nixon, who had made his name as a rabid anticommunist, met productively with Zhou En-lai and even with Communist Party chairman Mao Zedong, a reviled man in American conservative circles. It was a bold, even a revolutionary act.

Nixon understood the need for balance in foreign policy. He knew that the Soviet Union would look with suspicion and distaste at the warming of our relations with China. He knew that even a major breakthrough in relations with China could not be justified if it did deep and lasting damage to our relationship with the Soviets. So Nixon also announced plans to visit the Soviet Union in the spring of 1972. His goal was nothing less than to achieve a fundamental revision of the strategic relationship between the United States and the Soviet Union.

There was a second, equally critical foreign policy issue on which Nixon's timing and substance were impeccable. Although he had been a prominent advocate of nuclear superiority, he understood that the old goal of one nation's achieving nuclear superiority was destabilizing.

For years I had been fighting against testing and deployment of weapons called Multiple Independently-targetable Reentry Vehicles, or MIRV missiles. This controversial program was advancing at the same time as the Johnson administration's proposal to deploy the Sentinel antiballistic missile system near a dozen or more U.S. cities. The first land acquired for this purpose was near Boston, and both cost and safety were major concerns. Although Nixon finally scraped the Sentinel system in favor of a limited Safeguard system in February 1969, I joined a bipartisan group of senators who warned that deployment of the ABM system could hurt our chances for substantive arms control talks and could speed the arms race.

On May 23, 1969, I had an emotional talk with Henry Kissinger. I told him that if the tests on MIRV were completed, the genie would be out of the bottle. I said this was a matter of conscience. I was convinced that the United States should take the lead in proposing a halt to the arms race, and that absent such a halt, new technology would propel the arms race to new and infinite danger. On June 17, I filed a Senate resolution calling for a moratorium on testing of offensive multiple-warhead missiles. My thirty-nine cosponsors included Michael "Mike" Mansfield and Ted Kennedy. Kissinger was displeased, and we spoke again. I told him that my legislative assistant and nuclear expert Alton Frye, whom he knew and respected, had lined up at least ten other senators, besides the cosponsors, to vote for the resolution. A few senators, notably Albert Gore Sr. of Tennessee, who chaired the Foreign Relations Arms Control Subcommittee, were wary of focusing on MIRV for fear that it would divert attention from the ABM issue. For that reason, even though a Senate majority supported a mutual suspension of MIRV testing by the United States and the Soviet Union, we were unable to get a hearing on the resolution for many months. Meanwhile, the tests proceeded.

In October 1969, I called for a complete missile test ban, and in March 1970, I introduced a resolution asking Nixon to propose to the Soviet Union a joint suspension of MIRV flight tests. The resolution was referred to the Foreign Relations Committee. When the administration announced in March 1970 that deployment of MIRV missiles would soon begin, the Gore subcommittee convened a hearing on my resolution. In adopting the call for restraint on MIRVs, the committee broadened the language to urge a mutual suspension of deployment of all strategic weapons, both offensive and defensive. On April 9, the Senate adopted the far-reaching resolution by a vote of 72–6.

In August 1970, I proposed an amendment to a military procurement bill that would authorize the secretary of defense to develop a single warhead for the navy's Poseidon and the army's Minuteman III missiles, both then scheduled to carry MIRVs. In the event that an agreement was reached with the Soviets to limit MIRVs, we would thus have had single warheads both for our land-based defense Intercontinental Ballistic Missile (ICBM) system and for our nuclear submarines. The Senate on a voice vote adopted the amendment.

Years later, Henry Kissinger said he wished someone had warned him how hard it would be to preserve strategic stability in a MIRVed world. In fact, an overwhelming Senate majority had told him so. Our initiatives did not immediately achieve the results we sought, but they added impetus to a process that lasted several years. Out of that process came the 1972 ABM Treaty that curbed deployment of such systems for three decades and other agreements that finally turned the strategic competition toward mutual restraint. Today the strategic nuclear dilemmas persist in altered form. But I still believe that an antiballistic missile umbrella—the so-called Star Wars proposals—could prove inherently destabilizing, economically wasteful, and only marginally protective.

Those dilemmas were first addressed in a significant way in the Strategic Arms Limitation Talks (SALT) that the United States and the Soviet Union began in Helsinki, Finland, in 1969. Negotiations continued throughout Nixon's time in office. In reality, all of the amendments and debates in the Senate during those years were attempts to influence the SALT negotiations. By demonstrating repeatedly that a majority of senators strongly supported efforts to moderate the dangerous competition in strategic weaponry, these congressional initiatives provided crucial support to the nuclear bargains that every successive president, including George W. Bush, would pursue.

Nixon's visit to Moscow in May 1972 was a watershed in Cold War relations, producing both the historic antiballistic missile treaty and an interim agreement limiting strategic offensive forces. These agreements, for the first time, placed limits on the growth of American and Soviet arsenals. Politically and psychologically, they marked an extraordinary turning point. Both superpowers accepted the vital paradox that mutual vulnerability, not one-sided superiority, was the greatest deterrent to nuclear war between our nations.

Like the "opening to China," this historic accord could only have been achieved by someone with conservative credentials. Richard Nixon did more than any president in history to advance the cause of arms control, and for this he deserves full credit. Yet Nixon's foreign policy had huge flaws. He had ravaged Cambodia with a secret bombing campaign; he prolonged the war in Vietnam far too long; and by his plot to destabilize Salvador Allende, Chile's first democratically elected president, he put the CIA and America in disrepute in Latin America for years to come.

Richard Nixon was a man who aroused strong passions and was despised by many liberals, but I always thought of him as a pragmatist, not an ideologue. He wanted power, and he was willing to move left or right in order to get and keep it. Once William Saltonstall, Leverett Saltonstall's son, asked me to take him to meet Nixon. The young man, having served in the Massachusetts state senate, was running for Congress and wanted the president's blessing. Two of the burning issues of the day were the ABM Treaty and whether eighteen-year-olds should be given the vote. I had advised him to oppose the ABM treaty and to support the eighteen-year-old vote. Those were not necessarily the positions that Nixon would have preferred, but he told young Saltonstall, "You do what Ed Brooke tells you to do. I'd be happy to see you in Congress, and he knows how to get you there. Don't worry about me." To a great extent, Nixon felt the same way about me. He accepted the times I voted against him and was glad for the times I was with him. He was, as I said, a supreme pragmatist.

Despite our differences, I backed President Nixon in the 1972 election. Impressed by his foreign policy triumphs and trying to be loyal to my party, I carried the president's banner at colleges and in Democratic precincts where other Republicans would not go. I was also running for reelection myself, and my support of the president cost me many liberal Massachusetts voters, who strongly supported the courageous antiwar Democratic candidate Senator George McGovern.

The break-in at the Democratic headquarters on June 17, 1972, came as a complete shock. It was not only morally repugnant, it was incredibly stupid. Nixon already had the election won. I doubted that he ordered the break-in directly. But the scorched-earth tone he set made his more zealous followers consider such an act acceptable. Nixon should have admitted promptly that there had been a burglary, taken the blame for it, and possibly saved his presidency. Instead, within days he was orchestrating the cover-up that would bring him down.

Despite Nixon's overwhelming reelection in 1972, the Watergate controversy would not go away. Congress, the press, and the American public were demanding the truth. The Watergate hearings opened in February 1973 and continued for months, with almost daily revelations. On August 15, President Nixon, rather than addressing the serious questions surrounding him, told a nationwide television audience that " . . . the time has come to turn Watergate over to the courts, where the questions of guilt or innocence belong. The time has come for the rest of us to get on with the urgent business of our nation."

He satisfied no one. His administration was falling apart. On October 10, Vice President Agnew was forced to resign in disgrace to avoid prosecution for illegal financial dealings. He had been a disaster as vice president. Nixon had used Agnew as his point man in attacking liberals and the media and for currying favor with the most reactionary elements in our society. As far back as 1970, I had said of Agnew's role in the southern strategy, "I can't understand some of the things the vice president has said or why he has said them unless, of course, it is part of this cold political decision that has been made." In the final days before his resignation, Agnew asked for—and was somewhat reluctantly granted—an opportunity to speak to our Wednesday Club of moderate Senate Republicans. His angry defense of himself and Nixon won him only looks of amazement from our group. If the White House was sending *him* to meet with *us*, we thought, they must be desperate. Fortunately, with Agnew gone, Nixon chose a decent and experienced Republican, House Minority Leader Gerald Ford, to take his place.

Then, on October 20, Elliot Richardson telephoned me. Elliot had replaced John Mitchell as attorney general. Nixon had just summoned Richardson to the White House and ordered him to fire Watergate Special Prosecutor Archibald Cox, my onetime special assistant in the Office of the Massachusetts Attorney General. Cox had demanded the so-called Watergate tapes, and Nixon was refusing to turn them over. Richardson, clearly in anguish, asked my advice. "Elliot, I don't see that you have any choice but to resign," I told him. That evening, the White House issued four announcements: Archibald Cox had been fired; Elliot Richardson had resigned; Deputy Attorney General William Ruckelshaus had been "dismissed"; and the office of Special Prosecutor had been abolished. This was the infamous "Saturday Night Massacre." Robert Bork, the last man standing—the one who was willing to carry out Nixon's order to fire Cox—remained as acting attorney general for a time.

The Saturday Night Massacre only increased the pressure for Congress to impeach the president. On November 4, on ABC's *Issues and Answers*, I became the first Republican senator to call for Nixon to resign. I said that I knew of no impeachable offense that he had committed and that I prayed there had been none. But, I said, the president had lost the nation's trust and was too crippled to lead. The country was suffering many painful consequences of Watergate. Every federal agency was marking time. Drift was the order of the day.

The following week the president went on national television and declared, "I will not walk away from the job I was elected to do." Nixon held a series of meetings with members of Congress. Even though I had called for his resignation, I was invited to one of these meetings held on Tuesday, November 13, in the family quarters of the White House. It was the first of several sessions Nixon planned with small groups of Republican senators, who were invited in alphabetical order. My group included Senators Gordon Allott of Colorado, Howard Baker of Tennessee, James Buckley of New York, and Carl Curtis of Kansas.

"This Watergate thing has gotten out of hand," the president said, and he asked our advice. I sensed that what he wanted was encouragement. When it was my turn to speak, I told Nixon that the break-in had become the worst scandal in American political history.

"Mr. President, I think you have lost the trust and faith of the American people. For the good of yourself and your family, for the good of the Republican Party, and more important, for the good of the American people, I think you should resign."

With hands clasped together just below his chin and staring straight into my eyes, the president responded solemnly: "Ed, that would be taking the easy way out, the cowardly thing to do."

"Mr. President," I replied, "I know how hard you worked to get elected. I certainly don't believe that resignation is taking the easy way out. I know how much being president of the United States means to you. And I think that voluntarily giving up the most powerful office, not only in the United States, but in the world, is not taking the easy way out."

Carl Curtis and Howard Baker jumped in and gave the president the encouragement he wanted: "I support you fully, Mr. President." "Stick it out, Mr. President." "Don't listen to Ed." "You have done nothing wrong." "Stay right in there and fight."

I received support from James Buckley, the brother of conservative icon William F. Buckley, who said simply, "Mr. President, I think Ed is right. I think you have lost the trust and faith of the American people, and that you should seriously consider stepping down."

"And if you don't step down," I added, "I think the House will instigate impeachment proceedings against you. I'm sure you don't want to put the country through such an ordeal as that."

On my way out of the White House that evening reporters pressed me for comment, but I declined. I had spoken my peace and had no wish to place further pressure on the president.

It was late when I returned to my apartment in Watergate. Soon someone knocked on my door. It was Rosemary Woods, Nixon's longtime secretary and a trusted member of his inner circle. She lived on my floor in the Watergate, and we had been friendly. But this night, she was livid. Word of my call for her boss's resignation had clearly been relayed to her. Rosemary had worked for Nixon for twenty-five years. She was utterly dedicated to him, and now she was bitterly angry. Standing at the threshold of my apartment, she castigated me in a profanity-laced tirade. It was a shocking display from a woman I respected.

I finally said, "Rosemary, You don't understand. I have nothing against the president personally. I only said what I believed, and I only gave him the advice I would give myself. It was not mean-spirited. I really believe resigning will be in his best interest, as well as that of the country." She continued to take vehement exception. Finally, I closed the conversation by saying, "Rosemary, I'm sorry you feel that way. I hope you will understand." She gave me one last choice epithet and stalked off.

The next morning, in the Watergate garage, I found a long, deep scratch on the door of my blue 1973 Mercedes-Benz convertible. Everyone who knew me knew how I prized that automobile, which I still own and drive to this day. I had recently bought it for only $10,000, a great bargain, because it had been a demonstration model. The car was parked on the lower level of the garage and could only have been damaged by someone who had access to the controlled area. Had Rosemary done it? I have no proof. But her tirade at my apartment door and that deep scratch on my car are a reminder of the weird, ugly legacy of Watergate.

If the Republican Party was to survive the Watergate debacle, Democratic and Independent voters had to know that Republicans were also appalled by it. By May 1974, the Republicans had already lost four of five special congressional elections. To many Republicans, Richard Nixon was the Republican Party. They backed him with every fiber of their being and called Watergate a witch hunt. They found dissent treasonous. My call for Nixon to resign prompted a deluge of letters, postcards, and telegrams. Most of them were angry missives from loyal Republicans, some old supporters of mine. Some impugned my motives and even my patriotism. Over the next seven months, I responded to their messages personally, one by one, using a basic premise: "Richard Nixon is my president as well as yours. I have campaigned with him and for him in two presidential elections. Thus, the events of this year and his response to those events have made me think, study, and pray as nothing else in all of my political life."

On July 27, the House Judiciary Committee overwhelmingly voted the first of two articles of impeachment. The end was near. To encourage Nixon to resign, I introduced on August 7 a "sense of Congress" resolution that if he resigned, neither the U.S. government nor any of its officers would initiate criminal or civil proceedings against him. Two days later, before the resolution could be debated, Nixon resigned.

I felt strongly that President Ford should grant a pardon to former President Nixon, but only if Nixon admitted wrongdoing during Watergate and apologized to the nation for his mistakes. My thought was not to protect Nixon but to protect the nation from the awful spectacle of a former president being put on trial. Instead, Ford pardoned Nixon and got nothing in return. If he had demanded—and received—an admission of wrongdoing and an apology, it would have defused one of the major issues against him in his 1976 presidential campaign, and he might have won his close contest with Jimmy Carter.

The Watergate affair was a disaster for everyone involved. We may never know the exact extent of Richard Nixon's complicity in the break-in and cover-up. But we do know that both his gifts and his faults were prodigal, and his political career was remarkable in its length and scope. Its abrupt end, although necessary, was tragic for Nixon, his family, and the country.

15

"The Freest

Man in

the Senate"

Despite the turmoil at the national level, 1972 found my own political fortunes riding high. As I approached reelection, no Republican of any stripe challenged me in the convention or primary. The nomination was mine without a fight for the first and only time. In the general election, we took my campaign slogan from the *Washington Star* columnist Mary McGrory, who had called me "the Freest Man in the Senate." She went on to say of me, "He approaches the major issues of the day, not with any preordained ideological bias, but with clear, uncommitted and independent judgment." We gladly borrowed McGrory's "freest man" phrase for campaign materials that emphasized my independence.

On the Democratic side, John Kenneth Galbraith, the distinguished Harvard economist, had for a time sought the nomination, at Ted Kennedy's urging, and had made an issue of my support of Nixon. But Galbraith withdrew, and Middlesex County District Attorney John Droney became my opponent. He spent very little money, and that enabled me to cut back on my own expenditures. On Election Day, Massachusetts was the only state where George McGovern beat President Nixon, but enough voters split their tickets to reelect me by a plurality of 682,654 votes, a considerably larger margin than I won by in 1966.

As easy as my reelection had been, there was no rest once the Senate reconvened. Once elected, a senator has many choices: there are far more issues and demands on his or her time than can possibly be addressed. This was my second term, and with increased seniority came more responsibility: I had to choose my issues carefully. Some I picked because I cared deeply about them; others I became involved with because they deeply affected the welfare of the people of Massachusetts. In most cases the two concerns overlapped. I have selected a few of these issues for discussion in the following pages, in large measure because they clearly demonstrate how even in a collaborative body, one person can make a difference.

The first issue was also the most emotional, and the one that would occupy me throughout my second term: it was the fundamental question of a woman's right to choose to have an abortion. On January 22, 1973, at the very beginning of my second term, the Supreme Court ruled in *Roe v. Wade* that women, as a matter of privacy, have a qualified right to terminate an unwanted pregnancy. The ruling galvanized both opponents and proponents and touched off a firestorm of debate that rages unabated to this day.

Abortion touches deeply emotional issues about the sanctity of life, the sexual freedom of women, the love that we all feel for babies, and the loving but often heavy hand of the church. Many opponents of abortion, far from accepting the Supreme Court decision, believed that it legalized the murder of innocent children and only redoubled their efforts to stop or at least reduce the practice any way they could. Their zeal led to endless, increasingly bitter legislative battles.

My position as the ranking Republican on the Appropriations Health Subcommittee put me in the middle of the debate. My support of a woman's right to make her own medical decisions about continuing or terminating her pregnancy had me at odds with my party, which was adopting an ever more strident position on this inherently private decision. The subject of abortion was abhorrent to a Senate that, with the departure of Margaret Chase Smith, was again 100 percent male. My colleagues were far more comfortable talking about missile defense systems than about conception and the right of women to control their own biological destiny.

I found it hard to understand how many of my colleagues, who so often railed against government involvement in the lives of Americans, were willing to go into America's bedrooms and dictate reproductive policy. No law can prevent abortion. Laws can only make abortion more difficult, more expensive, and more dangerous, especially for the poor. Who were we, an affluent all-male legislative body, to decide what women could do and could not do with their bodies?

A major battle began in 1976 with the annual appropriations bill for the Department of Health, Education, and Welfare. Freshman Representative Henry Hyde, a Republican from Illinois, offered an amendment to the bill that would ban all federal Medicaid funding for abortion services, with no exemptions. Although the Senate rejected his provision, it passed in the House, and the issue had to be resolved in a House-Senate conference. At the request of Appropriations Committee Chairman Warren Magnuson, I served as manager of the bill. For six brutal months, Hyde and I fought over compromise language for it. Although unerringly gracious in his manner, Henry Hyde was a man of firm resolve, and he had far more reliable support behind him on the antiabortion side than I had on the pro-choice side. In many ways, I was on my own. My closest allies in the Senate, Jacob Javits, Clifford Case, and Birch Bayh, were not on the appropriations committee where these battles were being waged.

Compromise language was reached in 1976 but quickly overturned by court action, setting the stage for another battle in 1977. The House again passed the Hyde Amendment, on June 17, 1977, and we again found ourselves in a House-Senate conference on how the ban on Medicaid abortions should be defined. Henry Hyde and I went back and forth tirelessly, both convinced of the rightness of our positions, and for the most part worked without rancor. When the now-famous language, "in the case of rape, incest, or when the life of the mother is endangered" was finally hammered out, neither of us was satisfied. But it was the best we could do. The votes for either of our preferred positions were not there. And so we compromised. That phraseology, so painfully arrived at nearly three decades ago, is still the law today.

Surprisingly to me, the "life of the mother" clause was the sticking point. While rape and incest were reluctantly viewed by the hardline antichoice faction as possibly acceptable reasons to terminate a pregnancy, they vehemently opposed abortions to protect the life of the mother. They argued that this was a loophole allowing women, in collusion with their doctors, to escape the restrictions on abortion by claiming it was "medically necessary" to protect their lives. I thought their position insensitive, condescending, paternalistic, and hypocritical. At one point in 1977, a version of the Hyde Amendment passed the House that would not even permit a Medicaid-funded abortion to save the life of the mother—the "pro-life" forces would sacrifice a mother's life to save her fetus. That was when Republican Congresswoman Millicent Fenwick of New Jersey said, "Those who are helpless are condemned."

These were extremely complicated negotiations. The courts increasingly gave support to the antiabortion forces, as did the Carter administration. Federal funding was being delayed on unrelated matters. Countless hours were devoted to hair-splitting. For example, should abortions be granted to avoid "severe *or* long-lasting physical illness" or "severe *and* long-lasting physical illness"? At one point, I was involved in a Senate debate over whether a colon in a House version of the bill was simply a typographical error or was part of a scheme to change the meaning of the law. As I noted, "One might wonder why I raise this question. We have been back and forth with the House on many occasions with respect to one word and now with respect to punctuation marks. I want to make it crystal clear, and I want to make it certain for the record, as to what was intended by the Senate." In other words, no one trusted anyone by that point.

As Laurence H. Tribe wrote in *Abortion: The Clash of Absolutes* (New York: Norton, 1990), "By sending approving signals on the Hyde Amendment, the Supreme Court and the Carter White House together did much to legitimize what had not previously been established as a legitimate political position. In a very short time, the political landscape had been altered. In 1977 a Democrat who wished to oppose the Hyde Amendment had to oppose not only a growing anti-welfare sentiment and a vocal pro-life lobby, but also a Democratic President."

By 1978, it was an open secret that some of the antiabortion strategists hoped that, facing reelection in a largely Catholic state, I would tone down my battle against the Hyde Amendment. In that, they were disappointed. But I could see our support slipping away. We lost people like Ted Kennedy and Hubert Humphrey. More and more liberals accepted support of the Hyde Amendment as the price they had to pay for their support of abortion rights in general—rights, that is, for women who could afford to pay a doctor.

I was outraged when Hyde proposed amending the bill to include the provision that no federal funds could be used to pay for abortions, or even to offer abortion counseling. Equally outrageous was a ban on Medicaid financing for abortions and the refusal to pay for abortions for women in the military or who were military dependents. Here was the basic question of fairness. Why should those without financial resources be denied the services that those with resources could secure? The ban was economic discrimination, pure and simple. Some staff members, angry at this harsh provision, referred to it as "Raw Hyde."

It took two long years to work out a compromise on the use of federal funds for abortion-related purposes. The language that was finally agreed on forbade the use of Medicaid funds for most abortions but allowed exceptions in the case of rape or incest, or where the life of the mother would be endangered "or her long-term health severely damaged." I still regard it as too restrictive, but this language, too, prevails to this day.

No one was questioning the ability of most American women, who had the money, to go to a doctor for an abortion. The issue was Medicaid abortions, abortions for poor women who did not have several hundred dollars to end a pregnancy. The abortion opponents, having lost the larger battle, focused their wrath on the most helpless women in our society. Having refused abortions to poor women, of course, they would go on to oppose various programs that would help those women raise their children. It was an ugly, unworthy fight. But the opponents of abortion won it because their zeal was greater than that of many liberals and moderates who were not willing to keep fighting on behalf of poor women year after year.

Ralph Neas, now president of People for the American Way, and my legislative assistant in those days, was at my side throughout these battles. He often expressed his amusement at Majority Leader Tip O'Neill's oft-repeated comment that the antiabortion bills would have been law "a long time ago, except for Senator Brooke and his fistful of proxies." I took that line—inspired, I assume, by the movie *A Fistful of Dollars*—as a compliment to our ability to marshal strength among moderate Republicans and block antichoice legislation.

But ours was a losing battle. In 1980, by a 5–4 vote in *Harris v. McRae*, the Supreme Court upheld the Hyde Amendment. Congress proceeded to eliminate the exceptions for rape and incest, leaving Medicaid coverage for abortion services only in cases of life endangerment. In 1993, President Bill Clinton proposed the complete elimination of the Hyde Amendment. The House and Senate both rejected this proposal, whereupon the administration and Congress did add exceptions for rape and incest. The battle continues to this day, as antiabortion forces use Congress as an arena in which to demonstrate their opposition to the right of women to control their own bodies and destinies.

Even as the abortion debate raged on, the Senate took up another extremely important issue: extension of the 1965 Voting Rights Act. The act had been extended once before, in 1970, over President Nixon's objections. But the debate in 1975 was even more bitterly fought, because for the first time, the extension would potentially cover every state in the union. The original Voting Rights Act had provided for federal supervision and control of the voting process in those states that employed a literacy test as a condition for voting, or in which fewer than 50 percent of the population of voting age was registered to vote. All were in the South. The 1975 extension of the act proposed to extend federal power to any jurisdiction in the country where fewer than 50 percent of voting age citizens had registered to vote in the 1972 presidential election; or to any jurisdiction that the census showed to have more than 5 percent non-English speaking minority citizens in areas where voting materials were distributed solely in English. This provision was designed to protect

Hispanics, Asian Americans, and Native Americans whose voting rights had often been infringed.

This was probably the only time that I found myself in opposition to the legendary NAACP lobbyist, Clarence Mitchell. Clarence and I had fought many civil rights battles together. But in this instance he feared that widening the provisions of the bill might dilute its ability to protect black voters in the South from white officials who might change the time the polls were open, or their location, or even change local boundaries in order to maximize white strength. I understood Clarence's concerns, but I strongly supported the wider provisions of the bill. All Americans should be able to vote, and all deserve the same protection under the law. We African Americans were not the only minority at risk.

The law was due to expire on August 6, and it was not until July 17 that the Senate received a new bill from the House. Not trusting its own Judiciary Committee, under the chairmanship of James O. Eastland of Mississippi, a longtime opponent of civil rights, the Senate Democratic leadership had the bill "held at the desk," a procedure that allowed the majority leader to call it up for debate without committee consideration. With the August 6 deadline fast approaching, and with Congress poised to begin a month's recess, the opposition skillfully employed every parliamentary and public relations tactic to prevent the bill from being considered. They tried to call up other measures. They offered amendments to weaken the bill. On July 23, opponents attempted a filibuster, and a cloture vote was taken. Seventy-six Senators voted to limit debate, nine more than the sixty-seven needed. It was an encouraging sign.

The southern senators proposed complex amendments in the hope of confusing and wearing down supporters of the bill. The most serious threat came in an amendment offered by Senator John Stennis. Stennis was a lawyer, and his language was so deceptively fair on the surface that he fooled some people. His amendment would have stricken section 5, the enforcement provision of the original Voting Rights Act, and would have required every state and political jurisdiction in the entire country to submit all changes in its electoral laws and procedures to the attorney general for approval. Under the existing law, preclearance was required only for those jurisdictions that had been held in violation of the civil rights of their citizens. Stennis argued that all jurisdictions in the country should be treated the same. But the provision, if enacted, not only would have created an immense backlog in the Justice Department, it was almost certainly an unconstitutional intrusion into state and local affairs where there was no history of voting discrimination.

Until then I had not entered the debate, deferring to senators who served on the Judiciary Committee. But the threat was so critical that I could not remain silent. I engaged Senator Stennis and his supporters in a debate that went on for hours. Our exchanges were often heated, and it was with deep emotion that I told the Senate that I could not believe that in 1975, on the floor of the United States Senate, we were ready to say to the American people, black and white, red and brown, that they could not be assured of the basic right to vote. My motion to table the Stennis amendment carried by 58–38. The next day, the Senate voted 77–12 in favor of extending the Voting Rights Act to all Americans. The bill went to President Gerald Ford who signed it on August 6, right on time.

Another issue I felt deeply about was smoking. Long before the surgeon general's warning about the hazards of cigarette smoking in 1963, I was repulsed by the idea of inhaling tobacco smoke into your lungs. My fourth-grade teacher, Miss Lillian Tanner, on whom I had a schoolboy's crush, lit up a cigarette in class one day and exhaled into a clean white handkerchief. I was appalled by the sickly yellow film that clung to the cloth as she held it up to the class. I never forgot her message: "This is what happens to your lungs when you smoke." At that moment I vowed never to smoke. It was a promise I kept even during combat in World War II, when the army encouraged smoking as a way of keeping us calm.

I could not escape smoke at home. Remigia continued to smoke despite the best efforts of Remi, Edwina, and me to dissuade her. As attorney general and later as senator, I forbade smoking of any kind in our office suites. At the time, prohibitions against smoking were unheard of, and my aversion to smoking was seen by many as perverse, if not eccentric. Later, staff members thanked me for helping them kick the habit.

In 1976, nearly fifty-five million Americans were addicted to cigarettes, and more than eight hundred died each day from smoking-related causes. It was incomprehensible to me that the U.S. government would spend $65 million a year to subsidize the cultivation and sale of tobacco, yet spend only $8 million a year for research on the hazards of tobacco. During my time in the Senate I sponsored, cosponsored, or supported nearly 150 bills that would have banned federal tobacco subsidies or otherwise discouraged the tobacco industry.

I was a strong supporter of the National Institutes of Health, especially the Cancer Institute. I fought for generous funding for cancer research programs, including the world-renowned Dana-Farber Cancer Institute in Boston, and Howard University's Cancer Center. My efforts were made possible by the unequivocal support of Chairman Magnuson. Though he smoked "the cheapest, rottenest cigars known to man," he took health issues seriously. "Maggie" and I spent a great deal of time fighting to ensure that health issues got their fair share of the federal government's attention.

––––––

Another very emotional issue I had to deal with in my second term arose not in the Senate chamber but in the streets of Boston. Racial tension increased dramatically in the early 1970s, when the issue of forced busing of schoolchildren brought resentments to a boil. The "separate but equal" doctrine established by *Plessy v. Ferguson* in 1896 had been a tragic mistake. It was fifty-eight years before the Supreme Court reversed itself, in the 1954 *Brown v. Board of Education* decision, and struck down racial segregation in public education. I was a young lawyer in Boston when I heard the news, and I recall my joy, thinking that this was one of America's finest days.

Segregated public schools implanted in the minds of generations of minority children the idea that they were second class. Segregated education leads to separate societies, driven by ignorance and suspicion. In an increasingly global world, where whites are a small minority, it is imperative that children grow up feeling some personal connection to people of other races. By 1972, 92 percent of black children in the South were in integrated schools, a dramatic change in just a few years. But little had changed in Boston. Nineteen years after the *Brown v. Board of Education* decision, 160 of Boston's 201 public schools were still segregated by race.

The Commonwealth of Massachusetts was enlightened on the issue, even if Boston was not. In 1965, the state adopted the nation's first statute to reduce racial imbalance in the public schools. The Massachusetts law declared that any public school whose student body was more than 50 percent black was de facto "unbalanced" and could lose its state funding. As attorney general of Massachusetts, I worked with state legislators in crafting that law and guiding it past legal challenge. It became a model for the nation. But it was a model that was flouted by its own capital and largest city, Boston. In 1966, one of my last tasks as attorney general had been to serve as counsel to the State Board of Education when the Boston School Committee challenged the law's constitutionality. The Massachusetts Supreme Judicial Court unanimously upheld the law, and the U.S. Supreme Court declined to review its decision.

It was painful to see so many people in Boston acting out of racial prejudice. It reflected a profound failure of white leadership. The Boston School Committee was dominated by strident, politically expedient leaders who played on the fears and worst instincts of their constituents. Louise Day Hicks, its chairman, was foremost among them. She and others insisted that segregation was the result of voluntary decisions by parents who wanted to send their children to neighborhood schools. She denied that *Brown v. Board of Education* had any relevance to Boston schools.

Boston school officials launched a bitter fight for segregated public schools. When forced busing of Boston's schoolchildren occurred in October 1974, white citizens responded with violence, and federal marshals were ordered into the city. In an attempt to help reconcile the issue, I made many trips to Boston and reached out to those on both sides. I attended long, emotional meetings with black community leaders and old friends, as well as with members of the Massachusetts

Citizens against Forced Busing, who demanded that I support a constitutional amendment ending forced busing. I reminded them that throughout our history, our Constitution has been a vehicle for protecting and expanding the rights of our citizens, not for limiting them. It took many years of conflict, threats of withdrawal of state and federal funds, and courageous court rulings, particularly on the part of U.S. District Court Judge Arthur Garrity, before desegregation began and Boston public schools could regain their reputation for excellence.

Meanwhile, the historical civil rights coalition in the Senate was weakening. As with abortion, some liberals and moderates grew weary of supporting a cause that was unpopular with many of their constituents. My like-minded colleagues and I constantly had to fight antibusing amendments, often by adding a phrase like "as consistent with the Fourteenth Amendment to the Constitution." We called these "perfecting amendments." But in time we simply did not have the votes to defeat the amendments, and federal agencies were denied the power to support local busing programs.

One victory came not in the Senate but in private negotiations with the Ford administration. I had learned that officials at the Department of Justice led by Solicitor General Robert H. Bork were considering filing a "friend of the court" brief in support of the Boston School Committee. This would have led to a reversal in official administration policy on the busing issue. I sought an immediate meeting with Attorney General Edward Levi; the meeting was also attended by Bork, my legislative assistant Ralph Neas, and by my friend Stan Pottinger, who was then assistant attorney general for civil rights. I made my case verbally and followed it up with a written memo, at the same time appealing to other administration officials whom I knew to be sympathetic to our cause. President Gerald Ford is a decent man, and I suspect that when the issue reached him, he fully understood its implications and made a decision to do the right thing.

Like Sherlock Holmes's dog that did not bark, our victory was simply that nothing happened. If the Justice Department had given aid and comfort to opponents of school busing at that critical moment, Boston's controversy could have spilled out across the country. Any waffling on the part of the United States government would have enflamed the debate over educational equality for all our children and strengthened an already outmoded and immoral system of separation. Having fought this battle, it was no surprise to me in 1987 when Robert Bork's nomination to the U.S. Supreme Court by President Ronald Reagan aroused such controversy and his views on civil rights cost him the appointment.

My commitment to equal rights for women extended far beyond matters of health care. Women on my staff always had equal opportunity for advancement and responsibility, and I believed in paying equal wages for equal work. I employed women lawyers in the attorney general's office in the early 1960s, and in the late 1960s I had one of the first women legislative assistants in the history of the U.S. Senate. I did, however, have one policy that some on my own staff regarded as discriminatory: I did not permit women on my staff to wear slacks or pantsuits to the office. The only time this rule was waived was during the Great Blizzard of 1978, when staff members in the Boston office made heroic efforts to help with disaster relief in Massachusetts.

Most people regarded this policy as one of my "eccentricities," like my prohibition of smoking. But just as my aversion to smoking was rooted in a firm belief that we should protect our health, my dress code was grounded in an equally firm belief that the way we dress is a measure of our self-respect and our respect for others. The code did not apply just to women; men were required to wear coats and ties in the office. As a measure of my own respect for the office I held, I never took my jacket off in the office, not even when alone at my desk.

Other members of Congress had a different policy. Even the president of the United States had a different policy. I will never forget my first visit to the White House after Jimmy Carter took office. Passing through the West Wing, I was appalled by the chaos and disarray. The blue jeans, piles of paper, trash and debris, and general poor housekeeping, I believed, showed a lack of respect for what I regarded as sacred ground, and I said so. My comments, in response to a reporter's questions about my White House visit, which appeared in the *Boston Globe*, the *Washington Post*, and other newspapers, apparently offended Carter's mostly young staff. Not long afterward, I was depicted in a political cartoon as a comic black caricature in suit and tie getting the boot out of the White House gates. The caption read, "Guess who WON'T be coming to dinner."

Nonetheless, I hold President Carter in the highest regard in his years since leaving the White House. He has been an inspirational force for good in his postpresidential years, a man of great humility and dedication, who with his wife, Rosalynn, has done much to promote democracy worldwide and to provide housing for the poor through the remarkable program Habitat for Humanity. He has dedicated his life to bringing peace to our troubled world.

Although I kept my jacket on in my office, I did not otherwise concern myself greatly with my dress, so I was quite amazed when a magazine voted me the best-dressed man in the Senate. I owned only two suits, one blue serge, the other gray flannel, along with ten neckties and a handful of white shirts. The irony was that there were at least two real sartorial dandies in the Senate at that time, Mark Hatfield of Oregon and Gale McGee of Wyoming, who were always sharply dressed. I can only assume that keeping my jacket on set me apart from my more clothes-conscious colleagues.

Dress code aside, I believe my staff appreciated my support for women's rights on many issues that came before the Senate. In addition to championing a woman's right to choose and supporting the Equal Rights Amendment, I also fought for Title IX, the celebrated amendment to the 1972 Education Act, which guaranteed equal rights for women in education. The most visible and controversial result of this provision was to require that women's sports should be funded equally with men's sports. Because men's football dominated most colleges' sports budgets, this caused some less visible men's sports to be cut back or eliminated. As a result, there was in 1974 a serious effort to weaken Title IX. Birch Bayh and I led the fight that spared Title IX any cutbacks that year.

The battle for equal rights for women had many fronts. In 1977, we were able to pass the Equal Credit Act, which guaranteed equal credit opportunities to women, who for too long had been treated by bankers and other lenders as second-class citizens.

Another of my priorities in those years was the annual fight to keep conservatives from gutting or eliminating the federal Legal Services program, which they hated because it empowered poor people to stand up against the rich and powerful. Jesse Helms used to express bewilderment at our support for Legal Services. Did we not understand that these people were using the taxpayers' money *to oppose the government*? Of course we did, and we thought it a good thing for the poor to have access to lawyers, just as their bosses and landlords and creditors and the police did. Year after year, a few of us would fight to keep Legal Services alive. After I left the Senate, another Republican who had previously been attorney general of his state, Warren Rudman of New Hampshire, took up the cause.

Another concern of mine had to do with the interest that banks paid or did not pay on checking accounts. When I was growing up, banks offered "Christmas Club" savings accounts. You would put money in week after week and then withdraw it in time for your Christmas shopping. The catch was that you received no interest and you could not withdraw your money early. When I was a child my father complained bitterly about the unfairness of those accounts, but there was nothing to be done about it. As a member of the Senate Banking Committee, I fought for the creation of the currently ubiquitous but at the time quite revolutionary NOW (negotiable order of withdrawal) accounts to ensure that people received interest on their checking accounts and Christmas savings accounts. The banking industry, needless to say, fought me tooth and nail. The best I could do at that time was a trial program whereby people in the Northeast received interest on their checking accounts. Later that was expanded to the entire nation.

My somewhat unlikely ally on some banking issues was Senator John Tower of Texas, a conservative Republican who favored Armed Services Committee meetings over Banking Committee sessions and would give me his proxy to vote as I thought best. I had first met Tower on the campaign trail in 1960, when he was a political science professor running against Lyndon Johnson, who had rigged the rules in Texas so that he could run for reelection to the Senate and for vice president at the same time. We met at a Republican rally, and Tower immediately led me backstage, pulled out a silver flask, and offered me a shot of whiskey. I declined, but he proceeded to wet his whistle and tell me about his political ambitions. He lost to Johnson that fall, but the next year, when Johnson vacated his Senate seat, Tower was elected to replace him, its youngest member at age thirty-six. There was a certain Bonapartism about John Tower. He was small in stature but big in ambition.

Not long after I entered the Senate, Tower briefed me on Vietnam. He had a map of Vietnam that covered one large wall of his Senate office. Figures on the map represented our troops and the Viet Cong. He moved them around with alacrity, and used a long wooden pointer for emphasis. When I asked him a question about the location of artillery and the use of air power, he looked surprised, and I explained that I had some experience in military tactics while serving in Italy during World War II. John, who had served with the navy in the Pacific, loved the military, and our shared service in World War II was the basis of our warm if somewhat improbable relationship. John, an expert on defense issues, became chairman of the Armed Services Committee and was able to hobnob with generals to his heart's delight.

—————

With Remigia living in Boston, I was a nominal bachelor in a city that often needed a single male to balance out dinner parties. Some of the most highly coveted invitations were those extended by Senator John Sherman Cooper of Kentucky. John and his wife, Lorraine, entertained luxuriously in their home in Georgetown, where I spent many a pleasant evening.

The governments of oil-rich nations such as Iran, Saudi Arabia, and Nigeria often gave lavish parties that I attended, as well as those of Israel, Jordan, Britain, and Italy. One of the most popular hosts was my friend Ardeshir Zahedi, the Iranian ambassador to the United States. Ardeshir was a serious, effective, and visionary diplomat, who negotiated the release of 165 hostages who had been captured and held at gunpoint by Hanafi Muslim terrorists in Washington, D.C., in March 1977. It was at one such party that I met the shah of Iran and his wife, Empress Farah Diba Pahlavi. The shah and I discovered that we had been born on the same day and at very nearly the same hour. With some irony I later noted that the shah eventually left his throne the same year that I left the Senate.

At one gathering at the Iranian Embassy in 1976, I danced with Elizabeth Taylor, whose beauty overshadowed her keen intelligence and knowledge of public issues. Someone snapped a photo of us that ran in newspapers around the world. The photograph did not play well in Boston, where it raised eyebrows and suggested that my life was far more glamorous than it was. Elizabeth Taylor aside, some of my advisers were concerned that photos of me dancing at a Muslim country's embassy would alienate our Jewish supporters, even though Iran was one of our strongest allies at the time. Remigia was one of the few who had no immediate reaction.

A few days later, I invited Miss Taylor to my Senate office for breakfast. She was gracious and charming as could be. My staff fell all over themselves trying to get a glimpse of her. Some time later, Ardeshir Zahedi and I claimed credit for introducing her to her future husband, John Warner, whom I had met in 1975 when I served as chairman of the board of the American Revolution Bicentennial Administration and John was its able administrator. Soon he was elected to the Senate from Virginia.

Fully 90 percent of the work of the Congress takes place in committees and subcommittees. As I achieved seniority, I acquired committee assignments that both served the needs of my constituents and satisfied my own interests. I had risen to be the senior Republican on the Senate Banking, Housing, and Urban Affairs Committee's Housing Subcommittee. On the Senate Appropriations Committee I became the ranking Republican on the Labor, Health, Education, and Welfare Subcommittee as well as holding the same position on the Foreign Operations Subcommittee, which oversees U.S. foreign aid.

Foreign aid has long been unpopular with the American people, largely because it is so poorly understood. Every year, attempts are made to reduce or eliminate funds for this vital program. In the spring of 1974, a major effort was mounted to terminate our aid program to Haiti, a desperately poor country with a tortured history of dictatorship, corruption, and political unrest. Critics said the U.S. aid had been used for inappropriate purposes and that the government of Haiti was so corrupt that it was a waste of money to send funds there. While conceding some truth to both points, I countered that Haiti was our neighbor and that we had a national interest in relieving poverty that would only breed violence. My colleagues were adamant: aid to Haiti would have to stop. In desperation, I volunteered to go to Haiti to review our aid program and to report back before the committee made a final decision.

Together with my aide David Rossiter, I set out on a four-day visit to Haiti. I met first with President Jean-Claude Duvalier, son of the infamous "Papa Doc," the brutal president-for-life who had ruled the country for fourteen years. I had meetings with Haitian cabinet officials; our respected ambassador, Heywood Isham; and with private aid organizations such as the Haitian-American Community Help Organization, CARE, and Catholic Relief Services, all engaged in the heroic work of assisting the poor. We flew by helicopter to visit the Albert Schweitzer Hospital at Deschapelles and traveled by car to agricultural projects in the Artibonite Valley.

On my return I reported to my colleagues that, regrettably, the primary interest of the Duvalier government was perpetuating itself in power. The local economic institutions could not foster meaningful development. Yet Haiti needed foreign aid to develop roads, improve irrigation systems, and provide rudimentary health care. I recommended that our aid be continued for those purposes. The program was funded, but questions persisted, so in 1977, I returned to Haiti for a second look. I concluded that the Duvalier government continued to put its own interests ahead of those of its people. Corruption flourished. Inadequate accounting for U.S. aid dollars made it impossible to judge what had been done. Changes of regime and decades of conflict have only perpetuated these sad conditions, and Haiti to this day remains one of the poorest countries on earth. Yet, the potential for economic growth is there, both in the country's natural and human resources. Though impoverished, it has produced the greatest artists in the Caribbean, noted throughout the world for vibrant carvings, paintings, and crafts. I continue to hope that one day this land will have a government worthy of its people.

The most far-reaching trip of my second term was to the Soviet Union in February 1976. Because of my position on the Housing Subcommittee, I was invited by the United States Information Agency to Minsk to open their exhibit "Technology for the American Home." I was proud to be a part of bringing this glimpse of American life to the Soviet people. David Rossiter accompanied me on this trip, too, along with Jerry Buckley and Carl Coan of the Banking and Housing Committee staff. We arrived in Moscow in the snow. On our first evening we ventured out of the Rossiya Hotel and were awed by the sight of the nearby Kremlin, truly one of the most magnificent buildings in the world, covered in snow and lit by floodlights.

I was determined to learn as much as I could and to engage in as much dialogue with the Soviets as possible. I met with Soviet officials to discuss the potential for improving relations between our two nations. The Strategic Arms Limitation Talks (SALT) were high on my agenda, as were conventional force reductions in the Warsaw Pact and the U.S. military presence in western Europe.

Also of concern to me was the plight of "refusniks," Soviet Jews who had applied to emigrate to Israel and were instead being held as virtual prisoners in their own country. With the help of the U.S. Embassy, I was able to arrange secret meetings with such noted refusniks as scientist Anatoly Shcharansky, Vladimir and Mariya Slepak, and Colonel Yefim Davydovich, a hero of World War II. They and others had been trying to get to Israel for years and had been subject to loss of jobs, harassment, and constant surveillance. Soviet officials were unmoved by my arguments on behalf of these individuals, but I believe my efforts helped convey the depth of American concern over their plight. For my own part, I gained a deeper appreciation of the innate strength of the Soviet people, as well as great sadness that their government was unwilling to grant their individual rights and freedoms.

In January 1978, I had the unique opportunity to carry a message of racial brotherhood to the Mormon Church, one of the last institutions in America to specifically exclude nonwhites from positions of responsibility. Through the good offices of Senators Wallace Bennett and Orrin Hatch of Utah, both Mormons and Republicans, I was invited to address the students and faculty at Brigham Young University in Provo. Following the speech I would meet privately with the leadership of the Mormon Church: President Spencer W. Kimball, Marion G. Romney, and Gordon B. Hinkley, who is now president of the ten million–member Church. It was a rare opportunity for any non-Mormon, and particularly for an African American.

In my speech to the more than six thousand students, on January 12, I focused on Africa. Cold War tensions were then being played out on the African continent in civil wars and in economic competition. I argued that Africa ought not to be the setting for a superpower confrontation. I called for an embargo on trade with Uganda to protest the violence in that ravaged land, and I decried the evils of apartheid. As I spoke, I was aware that there were no minority faces in the audience. I knew that this was one of the few times that some of these students had even seen an African American, let alone been addressed by one. After expressing the hope that white South Africans would find the way to open up their society to other races, I turned to the Mormon Church's own exclusionary policy.

"You and I know that the relationship between black Americans and Mormonism in general is not all that it could or should be," I began. "This is distressing to me personally, for I find that the two groups have much in common. Black Americans and Mormons have a common heritage of persecution at various points in their history in this country. . . . Both groups have been sustained in times of adversity by their seeking to know the will of God and to carry it out," I continued. "Even though these affinities exist, we know that black Americans and Mormons have only begun the process of understanding that can result in greater empathy for each other." I told the audience that I did not seek controversy but hoped that honest discussion of differences could lead to "a closer association between the Mormons and my people" and that "what I have said here today will be conducive to helping bring that about." I was astonished and more than pleased to receive a lengthy standing ovation, which suggested that these young Mormons were open to my message of tolerance and change.

Next I met with the church leaders. We discussed the church's position regarding African Americans. I knew that for them a change in church policy could only come as a revelation from God. But the meeting was cordial, and I could not help wondering if my words had done any good. Six months later, President Kimball stunned the Church with his latest Revelation, reversing a 148-year-old church policy. Front-page headlines reported the startling news: "Mormon Church Strikes Down Ban against Blacks in the Priesthood." I knew I had not caused the change. Many Mormons had been working and praying for years for their church to abandon its exclusionary policy. But I may have helped prepare the way for acceptance of such a dramatic policy change.

The next great challenge of 1978 came just weeks after my return from Utah. On February 6, the Northeast was hit with one of the biggest blizzards in history. The storm smacked right into Boston and Cape Cod. It raged for thirty-three hours and dropped nearly three feet of snow on some areas that already had twenty inches on the ground. An area that prided itself on being able to deal with horrific weather was crippled. Thousands of motorists were stranded. Thousands of residents were left shivering in the dark when power failed. Worse yet, a deadly storm surge from the Atlantic destroyed much of the coastline, ravaging the coastal towns of Scituate and Revere, Winthrop and Hull, washing away homes and businesses in one powerful sweep up the coast. The ocean crested at six feet above normal.

Helping the people of Massachusetts get through that storm and its aftermath was the greatest logistical challenge I ever faced. On February 8, I flew by military transport to Boston with William Wilcox, the administrator of the Federal Disaster Assistance Administration, and White House aide Greg Schneiders. We flew over those coastal areas most seriously damaged by the storm and met with Governor Michael Dukakis to coordinate our efforts. The next day we took a helicopter to the South Shore and the Fall River and New Bedford areas to assess the damage there.

Marshaling staff and volunteers, I used all the means at my disposal to offer assistance to victims of the storm and spent hours on the phone trying to coordinate relief services. I asked President Carter to declare the region a National Disaster area, paving the way for federal assistance. My staff and I enlisted the army and National Guard troops to help move the snow. We helped make sure that groceries got delivered to elderly shut-ins. I was able to arrange for federal relief to cover ice and snow damage for the first time in our nation's history. In the storm's aftermath, millions of dollars came into the commonwealth in relief funds.

There was a wonderful outpouring of individual heroism. A movie house was hastily converted into a shelter where people ate beef stew and slept in the theater seats. In Cambridge, a surgeon raced down the frozen Charles River on skis to reach a Boston hospital and perform emergency surgery. State troopers rescued motorists from their cars. St. Bartholomew's Church in Needham alone took in 1,500 people. People traveled by sled or snowshoes or hitched rides on snowplows. Firefighters traveled by snowmobile. Store and restaurant owners kept their establishments open and often gave away their dwindling provisions to those in need. For all of the storm's damage, and the death of twenty-nine people in Massachusetts, the Blizzard of '78 brought out the best in our people.

———

The same week that the blizzard struck New England, another kind of storm erupted in the Senate. President Carter sent the Panama Canal Treaties to the Senate for ratification. Few issues have aroused national pride more than "giving up" the Panama Canal. Almost all Americans had a sense of pride in the monumental engineering feat that the canal represented. Yet many people recognized that the canal rightfully belonged to the Panamanian people and that turning over the canal was not only right but essential to good international relations. President Carter put his prestige on the line in an uphill battle to secure ratification of the treaties in the Senate. My

Massachusetts constituents overwhelmingly disapproved of the treaties. They were concerned about national defense and our national security should the canal ever be controlled by others. "We built it and it is ours," was the prevailing view.

There were two treaties under consideration: the actual Panama Canal Treaty, signed by President Carter on September 7, 1977, which turned the canal over to Panama, and a corresponding Permanent Neutrality Treaty, which provided that the canal itself would remain neutral territory in perpetuity. Neither treaty addressed the primary concern of many senators and their constituents, the guarantee of U.S. access to the canal at all times, especially in times of war. The debates and the voting began on February 22 and continued for almost two months. Altogether, eighty votes were taken on amendments, reservations, and procedural matters. For much of that time, the Senate conducted no other business. Approval of a treaty required two-thirds vote of the Senate for ratification, sixty-seven members out of one hundred. As the debate opened, the Senate leadership counted sixty-two senators in favor of the treaties, twenty-eight senators against, and ten in the "undecided" category. I was one of those. I was also among the thirty-four members of the Senate up for reelection that year.

My habit of gathering all the facts and hearing all the arguments before making important decisions inspired criticism that I was stalling. The conservative wing of the Massachusetts Republican Party was encouraging radio personality Avi Nelson to challenge me in the primary. I knew that a vote in favor of the treaties would give the right-wingers fresh ammunition. But my hesitancy had far less to do with politics than with specific provisions of the treaty, including financial arrangements, defense of the canal, and the waterway's continued neutrality.

The first key vote came on March 16, on ratifying the Permanent Neutrality Treaty. All one hundred senators were present. The gap had closed in the final days, and the leadership believed that it had the votes for passage. The day before, I had declared my intention to support the treaty, thus becoming the sixty-fifth senator to announce in favor. When the vote came, it was 68–32, one vote more than needed for passage. The breakdown by party was fifty-two Democrats and sixteen Republicans for the treaty, ten Democrats and twenty-two Republicans against.

It was another month before the other treaty, returning the canal to Panama, was approved, after much debate and many amendments, including provisions allowing the United States to step in and guarantee access to the canal if conditions ever required it. The second vote, on April 18, was identical to the first: 68–32. The treaties would have passed without my vote. It provided a ready target for those already unhappy with my positions on abortion rights, desegregation, and other issues, and I could have ducked it. But I believed I was making the right decision, and I did not believe in ducking hard issues.

My second term had been even more exciting than my first. I knew my way around the Senate and official Washington. I knew how to get things done, and with my seniority and experience, I often had the power to advance causes about which I cared deeply. I had almost unlimited opportunity to indulge my wide range of interests, both foreign and domestic. I began to feel like "the freest man in the Senate."

In my personal life, however, I was anything but free. I wanted a change, and it soon came.

16

A Private

Matter

In 1975, my life looked good. Secure in my second term, I enjoyed Washington, relished my growing seniority, and was proud of what I had achieved in the Senate. It was frustrating that my party had never been in the majority while I was there, but I was the ranking minority member of a full committee and several subcommittees and I was often able to advance causes I cared about deeply.

But storm clouds had been brewing over my life for a long time. My visits to our home in suburban Boston were important to our daughters and to me, but time spent with Remigia was increasingly strained, and I would often retreat to my room. Remigia and I had spoken about divorce since the mid-1960s. I knew that divorce was foreign to her way of thinking, but our lives were changing, and the realities could not be denied.

In 1970, when I purchased a property on the French side of the island of St. Martin, both as a vacation home and as an investment, I had no idea how it would change my life. The first time I heard of St. Martin was in 1962 when I was staying in St. Thomas in the U.S. Virgin Islands. My dear friends from Boston, Herb Feld and Irene and Ben Bayne, were living on the island. Ben and Irene had lost their son during the war, and in many ways I became like a son to them, benefiting for years from their affection, advice, and generosity. When they suggested I look into the island of Anguilla as both a vacation and investment opportunity, I took their advice. In April 1963, accompanied by my friend Norman Cohen from Toronto and a friend from Massachusetts, I set out on a visit to Anguilla.

The small plane landed on a grassy strip leading to a hut, where two colorfully garbed soldiers greeted us and a clerk approved our passports. We took the only cab to Rendez-vous, a small, secluded resort owned by the Gumbs family on a beautiful beach called Rendez-vous Bay. Jerry Gumbs, a big, good-looking native son with a quick wit greeted us, along with his sister, Aunt Bea, who turned out to be a talented cook. She prepared three meals a day with fresh fish, lobsters, carrot cake, Johnnycakes, stuffed crab backs, and fried plantains—all of this plus your room and all the Heineken beer you could drink was ten dollars per person, per day! Anguilla is blessed with the whitest sandy beaches in all of the Caribbean, and the water is so clear you could literally find a dime at a depth of six feet. The three of us spent a glorious week swimming, eating, reading, and exploring the island.

In order to return to the States, my American friend and I had to get a smallpox vaccination, which was not available in Anguilla. So we chartered a fishing boat and went to St. Martin, twelve miles across the channel, to the St. Rose Hospital. The boat was navigated by an old sea captain, "Uncle Ben," a man with a very dark complexion, gray hair, and beard, piercing eyes and a warm face with many wrinkles. As we approached the wharf in Marigot, the capital of the French side of the thirty-seven-square-mile island, we saw a house under construction on a cliff overlooking a lovely deserted beach. I could not help but think how wonderful it would be to live in such a beautiful setting.

When we pulled up to the dock, the first man we met was Jules Petit, a silver-haired gentleman who was sitting in a chair in the ground floor window of a store overlooking the harbor. Mr. Petit ran one of the island's grocery stores, and from his bay window he could survey the whole harbor. Years later, my daughter Remi would marry his grandson Roger Petit, and Edwina would marry his grandnephew, Michel Petit. We found a ride to Philipsburg, where we got the required inoculation. Then we headed back to the wharf where Uncle Ben was waiting for us. We had seen little of St. Martin, but I vowed to return.

Six years later I did so, as a vacationer with an eye for real estate development. I rented a car and drove around the island, talking and mingling with its friendly people, admiring its small towns, high hills, and shimmering beaches. I noted the absence of middle-income housing and thought perhaps a housing development would be a good business opportunity and would also benefit the island. I was interested in real estate and wanted to invest outside of Massachusetts to avoid any perception of conflict of interest. The Caribbean was a perfect place to explore.

The next year I again returned to St. Martin. While there, I was invited to cocktails by Janet Hanson, a well-known real estate agent. Janet raved about a house she had for sale. But the house and grounds carried an asking price of $280,000, a sum that I said to me was as big as the national debt. We both laughed, but she insisted that I at least *see* the property. So I drove up to the house, which was rundown and boarded up but was shown to me by caretaker James Carty, a native of St. Martin. The house rose forty-two feet above the sea and had two thousand feet of ocean frontage. It was nestled into the top of a hill with stone steps running down to Friar's Bay, the isolated beach below. The views were breathtaking. I realized it was the very house I had seen from Uncle Ben's boat on my first visit to St. Martin.

The house sat on five acres and was even more extraordinary than I had imagined. It had twelve rooms, a master bedroom with a sunken shower and walk-through cedar closet, a mahogany-paneled study, a lily pond running the length of the large living room, and a lanai filled with banana trees and orchids. The six thousand–square-foot house, designed by Miami architect Wahl Snyder, featured Italian marble floors and mosaic tile and was equipped with a walk-in freezer, a wine closet, drive-through double garage, and a fully equipped guest cottage. The owners were in the midst of a prolonged divorce, and though the house had been sorely neglected, I still could see how beautiful it had been and could be again. The grounds were landscaped with hibiscus, palms, frangipani, bougainvillea, orchids, and orchards of oranges and grapefruits. The driveway was lined with flamboyant trees. I fell in love with the house and began to dream the impossible dream of purchasing and restoring it.

The owner, D. Reginald Tibbetts, was living in California. He and his wife, Louise, an artist, had invested a lot of themselves in the property in happier days. When I called him and identified myself, he asked, "You wouldn't be related to the senator from Massachusetts?" I admitted I was that Edward Brooke, and I told him that I was interested in buying the fine house he had built, but that his asking price was out of my league. When the moment came to discuss the price, I told him the most I could afford to offer him was $190,000. After a silence, he said, "Maybe I didn't hear you correctly, Senator. I want to sell my house, not give it away!" He added that he had invested more than $450,000 in the property and he had already reduced his price substantially. I told him I certainly understood his position, but asked him not to reject my offer out of hand.

I called my friends Al Gammal and Herb Tucker in Massachusetts and asked to borrow $5,000 from each of them. This money along with $9,000 I had in the bank made up the $19,000 good-faith deposit that I rushed to Mr. Tibbetts along with my written offer of $190,000. Al and Herb thought I was crazy to consider such an obligation. I made application for and received mortgages of $125,000 from the Commonwealth National Bank in Boston and $75,000 from the South Boston Savings Bank, both at the going interest rate, to cover the purchase price and closing costs. Mr. Tibbetts finally accepted my offer, and on December 31, 1969, I became the owner of what many considered the most beautiful home on St. Martin.

I renamed the house "La Batterie" after I learned that the French had referred to the area as Batterie when they had defended St. Martin against invasion by the British from Anguilla two hundred years before. Old remnants of the fortifications remained, and I restored an old rusted battery piece and had it mounted on rocks in front of the house. Remigia, Remi, and Edwina and their friends thoroughly enjoyed La Batterie. They often spent Christmas and summer vacations there. In January, February, and March, the house was usually rented, except for my brief trips when the Senate was in recess. The house was perfect for entertaining, and we hosted wonderful parties with flickering torchlights, calypso bands, and French champagne.

Part of my plan for the house was that I would help meet expenses by renting it when my family and I were not using it. Our first tenants included Henry Ford II and his beautiful, Italian-born wife,

Christina. Ford had business to conduct while on the island, and his wife liked to swim in the altogether in the waters below the house. We were told that they hired a local man called Tall Boy to stand guard and make sure no one caught a glimpse of Christina while she swam. It was never clear who stood guard over Tall Boy. But Christina was a lovely woman, and she and Remigia, with their shared Italian heritage, were friendly for some years.

Public electricity did not extend as far as La Batterie, so a pair of diesel generators provided our power. To purchase the diesel fuel, I opened an account with the L. C. Fleming Company, the Texaco agent, owned and operated by Mrs. Yvette Fleming. Mrs. Fleming was the widow of the revered mayor of French St. Martin, Louis Constant Fleming. He had died in 1949 at the age of fifty-one, leaving his thirty-two-year-old widow to run his many businesses and raise their two young children, Louis-Constant, then two, and Yvette Anne Frances, only three months old. Mrs. Fleming and I became close friends. When I was in St. Martin, I would stop in her office in Marigot to talk. She was intelligent and articulate, and she knew just about everything that happened in French and Dutch St. Martin. Her father had also been mayor of French St. Martin, as had his father before him. She was the matriarch of the island. She often spoke of her two children, who were then in private schools in Canada.

It was the custom for well-to-do families on the island to send their children away for higher education. Some went to Europe, but Mrs. Fleming sent hers to French-speaking Montreal. Louis-Constant went to Jean-de-Brebeuf, a Jesuit college, and Anne attended Villa Maria Convent and later Marianopolis College, affiliated with the University of Montreal, from which she earned a B.A. degree cum laude. As the years went by, I learned all about their birthdays, graduations, and marriages: Louis to a medical student from France and Anne to a French-Canadian lawyer, a former college roommate of her brother. Louis and his lovely bride, Hélène, came back to St. Martin to live. But Anne and her husband stayed in Montreal where he practiced law. I met them for the first time at a party Remigia and I gave for my mother at La Batterie in 1972.

In 1975, Edwina chose La Batterie as the site for her wedding to Dr. Michel Petit. Remigia and I were then talking about divorce. We had agreed to wait until after the celebration, but I thought it would be awkward if I stayed in the house during the wedding. However, Edwina called me in Washington and insisted that I stay at La Batterie to prevent gossip from marring her special day. Knowing my love of ceremony and my attention to detail, Edwina asked me to take charge of the wedding arrangements. So my mother and I stayed at La Batterie, and everyone put on the best face possible.

I had arranged bouquets of red and white bougainvillea on the steps leading to the highest point on the property, a spot surrounded by bright red flowering flamboyant trees. It was there on the wide steps that Edwina exchanged vows with Michel Petit, the eldest son of the then mayor of French St. Martin, Dr. Hubert Petit. Many guests had flown in from Washington and Massachusetts, and others came from both the Dutch and French sides of the island. I had wanted to have more of an island wedding, with a night of calypso music, torch-light, roast pigs, and West Indian fare. But Remigia insisted on a for-mal sit-down dinner at the Mullet Bay Resort.

Edwina's wedding was scheduled for 5 P.M., to avoid the heat and to make the most of the late afternoon light. Just moments before the ceremony, Mrs. Fleming, her son Louis, daughter-in-law Hélène, and daughter Anne arrived. Anne, then in her mid-twenties, had re-turned to St. Martin unexpectedly, and Mrs. Fleming had asked Remigia if she could bring her. I could not help but notice that Anne was prettier than I had remembered from the one time I had seen her before.

After ushering in the latecomers, I proudly escorted my daughter out onto the terrace and up to the altar before the hundred or more guests. The ceremony brought tears to my eyes, yet, even as I walked with Edwina up the aisle, I felt the presence of the pretty young woman who stood in the back of the terrace with her family. After the ceremony, I saw Anne on the terrace, chatting with friends and drinking champagne. I commandeered a bottle from one of the white-gloved waiters and filled her half-full glass. I took the crystal flute from her hand and drank from the rim where her lips had been and passed the glass back to her. She flushed, glanced down, and said nothing. After the reception at La Batterie, we all traveled across the island to Mullet Bay for the formal wedding dinner.

Seated at the head table with Remigia, I could not keep my eyes off Anne. I knew what I must do. After my first dance with Edwina and after moving from table to table to greet guests, I made my way to Mrs. Fleming's table, greeted her and her family, and asked Anne for a dance. She glanced quickly at her mother, who just as hesitantly nodded her approval. We danced and danced but did not speak. I sensed there was a connection between us. Mrs. Fleming must have sensed something too. She came over to us and told Anne it was time to go.

The next night, the groom's father, Mayor Petit, gave a party at Le Galion Beach Hotel for the newlyweds. I had hoped to see Anne again at the party. But the Petits had invited nearly everyone on the island *except* the Flemings. The two families had been political rivals for years. But I had to see her again. The next day I drove all over the island to all the places I thought she might be, without success. I tried to put her out of my mind. I was troubled by my feelings for a woman who was married and had a child. I heard later that her marriage was in trouble, but I took no delight in the news. On the contrary, with my own marital difficulties, I felt sorry for her and her daughter. But I wanted to see her again.

At the end of February 1976, I telephoned her in Montreal. She seemed pleased, which encouraged me to ask her to dinner. We met in Montreal on March 19, at the restaurant in the Hotel Chateau Champlain, which offered candlelight and a harpist. We had a delightful evening, and I spent the long plane ride back to Washington thinking of her. Anne came to Washington in June. The Ford White House arranged for me to use the presidential box at the Kennedy Center. Prior to the performance of the ballet *Manon Lescaut* with Natalia Makarova, we had caviar and champagne at my apartment in the Watergate. From that weekend onward, we saw each other as often as we could, meeting in Washington, Montreal, Martha's Vineyard, St. Martin, and St. Barts.

In 1976, the Massachusetts General Court passed a no-fault divorce statute. Couples could attribute the end of their marriage to "irreconcilable differences" instead of ascribing blame for the failure of the marriage to one or the other partner. I thought this was the perfect opportunity for Remigia and me to begin new lives. We would not have to go to court and make cruel statements about each other. We could cite profound differences, equitably divide our property, and quietly end a marriage that had not been a marriage for decades. We had waited until the girls were grown and had lives of their own. Why did we have to wait any longer? I knew Remigia was reluctant, but I thought she had finally come to the conclusion that it was best for us both. Finally, she said, "It's okay, if that's what you want." I told her that I had retained a lawyer and that she should do the same, and that the papers would be filed soon.

My political advisers were not so sure. "Are you certain Remigia will agree to a divorce?" they insisted. "Why not wait until *after* the election?" Holding off filing for more than two years, until after the election in 1978, did not seem right to me. I had no intention of rushing into another marriage. I just wanted to be free. I wanted an open life. I also wanted happiness for Remigia and hoped that she could find someone who could bring her that happiness. "Don't worry, it will be all right," I assured my friends. "It won't be a public matter. Just a quiet, personal divorce. The election is two years away, and this will long be over by then."

I could not have been more wrong.

17

Stormy

Weather

Once the decision to file for divorce was made, and believing that the divorce would be routine, I retained a reputable Boston divorce firm, known for its success in working out amicable financial settlements. On June 4, 1976, my attorneys filed divorce papers in Middlesex County Probate Court. I believed that Remigia would live up to our verbal agreement for an uncontested, no-fault divorce. I was prepared to enter into a fair settlement agreement. With the proceedings underway, I called my staff into my office and told them the news. No one was surprised.

At the time the papers were filed, Remigia was vacationing at our home in St. Martin. Remi was also living on the island with her husband, Roger Petit, and their infant daughter, Tamara. A reporter from the *Boston Globe* reached them and asked them to comment. Reading the newspaper the next day, I learned that Remigia and Remi had said they were shocked by the news and had given the reporter outrageous statements about me. They claimed that I had failed to give my wife adequate monetary support during our marriage and that I was abandoning a poor, sick woman. Although Remigia expressed her shock at the news of the filing, I was the one who was shocked, for I had alerted her before she flew to St. Martin that the divorce papers would be filed.

The *Globe* had not contacted me in preparing its story. Nor did it contact other family and friends. My Boston press secretary, Hap Ellis, called me in Washington, dumbfounded by the front-page story. I was humiliated, embarrassed, and saddened—even more so when other newspapers picked it up. At first I did not know what to make of Remigia's charges. Friends begged me to correct the impression of Remigia as a martyr, but I could not bring myself to say anything publicly. I could not strike out against my own wife and daughter, questioning their veracity and motives, even to prove that the charges were untrue. I made a decision not to respond, believing that coverage of the divorce would soon die down. It was a private matter, I told myself, that had nothing to do with my Senate responsibilities. As awful as the allegations were, at least they had said nothing that would impugn my integrity as an elected official. I did not realize this would be the beginning of a two-year barrage.

I had charted a lonely course. It was then that Anne began to take on a much larger role in my life. She had by then separated from her husband, and we had been in frequent contact. As the controversy swirled around my campaign, I found more reasons to get away from it. My lawyers complained, with some justification, that they could not get me to focus on the divorce proceedings, and in part I did not do so simply because they were so increasingly unpleasant. During President's Day recess in February 1977, Anne invited me to a friend's chalet at the resort Lac Achigan, one hundred miles north of Montreal. Anne met me at the airport with her navy blue Volvo's large trunk packed with delicious meals she had prepared. We drove up through the snow-capped mountains to the cozy chalet, with its huge fireplace. Heavy snow had fallen, and the lake was frozen. It was a crystalline wonderland. We spent the days cross-country skiing, taking long walks, and sitting for hours in front of the fire. For the first time in months I felt as if I had left my troubles behind. It was then that I thought I could live the rest of my life with this young woman.

After that we saw more of each other. Her high spirits lifted mine. She was a good listener as well as an intelligent and insightful woman. I began to confide in her and she in me, telling me more about her troubled marriage and her own divorce proceedings. During the worst days of my divorce, she offered understanding and comfort. Her maturity amazed me. From her I drew strength and courage to carry on with the divorce and my campaign for reelection.

On July 21, 1977, Remigia's mother, Teresa, died after spending the last years of her life in a nursing home. Remigia was vacationing in Italy at the time, and I flew to Boston to arrange the funeral. I was deeply saddened. We had tried to spare her any involvement in our increasingly acrimonious divorce, but her last years had been hard for her and for all of us who loved her. At Teresa's funeral I had the first direct contact with Remigia, Remi, and Edwina since the divorce proceedings began. At our Newton home after the funeral, Remi asked, "Daddy, why are you divorcing *me*?" "Remi, you are my daughter. I could not divorce you," I told her. "Your mother and I are divorcing each other, not you and not Edwina. We both love you and your sister." I meant that wholeheartedly, but Remi did not seem convinced.

The stories about my divorce grew worse as the case entered the courts. It seemed that almost every day a new charge more ridiculous than the one before surfaced. The most damaging was that I was abandoning my poor sick wife of thirty years while she was stricken with cancer. When the divorce papers were filed in 1976, Remigia did not have cancer. Her physician, Dr. Howard Trafton, had informed me in 1969 that Remigia had benign polyps, not uncommon in women her age, and he had kept me apprised periodically about her health. When I called him a week or so before papers were filed, he again assured me that Remigia was doing well, but that if she did not stop smoking she could die from smoking-related cancer.

The coverage was most intense in the *Boston Globe*, which seemed to be receiving leads from one or both of my daughters. Its front-page "Spotlight" feature was repeatedly devoted to some new revelation about my supposed misdeeds. At one point the paper published aerial photographs of my Vineyard "estate," raising questions as to how I could afford such a luxurious property on my Senate salary. A reporter could have gone to the Dukes County Registry of Deeds and easily found out that I had paid $18,000 for the property in 1958, four years before I was elected attorney general.

When I purchased La Batterie I had applied for and received mortgage loans from two Massachusetts banks. Now the newspapers were falsely reporting that this was an unsecured loan, despite the fact that I had put up stock as collateral. They hinted that because of my status as a member of the Senate Banking Committee I had received special treatment. This was not true; the loans and their terms were a matter of public record for anyone who bothered to check. The press referred to the St. Martin house as a "multimillion-dollar estate," once more raising the question as to how I could afford it. Again, they could have gone to the French Notaire's office and learned that I had paid $190,000, or they could have simply asked me. They never did.

Helene and I tried to shield our mother from the headlines, but one day a reporter from the *Washington Post* telephoned her pretending to be a friend of mine. Naturally my mother greeted the stranger warmly. "Why yes, darling. Yes, I had a wonderful time in Europe. No darling, Edward didn't pay for my trip. Edward doesn't have any money to send me to Europe; I paid for my own trip." The reporter made several calls to her and even questioned Watergate management as to whether Mother had purchased her own apartment and paid her own monthly mortgage and maintenance payments or if I did.

In truth, Mother sometimes gave money to me, not the other way around. My father had left her financially comfortable, and she had paid $45,000 for a one-bedroom apartment at the Watergate, a place she loved because of its security and convenient access to services. Mother lived modestly; her trip to Europe with her friend Laura Carson, as part of a package tour, was one of her rare extravagances. She was bewildered by the questions, and I was outraged. Robert Waite, my Washington press secretary, was so distressed by this badgering of "Mother Brooke" that without telling me he called *Washington Post* editor Ben Bradlee. Ordinarily, he would have been intimidated by the legendary editor. But Bob was so angry that he got Bradlee on the line and stated his case forcefully. Bradlee finally told Bob, "I'm going to check it out. If it's true, I'll make sure it stops. Tell the Senator I'm sorry for any discomfort to his mother." The calls stopped. Even as I tried to shield Mother, I knew she never missed much. I suspected that she knew what was going on and tried to bolster my spirits just as I tried to bolster hers.

Of course, there was Remigia's family to consider. I remained on good terms with her mother during her lifetime, as well as with her sister Mina Jones and her husband Sam, and her brother Pino and his wife Germanna. At one point both couples came to court prepared to testify on my behalf and to rebut Remigia's blatantly false statements and implications about her alleged poverty. They were never called to take the stand, nor were they interviewed by the press, but they sat through the hearings ready and willing to testify. They did this not because of any anger at their sister, or because I asked them (which I did not), but because they wanted to tell the truth. Remigia and the girls never spoke to them again.

Near the end of the divorce proceedings, Remigia's attorney asked to speak privately with my attorney and me. He showed me a list of women he alleged were "more than friends" of mine and said he was prepared to go back into the courtroom, put Remigia on the stand, and ask her about each of the women listed. "This is blackmail," I said. "You said it, Senator," came the smug reply. Several of the names on the list were "more than friends," but most were not. Some were celebrities I hardly knew. Some I had met at social events. Thoroughly disgusted, I told my lawyers, "If they are going to stoop this low and are willing to wreck the lives of innocent people and their families, I want nothing more to do with them. Give them whatever they want. All I want is to walk out of here a free man." I felt sick to my stomach as I left the courthouse and caught the next plane to Washington.

The lawyers and I agreed on a settlement more favorable to Remigia than I believe the court would have awarded. I signed the agreement and thought that was the end of it. Under its terms I would keep my mortgaged apartment at the Watergate, a mortgaged, undeveloped parcel of land in St. Martin, and the mortgaged summer home in Oak Bluffs. Remigia would be full owner of our homes in Newton and on St. Martin, two cars, all the furniture in both homes, and she would receive $18,000 a year in alimony. I pledged to pay all of her future medical and dental insurance and maintain a life insurance policy on myself payable to her in the event of my death. I further agreed to pay $190,000 in mortgage debt on the Newton and St. Martin homes so that she would get both free and clear.

As terrible as the divorce had been, I at least thought that the worst was over. Then, in January 1978, at the beginning of the election year, Remigia repudiated our settlement and demanded more money. The allegation that drew the most public attention was the result of a disparity between two financial statements, one submitted to Remigia's lawyers in the divorce proceedings and the other in the Public Financial Disclosure Statement that I filed with the secretary of the Senate. This discrepancy, together with the other media allegations, triggered a review by the Senate Select Committee on Ethics that began in midsummer. Senator Adlai Stevenson Jr., Democrat of Illinois, chaired the committee and hired a special counsel named Richard Wertheimer to direct the investigation.

The financial statement filed in the Senate listed a loan from a family friend in the amount of $2,000 and an indebtedness to Remigia's mother of $47,000, the money held in my checking account at the request of Teresa and her three children. None of Teresa's money was ever used for any purpose other than as directed by Teresa or Remigia. The financial statement submitted to the Senate was correct, as the Senate Select Committee later concluded.

The financial statement provided to Remigia's lawyers and contained in the deposition, which is supposed to be confidential, listed a loan of $49,000 from our family friend without any mention of an indebtedness to Remigia's mother. This was obviously a misstatement. And I said so to the committee and publicly. Remigia knew about the loan and was party to this agreement, which was designed to keep her mother's name out of our divorce proceedings. There was never an attempt on the part of my lawyers or me to misrepresent my total liability, and Remigia and her lawyers knew that. The total liability of $49,000 was correct, and the misstatement as to whom the money was owed had no material impact on the divorce settlement, as found by former Massachusetts Supreme Judicial Court Justice Jacob J. Spiegel, who was asked by the Suffolk County District Attorney to review the matter. Nevertheless, the Senate Ethics Committee took me to task for misstating the source of the loan in my deposition taken by Remigia's lawyers.

Another media allegation concerned my mother-in-law, Teresa, being a recipient of Medicaid. It was suggested that, to qualify for Medicaid, she had hidden her money with me. The truth was that I was unaware that Teresa and other members of her family had obtained Medicaid coverage for her. It was even said that I had voted in the Senate to liberalize Medicare benefits in order to benefit my mother-in-law. That truly was laughable. Anyone who knew my record knew that I would have voted to liberalize Medicaid benefits even if I had had no mother-in-law. The Senate Select Committee on Ethics, in its final report concluded that "on the basis of the evidence obtained, it does not appear that Senator Brooke personally knew his mother-in-law was a recipient of Medicaid assistance and did not act improperly in casting his votes in the Senate relative to Medicaid." The Massachusetts Department of Public Welfare, after an extensive investigation, reached the same conclusion, that I had been unaware that Teresa was receiving Medicaid benefits.

Further allegations were made that I had improperly claimed my daughters as exemptions on my federal income tax returns from 1971 through 1975. The Senate Select Committee concluded that I "properly claimed" my daughters. In the end, all the allegations were dismissed. But by then the damage had been done. "Who steals my purse steals trash," Shakespeare wrote, "But he that filches from me my good name . . . makes me poor indeed." That was how I felt as these ugly stories continued on and on.

My defenders in the press were few and far between. The *Berkshire Eagle* was one newspaper that treated the allegations with balance. The *Eagle* even wrote an editorial taking the *Globe* to task for its biased coverage. Chicago-based columnist Mike Royko, saying that he did not think he had ever defended a politician before, weighed in with a column headed "Give Brooke a Break." I also received strong support from the *Banner*, an African American newspaper in Boston, and from its courageous editor Melvin Miller, who researched the charges against me and refuted them.

Speaker of the House Tip O'Neill had once given me an Irish blessing: "Somewhere along the line that sonofagun Ed Brooke kissed the Blarney Stone. He'll be in that Senate seat as long as he wants to be." Despite my cautious nature, I had been inclined to believe him. A year earlier, my reelection campaign had been shaping up to be as sleepy as my 1972 campaign. In spite of my controversial positions on such issues as abortion and busing, I was confident I could safely run on my record. Polls had shown that most voters saw me as a

principled and sensible senator who was working hard for Massachusetts and the country.

My campaign coffers were full. By October 1977, I had raised
more than half of the $750,000 I estimated I would need to run. No
major Democrat had announced. But in politics nothing is ever certain, and overconfidence can be fatal. As the hostile stories about me
continued, the media was not alone in smelling blood. Overnight,
potential candidates were springing up in both parties. One Democratic challenger, Elaine Noble, then America's only openly lesbian
state legislator, started calling the race "Looney Tunes Presents . . . "
Other candidates and possible candidates on the Democratic side
included a young Democratic congressman from Lowell named Paul
Tsongas and the Massachusetts secretary of state and former Harvard
football star, Paul Guzzi, who appeared at first to be my biggest threat.
My onetime protégé, Howard Phillips, now an archconservative, also
ran as a Democrat. Kathleen Sullivan Alioto, a member of the Boston School Committee, jumped into the race. Tip O'Neill's son, Thomas O'Neill, the lieutenant governor, and my old foe Kevin White
were rumored to be possible candidates.

But before I could take on the Democrats, I had to contend with
conservative talk show host Avi Nelson, who challenged me at the
Republican convention and later in the Republican primary. Avi had
a nightly radio show on WHDH, as well as a television show on WSBK.
A former electronics engineer and son of a Brookline rabbi, Avi was,
at thirty-five, a seasoned debater. Like many talk radio hosts, he could
be abrasive and outrageous; detractors called him a demagogue, but
conservatives loved him. Avi held a special contempt for affirmative
action and our "soft" criminal justice system. He ran a tough, skill-
ful campaign against me, making good use of the powerful pulpit of
his radio show to attack my support for the Panama Canal treaties,
federally funded abortions, and handgun control.

Even as my fundraising dried up, Avi got direct-mail fundraising
genius Richard Viguerie to raise money for him from conservatives
around the country and actually outspent me. He had no record to
defend and no Senate duties to interrupt his campaign. A growing
number of Republicans called for me to step aside and give the nomination to Elliot Richardson. I refused. I had no intention of handing

my Senate seat to Elliot or anyone else. Anyone who wanted it would have to fight for it.

I was trying to maintain my 90 percent voting record. When Congress was not in session, I would occasionally sweep through the state by helicopter and campaign from mall to mall. It was not unusual for me to cast a vote in the Senate in the morning, shuttle up to Boston for an appearance, and fly back to Washington the same night. On rare occasions I made two round-trip shuttle flights in the same day.

My efforts paid off in June when I narrowly won the Republican preprimary convention in Worcester. In my entire political career, the Massachusetts Republican Party never denied me the nomination for any office I sought. But at that convention I was booed for the first time by members of my party. To my regret, I lost my cool. I said angrily that the Republican Party was "lucky to have an Ed Brooke." I should not have said that. But in truth, the Republican Party in Massachusetts, captive of an increasingly far-right leadership, has never regained its position. More than a quarter of a century later, no other Massachusetts Republican has been elected to the United States Senate.

With the nomination secure, my campaign began to gear up in earnest. Five conservative senators issued a statement on my behalf. Unions supplied my campaign with volunteers. Former Federal Reserve Board Chairman Arthur Burns, Republican National Chairman Bill Brock, Secretary of State Henry Kissinger, Jesse Jackson, Coretta Scott King, and Senators Jacob Javits and Robert Dole all came to Massachusetts to support me.

Paul Tsongas won the Democratic nomination. While avoiding comment on my divorce, he charged that I was aloof from the voters. He skillfully handled the doubts about his qualifications. When someone derided him as "an obscure first-term congressman," Tsongas joked, "No, I'm an obscure second-term congressman." People could not pronounce his name, so he ran television ads about people struggling to say it. When the Democrats saw that Tsongas had a chance, big names began to campaign for him, including Tip O'Neill, Ted Kennedy, and President Carter. Kennedy's work against me stung. Of course, he was a Democrat and I was a Republican, but we had always gotten along well. I did not expect Ted to campaign for me, but I did not expect him to campaign as he did for my opponent either.

For a long time during and after my Senate years, I have been asked about my relationship with that "other" Massachusetts Senator, Ted Kennedy. I have usually made no comment. Ted was the senior senator from Massachusetts and I was the junior, ranked according to the date we took office: he in 1962, and me in 1967. When Ted was an assistant district attorney in Boston and I was chairman of the Boston Finance Commission, I did not know him or his brother Bobby, who lived mostly in New York. I did know Jack Kennedy, but not well. I always admired and felt deep sympathy for the Kennedys (especially Mrs. Rose Kennedy)—a family that had suffered such great tragedies. When Ted's mother died at age 104 on January 22, 1995, I wrote him a personal heartfelt note, expressing my sympathy, as he had done when my mother died in 1992 at age 100.

For a time, Ted's office was next door to mine in the Old Senate Office Building (now the Russell Building), but he never visited me nor did I ever visit him. As one might imagine, it was never easy to share power with a Kennedy. Our staffs rarely interfaced on Senate matters or socially. Also there was a generation gap: when I first took office, he was thirty-five and I was forty-eight. He was fiercely partisan. I was not. Some of my best friends were Democrats. With the exception of the enjoyable luncheon that he and Joan gave for Remigia and me prior to my swearing-in ceremony, I do not recall that we have ever broken bread together since. Though there was far more civility in the 1960s and 1970s than there appears to be now, the Senate is strictly divided along partisan lines. I suspect that there is bound to be "sibling rivalry" between same-state senators, particularly when they are of different parties, but it is also true when they are of the same party. Though we cosponsored many legislative bills and often voted together, we rarely collaborated.

In my early days in the Senate I looked at Ted as inarticulate and lacking in confidence. But he has grown in stature and performance during his more than forty years' service. He is now an accomplished, able, articulate senior member of the Senate and the unrivaled champion of social causes. Once he assured himself that the presidency was not going to be available to him, he seemed determined to be the best senator he could be. And he has.

I could feel my campaign sagging. I went to the same clambakes, Fourth of July picnics, and Labor Day parades that I always had. But the crowds were smaller and less responsive. The campaign lacked the zest and joy that had marked my earlier ones. I had lost my spark, and the crowds felt it. Many mornings I simply did not want to go out and campaign—and I had never felt like that before. I was embarrassed by the allegations made against me. I had always run as an honest man, a reformer. I felt that people looked at me differently, and I hated it.

Yet even in my faltering campaign, there were wonderful individual moments. There always are. In mid-September, I was in a Newburyport diner when an old man eating bacon and eggs looked up and assured me, "Jesus Christ couldn't beat you." I said, "You can bet I'm not going to take Him on." On Seven Seas Pier in Gloucester, a fishing boat had been lost for five days. I spoke to a crowd, some of them sailors standing on their weathered boats, about the need for prayer. I also promised to get the search extended, and did by placing a call to the Coast Guard. Outside a high school in Tyngsboro, I went to a picnic run by the Lowell Council on Aging. It was a traditional rally: a stage covered with bunting; an Air Force band playing patriotic tunes; politicians scrambling around, shaking hands, answering questions, and promising help. A thousand senior citizens at that picnic bathed me in applause, because they knew that I had fought for them.

Near the end, I felt my campaign began to pick up steam. I wound up traveling in a large motor home, on an old-fashioned whistle-stop tour of Massachusetts. It was time-honored street campaigning with advance men Brian Lees, later the Republican leader in the state senate, and Tom Reid, a longtime friend, scheduling appearances across the state, timing our arrival by walkie-talkie, and using a three-piece banjo band to play my theme song. Shaking hands, taking real questions from real people, was a refreshing change from having reporters interrogate me about my divorce. Making small talk with local mayors, touching on issues that mattered to them, and receiving thanks from mostly Democratic politicians whose cities I had been able to help with federal funding, reminded me what is best about politics.

On October 9, four months after beginning its inquiry, the Senate Select Committee said it could not make its report until after the election. Differences of opinion over the scope of the investigation were compounded by leaks from the committee. I kept my distance from the investigation. I never asked any Republican or friend of mine on the committee for special consideration.

Ironically, I had played a major role in creating the kind of aggressive ethics investigation that was now bedeviling me. A few years earlier, conflict of interest charges had been raised against another senator. The problem, historically, was that senators did not like to investigate themselves. Unless pushed hard by public opinion, they tended to be forgiving of one another, for obvious reasons. At that time I wrote a tough ethics-reform package that became law. The most important element was to create a special counsel, from outside the Senate, who would lead ethics investigations if there was probable cause of wrongdoing. The problem, of course, was the same that the executive branch had with its special prosecutors—how much independence do these independent prosecutors have?

On Friday, October 13, just three weeks before the election, Richard Wertheimer, the special counsel hired by the Senate Select Committee, resigned abruptly and alleged that my lawyers were delaying, altering, and withholding documents. More damaging than his resignation was the fact that it appeared on the front page of the *Boston Globe* before anyone in the Senate knew about it. Wertheimer surely knew that his charges, combined with his resignation, would gain great publicity. I thought it was an unprofessional and irresponsible act, and the reason for his sudden resignation was never explained to my satisfaction. It is impossible to write legislation that anticipates every problem that can arise, but our ethics reforms did not expect there would be a committee chairman who would permit his special counsel to run wild, as my lawyers and I believed Stevenson had permitted Wertheimer to do.

Incensed by Wertheimer's resignation, I rushed to the Senate floor to address my colleagues on a rarely used matter of "personal privilege." The timing could not have been worse. I was asking for the

Senate's attention just as its members were rushing to complete their business and adjourn for the session. But when your honor has been challenged, you ignore the Senate calendar. I denied that my lawyers had interfered in any way with the Select Committee's review. I said I would not be run out of office by false allegations, misstatements, and misconceptions. I wanted the committee to conclude this matter and make its report before the election now only three weeks away. I had always favored reason over emotion in my Senate speeches. But now I spoke passionately for twenty-three minutes. I told my fellow senators that "never in my life have I ever altered, given permission to alter or would I alter any document that would be given to any investigative committee."

I attacked the scope of the Select Committee's investigation, and waving a copy of the *Boston Evening Globe* that had run the story of Wertheimer's resignation the night before, I accused the committee of leaking it to the press. As my colleagues watched, Stevenson defended his committee's work, saying that no one was charging me personally with altering documents or asking my lawyers to do so.

Senator Joseph Biden, Democrat of Delaware and member of the Judiciary Committee, spoke in my support, decrying the fact that "all the special counsels we appoint think they are [Watergate prosecutor] Leon Jaworski. All see themselves as though somehow they are about to be knighted for uncovering great corruption. . . . It worries the heck out of me, as a U.S. senator, as an individual, that we seem to be falling into a situation where we can be tried in the press, we can be tried outside the normal channels of jurisdiction of both the Senate and the courts of law in this country."

On October 24, two weeks before the election, I testified before the Ethics Committee and again refuted charges that my lawyers had attempted in any way to obstruct the investigation. The Ethics Committee released a statement the next day stating that there was no evidence to substantiate the charge of obstruction. But the damage had been done.

It was a bright spot for me, late in October, when Gloria Steinem and Eleanor Smeal of the National Organization of Women came to Massachusetts and campaigned vigorously on my behalf. Neither was known for supporting Republicans, but they were thanking me for my years of fighting for abortion rights and for my leadership that year in gaining a three-year extension in the time available to pass the Equal Rights Amendment.

Not long before the election, I unleashed one final controversy on the Senate floor. In mid-October, as the Humphrey-Hawkins full-employment bill was being considered, I added an amendment that would have guaranteed for Senate employees the same protections against discrimination in hiring and firing, and other civil rights, that we had provided for many other American workers. The Senate was well known to be the last plantation—the senators were all-powerful, and the people who worked for them had few rights beyond those that came with their boss's good will. My amendment was not popular—nothing like it passed for another fifteen years. Once again I was challenging the Senate powers-that-be, but if I had to have one final cause, it was a good one.

Just days before the November 7 election I wanted to go on television in Massachusetts and speak directly to the voters. I wanted to tell them the facts and say, "In all of my years in public service I have always been honest with you. You have always given me your trust, and I have always kept it as your attorney general and as your senator." I wanted to tell the people of Massachusetts that all of this boiled down to very private matters that had nothing to do with my service in the Senate. I was not going to disparage Remigia or my daughters, but I was going to say that none of their allegations or those of the media were true. I felt I owed it to the supporters who had been with me for so many years. The media coverage had raised alarming questions, and I had given the voters no answers, only denials. I wanted to tell the voters that I was the same person they had voted for before, that nothing had changed, and that I wanted their confidence and support.

However, the well-known political pollster Robert M. Teeter of Market Opinion Research Company, hired by our campaign, had projected a ten-point lead in polls taken just days before the election. Because of this, my advisers felt strongly that the television spot was not necessary. They pointed to the polling data and discouraged me from doing anything that might backfire. I argued with them, but in the end I accepted their advice. My mistake was not following my own best judgment. They trusted Teeter's polls, but I had been out among the people taking my own poll and I knew better.

On Election Day I went through my traditional routine, ordering clam chowder and cherrystone clams on the half shell at the old Union Oyster House in the North End. But not with the old gusto. For weeks I had hoped for a miracle by which I would be reelected even by the slimmest of margins. I wanted to go back to the Senate. There was so much more to do. I expected to be chairman of the powerful Appropriations Committee if Republicans won control of the Senate, as they did two years later.

Campaign strategists Tom Trimarco and John Bottomly were still optimistic, buoyed by the Teeter polls. I told them, "This is one time you can't believe the polls. It's not out there. It's different." "I know what you are going through hurts," Jack said, "but believe me, Teeter's right." Early on Election Night, when returns began to come in, Roger Woodworth's instincts told him otherwise. He had too much political experience not to recognize the signs. The first clue came from the small town of Lexington, then a Republican stronghold that had always come through for me. In one precinct after another Roger saw that I had won by only ten or fifteen votes and in some cases had lost. "If that's happening in Lexington, it's over," he told me.

By 8:30 P.M., I knew he was right. I remember taking the elevator down to the ballroom at the Copley Plaza, for the first time without Remigia, Remi, and Edwina, walking through the glittering ballroom, mounting the platform and talking into the microphones. All three networks had declared Paul Tsongas the winner with 55 percent of the vote. Although I cannot recall what I said in my concession speech to the hundreds gathered there, I do remember the tears, not mine but those of my supporters. I remember a sea of hurt and disappointment, the sadness in the eyes of those who had worked hard and were unaccustomed to defeat. Many of them might have seen it coming. But hope is the fuel of political campaigns, both the ones we win and the ones we do not.

I could accept losing, but I hated to lose for the wrong reasons. If I had lost the nomination to Avi Nelson, at least I would have lost on civil rights, abortion, busing, gun control, the Panama Canal, and women's rights, issues that I felt passionately about. We learned much later that the Teeter poll results were skewed by the fact that many of the young people his firm hired in Detroit to make the calls in Massachusetts were identifiably African American. Many Massachusetts voters who answered their questions said that they would vote for me, even though they had no intention of doing so, because they did not want to appear racist. But when they went to the only poll that counts, they pulled the lever beside Paul Tsongas's name.

A few days after my defeat, the *Washington Post* published an editorial that said in part:

> . . . over the years, Sen. Brooke's voice was an important and wholesome influence in the Senate. Yes, as the drama-minded keep insisting, he was the only black in the Senate; but to say that is also in no way to begin to define his role there *as a black*. Sen. Brooke has been unyielding in his pressure for civil-rights advances of a very sturdy, conventional, even old-fashioned kind. He distinguished himself in this connection by his work on housing programs on the Banking Committee and his impassioned pleas for his colleagues not to turn the clock back on their own progress toward desegregating the nation's schools and other institutions. He was totally—immoderately—committed to pushing ahead for moderate solutions, for unrelenting progression of racial gains leading eventually to his ideal of the integrated community. . . . He was a good Senator.

Four months later, the Ethics Committee issued its report, absolving me of wrongdoing. But that was too late to matter. My political career was over.

18

Love and

Redemption

The winter of 1978–79 marked the lowest point in my life. My staff and I tried to carry on business as usual, to ensure a smooth transition for my successor, but defeat had hit us hard. The Senate was not in session during the holidays, so most of my energy was devoted to finding positions for my staff. Republican colleagues, particularly Jake Garn of Utah and David Durenberger of Minnesota, hired several. Our people were talented and dedicated, and placing them was not difficult.

The volume of mail and phone calls diminished. Invitations ceased. At the request of the Library of Congress, we filled several hundred cardboard boxes containing twelve years of Senate files and turned them over to the library. To some degree these immediate tasks occupied my mind. But I could not escape reality. I was fifty-nine years old, with no job, no money, and no solid prospects, and my divorce had left me hundreds of thousands of dollars in debt. To my discredit, all I wanted to do was to retreat to the shelter of my apartment, away from the scrutiny of others. I was hurt, embarrassed, and depressed. I prayed for strength to accept my circumstance with grace and to get on with my life.

Soon after I left the Senate in January my mother underwent cataract surgery and required care for several weeks. For several nights I slept on her living room couch, changing her bandages and administering her eye drops every few hours. It was a wonderful opportunity for us to be together. We laughed over old photographs and sat for hours recalling family stories. Her company gave me much needed distraction. The heavy January snowfall added to our isolation. For days the city was snowbound. I would make my way downstairs to the Safeway on the lower level of the Watergate complex and return to prepare our meals. Mother could not watch television, but she still managed to listen to soap operas and to Oprah Winfrey, co-host of *People Are Talking*, on Baltimore's WJZ-TV. Mother was a big fan of Oprah long before the rest of the nation discovered her. We played Mother's old records and listened to the radio. It was comforting to both of us.

My life had changed dramatically. In the Senate, I had a staff and a highly organized daily schedule. Now, for the first time in years, I had to do everything myself. When my mother's condition improved, I spent more time in my own apartment reading and doing chores. In the evening, I would put on a recording of *La Bohème, Tosca*, or another much-loved opera. Sometimes I listened to hymns and spirituals. As much as I love the written word, nothing provided solace more than music. I read books but stayed away from newspapers and magazines, fearful of further pain. Old friends telephoned, and I could detect their concern. We would talk about getting together, but I saw people rarely. For one who had lived a busy life full of issues, problem solving, and social engagements, I now uncharacteristically wanted to be alone.

My trips to Boston were especially painful. Flying into Logan Airport, I could not help but think that these were the people I had served and asked to continue to serve. I had done my best for them, and they had rejected me. I was hurt. I could not understand what I had done to merit their loss of faith. I had never committed a crime or violated my oath of office. I had endured a tragic marriage and a divorce that had gone wrong. I prayed for the strength to forget and forgive. Forgetting is not easy, but harsh memories eventually fade. Forgiving has always been difficult, but it should not be. It was much easier to understand and forgive Remigia, she was a wife who felt rejected.

But it was harder to forgive my daughters. I had loved them and provided for them as best I could. I tried to be a good father. I stuck with them through personal difficulties. That they wanted to see their mother protected in the divorce, I could understand. But that did not mean that they had to do what they did. I knew that my most difficult task would be to forgive them. And, I have.

Some of my friends encouraged me to seek psychological help. I told them, "God is my psychiatrist" and that He would help me with my inner self and being. It would take time. I prayed that He give me the wisdom, the strength, and the courage to endure. The words of the Twenty-third Psalm and the Prayer of Serenity were especially meaningful during this period of my life. For years, my mother had been a devoted reader of the palm-sized publication, the *Daily Word*, a compendium of scripture and inspirational anecdotes that has been published monthly since 1924 and has millions of readers around the world. Mother had often encouraged me to read it, but I was always too busy. Now she said with quiet insistence, "Edward, it has helped me so much, just try it and you will see." And I have, never missing a day since I first started reading it, finding guidance and comfort in its scriptural wisdom.

When I did return to Massachusetts, people were unfailingly kind. Many would come up to me and say, "We miss you. You should still be in the Senate." I would laugh and ask, "Where were you in 1978?" "Oh, I voted for you Senator Brooke," was the inevitable response. I often thought that if everyone who told me that he or she voted for me had actually done so, I would have won overwhelmingly. But I was not angry with the voters. If I believed what had been printed in the press, I might not have voted for me either.

I had never planned to spend the rest of my life in the Senate. I had thought about leaving after my third term and pursuing the interest in business that I had harbored for some time. I believed that the Senate was not a place to grow old. Once, during a quiet moment on the Senate floor, I discussed this with fellow Senators Jim Pearson, Robert Griffin, and Howard Baker. We talked about how wonderful it would be if we did not have to concern ourselves with reelection and could spend all of our time on the issues we cared most about. But we expected to leave the Senate voluntarily.

During that first wretched winter, Anne offered hope amidst my despair and gave me the courage to prepare for a new life. Once she had gotten a divorce in 1977, I began to think of the future, a future that included her. Although I was concerned about the twenty-nine-year difference in our ages, I put the issue aside. It never occurred to me that I would not ask her to marry me or that she would not say yes. On Valentine's Day 1979, I was ready. I hoped she was too. I made reservations for a table in a quiet corner of the Ritz-Carlton Hotel dining room in Montreal, where she still lived, and ordered a special flower arrangement.

Anne knew that something was up, and she leaned forward on the edge of her chair all evening, anticipating the inevitable question. We enjoyed a leisurely dinner, and as we lingered over dessert I could sense her impatience. But somehow I just could not get the words out. As we prepared to leave, I could tell she was dismayed that the proposal had not come. We walked out into the night and hailed a cab. As we settled into the back seat I talked about how cold it was, and in the middle of my rambling, I came to my senses and asked, "Anne, will you marry me?" "Yes, yes, yes," came her response. I kissed her and then turned to the cab driver. "Have you ever had anyone propose marriage in your cab before?" When he realized what I was talking about, he congratulated us in his broken English.

Only a few members of our immediate family and former members of my attorney general and Senate staff were present at the 5 P.M. ceremony in St. Luke's Episcopal Church in Washington on May 12, 1979. The Reverend William Vancroft presided over the traditional service. Anne wore an ivory, ankle-length dress with a lace neckline. She was escorted down the aisle by her brother, Louis-Constant Fleming, and carried a colorful spray of wildflowers, which we had picked in a vacant lot across from the gas station near the Watergate. My "like-a-brother" cousin Dr. Wilbur Jackson stood with me as my best man. I fought back tears as the church soloist sang the traditional "Ave Maria" and a special song from our courtship, "Evergreen."

Some predicted that our marriage would not last because our age difference was too great. Others thought that I had been carried away by her youth, beauty, and intelligence, or that after the battering I had received I was seeking safe harbor in the arms of a younger woman. But our closest friends knew that if we were taking this step, we had thought about it carefully and knew what we were doing. I did not have to *think* about marrying Anne. I had found my soul mate. We were meant to be together, and neither age nor adversity could keep us apart.

Our finances were so tight that instead of holding a reception at a Washington hotel, we invited a few guests back to our apartment at the Watergate, where Anne had prepared a simple but delicious dinner: shrimp cocktail, boeuf bourguignon, white rice, and a salad of mixed greens. To economize we had bought raw shrimp at the Maine Avenue wharf on the Potomac, which Anne's mother shelled over the kitchen sink. Anne even baked her own wedding cake. Our guests brought gifts of champagne that kept the party going for hours. In less than six months I had emerged from the lowest point of my life to its highest.

We had talked about a honeymoon cruise to the Greek islands. But with little money I chose instead the tiny island of Saba, which rose dramatically out of the sea across from St. Martin. Two people so in love could not have found a more idyllic honeymoon destination. The lush island is speckled with little houses, many with red tin roofs and bright green shutters. Its cobblestone streets often remind visitors of Ireland. Our four-poster bed was so high off the floor that we had to use a small step-up to reach it. The bathroom had no hot water. But the view was spectacular. Anne and I could not believe we could be so happy. We were buoyed by a sense of better days to come. I shook off my gloom and began to address the realities of my life.

Outgoing senators usually have a soft landing. Law firms, brokerage firms, and corporations vie for their services. For those interested in continued government service, ambassadorships or agency jobs are often offered. But thanks to the combination of my divorce and my defeat, my telephone was not ringing off the hook with lucrative offers. It was not ringing at all. Then out of the blue, David Stone, a supportive friend, who was a highly respected CEO of a private investment firm in Boston, and two of his friends offered to lend me money to pay off my debts. Very few people were even aware of my financial situation, but David and his friends, understanding it, offered me a conventional, interest-bearing loan of $300,000, which to me was a fortune. With the money I was able to pay off the mortgages on the two houses I had given to Remigia, as well as attorney's fees and other debts.

It was time for me to seek opportunities, and it was natural that I should return to the law. Friends set up meetings with law firms, and I met with several. The partners were all cordial and some offered interesting financial packages. But though I did not want to return to live in Massachusetts, I thought I should maintain some contact with the state that had been the center of my adult life.

A meeting with a senior partner of a Washington law firm finally led to an agreement. The firm would let me work at my own pace. The partners agreed to a salary of $100,000 a year and a percentage fee for bringing in business, and promised not to hold me to a strict schedule. They also agreed to the unusual arrangement of my being "of counsel" to a Boston firm, which agreed to pay me $25,000 a year with additional fees for business that I brought in. Both firms agreed that any fees I earned from corporate board directorships, books, speeches, and nonlegal consulting fees would be exclusively mine. The total package of $125,000 did not come close to what some former members of Congress were receiving from Washington law firms. But I was grateful.

Returning to law was exciting. It was like starting all over again. I began work for the firm in June 1979. One day I made my way to the firm's law library to do research for my first case, just as I had in the 1950s. A senior partner happened to see me. Aghast, he came over and whispered, "Senator, you're not supposed to be in here, that's why we have paralegals. This is *not* the best use of your time." My time was being billed at $250 an hour, which I found a bit shocking. As for paralegals, I soon found out how indispensable they are to present-day law firms.

I was happy to be working again, associating with sharp minds and addressing substantive legal questions, especially when they involved subjects close to my heart. But after nearly twenty years in politics, I found the practice of law somewhat boring. Nothing I was doing could compare with the excitement and challenge of the Senate. Accustomed to the more personal kind of law practice that I forged in my early days in Roxbury, I was uncomfortable with the minutiae of tracking billable hours and phone calls and strict adherence to fee structures. Although some of the legal issues were interesting, the overall practice lacked the thrill that comes from working on matters of importance to the nation. It seemed that everything I was doing was about making money. "Where?" I asked myself, "am I making a difference?"

I missed the action. I missed the Senate and the friends there with whom I had fought so many battles that truly were important. I was grateful for the opportunity to make money that would pay off my debts and give Anne and me a comfortable life, but I did not think I was making any real contribution to society. My first opportunity to continue to work on issues dear to my heart came from Cushing Dolbeare, a woman who devoted her life to the cause of housing for the poor. As president of the National Low-Income Housing Coalition, she asked me to serve as chairman of her board of directors. This private, nonprofit organization was established to help create safe, affordable housing for the nation's poorest citizens. At a time when we were seeing a hardening of sentiment toward the poor, I thought this provided an important opportunity for me to speak for those whose voices are too little heard in Washington. The volunteer position gave me purpose and showed that even though I was no longer in office I could still have a positive impact on the lives of others.

In the early days of our marriage, Anne and I did not talk about having children of our own. Anne had a lovely daughter, and the prospect of starting a new family at my age was daunting. In addition, I had been so devastated by my daughters' actions during the divorce that I wondered how I could open myself up to the potential for so much pain again. But after we had been married for a year, Anne said that she wanted a child. "You are a young woman and I understand your desire to have a child," I said, in what I thought was a reasoned response. I raised all the practical objections: she already had a child, I was too old to be a father again. She might have to educate and raise the child alone if something happened to me.

Her response was strong and clear. "I don't have *your* child; you don't have *our* child," she said. "I want our child." She added, "It's not the age; it's not the time. It's the quality of time that you're going to spend with the child. And if our child has anywhere near the beautiful relationship with me that you have had with your mother, then that in itself is reason enough to have a child. And if need be, I am perfectly capable of educating and raising a child alone." My debating skills failed me. I could not argue with her. She acknowledged that I might not be able to do all the things a younger father could do. "But a younger father wouldn't have the wisdom and all the experiences you have had, and the child would benefit from that," she said.

When Anne told me that she might be pregnant, I was elated far more than I had imagined. We began doing all the rearranging and buying that you do when a new life joins yours. We bought a crib and baby equipment for our apartment. We read everything we could find about pregnancy and child development. We took long walks on the Vineyard, always talking about the baby, like all couples preparing for a child.

My mother was thrilled. Friends, aware of the difficulties with my daughters, hoped the child would be a boy. Anne wanted a son, but I told her it mattered not to me as long as the child was healthy. We had the option of knowing the child's sex, but we opted to wait. Edward William Brooke IV was born in the George Washington University Hospital in Washington, D.C., at 8:09 A.M. on February 26, 1981.

The night before, Anne; her nine-year-old daughter, Melanie; and I had attended the musical *The King and I* starring Yul Brynner at Washington's Warner Theatre. It was a cold night, and after the show we walked almost home before we were able to get a cab. At 1 A.M. Anne awakened me and said her water had broken and she was ready to go to the hospital. I got up, made up the bed and shaved while Anne called Dr. William H. Cooper, who said he would meet us at the hospital. I unwisely suggested to Anne that we walk, as the hospital was only a few blocks away. She looked at me as if I were crazy. I drove her to the hospital and got her installed. Then I sat up with the doctor, talking politics. Dr. Cooper turned out to be a rock-ribbed conservative, and we had a spirited exchange.

Around six in the morning the doctor gave me green hospital garb and suggested that we look in on "our patient." He said that though he would have preferred that I had taken a Lamaze course, he presumed that a United States senator had reasonable intelligence, so we could proceed. I told him the presumption was rebuttable. For the next hour or so I held Anne's hand as her pains grew stronger. This was a new experience for me. When Remi and Edwina were born in Boston's Lying-In Hospital, I paced the hallways outside the delivery room. This time, I stood at the foot of the delivery table with the doctor, and together we were the first to see that Edward was unmistakably a boy. When Edward let out his first sound, I was moved by the reality that for the first time in my life I was witnessing the birth of a child!

The day of Edward's baptism at St. Luke's Church was one more happy memory in a sacred place that had meant so much to me. St. Luke's was where my sister and I had been baptized and confirmed, where my sister had married, where both my girls had been baptized, where my father's funeral service had been held, as well as that of my sister Helene's husband Bun, and where Anne and I had been married. At the baptismal font, Edward did not utter a sound when Reverend Vancroft poured water on his forehead and made the sign of the cross.

Fatherhood the third time around was a new adventure. From the beginning, Edward slept all night and awakened each day with a smile. We were blessed. As time passed, we took our son everywhere: to restaurants, to church, to the beach, to the tennis courts, to the zoo. These were wonderful days. As Edward grew into a rambunctious toddler, our apartment began to feel cramped. Anne began spending early May until November at the Vineyard, and I would travel back and forth on weekends when I could. I was able to take most of August off. I spent hours walking the beach on the Vineyard, playing with Edward in the surf, arranging wildflowers, attending island concerts, and playing tennis. But as Edward grew older and was ready to enter school, we knew we needed a more permanent home than the Watergate apartment. I recalled how much I loved the time I spent as a child in the green countryside and fresh air of my aunt and uncle's farm in Virginia. I began to wonder if Anne would consider living on a farm. When I broached the subject, she was enthusiastic.

In 1984, after looking at more than twenty properties in the northern Virginia countryside west of Washington, Anne and I purchased a 142-acre cattle and horse farm near Warrenton, in Fauquier County. Merging Anne's and my first names, I named it Edan Farms and did not care if people would mistake it for Eden. The three-story house was strategically placed on one of the highest points of the property. It was not a great house, and it needed a lot of work, but the land was spectacular. There is a small island with a weeping willow tree in the middle of a well-stocked, stream-fed pond. There are rolling hills and, given exceptional eyesight and a clear day, you can see the Blue Ridge Mountains in the distance. The farm is home to deer, Canada geese, herons, rabbits, turtles, wild turkeys, fox, an occasional bear, and a variety of birds. I sensed from the beginning that the farm and my life with Anne and Edward would bring me more happiness than I had ever known.

As beautiful as the property was, it was hard work, and I was still commuting five days a week to Washington. Returning home, I would throw on work clothes and my tattered Boston Red Sox cap and head down to the barn to begin my chores. I would go to the Fauquier Livestock Exchange in Marshall, Virginia, to buy young steers. At first we bought them in the spring, and after fattening them up, we sold them in the fall. But we found it more profitable, and more work, to switch to breeding. My good neighbor Clarence "Bunny" Gill took us under his wing and gave us tips on the care and management of cattle. Anne did the gardening, cooking, cared for Edward, and performed many farm chores as well. Her earlier life had done little to prepare her for running a farm. We learned that raising cattle is not a very profitable business unless done on a large scale. Thankfully our pastures were later rented to our friend Bunny Gill, who is a real cattle farmer.

When we moved to the farm, Edward was three. It was a wonderful place for a boy to grow up. He would ride in the back of our pickup truck with our yellow Labrador, Tuff, as I drove around the farm. We would run up and down the hills chasing cows to get them into the pen for fly tagging or transporting. I taught Edward to swim and to play basketball, soccer, and especially tennis. He became a reader, too, and loved the many spiritual, historical, and adventure books often given to him by his godfather, Joe McMahon, a former staff member and friend, who had become like another son to my mother.

In addition to our two adopted cats, Marilyn and Monroe (named by Edward), I purchased three riding horses—two thoroughbreds for Anne and Edward, and a quarter horse for me. At first the three of us rode together. Then Edward announced, "I don't want to ride anymore," and soon Anne joined him, so I rode alone until my eightieth birthday, when I gave it up.

Since my father first took me to the Preakness at Pimlico Racetrack in Baltimore, I have loved the Sport of Kings. I bought several young racehorses, hired a trainer, and began racing them at the tracks in Pimlico, Maryland; Charlestown, West Virginia; and Garden State Park, New Jersey. It was at Garden State where my first and only winner "Brookline Blade" won his maiden race with jockey Maryann Alligood up. My stockbroker and friend Peggy Forbes convinced me to buy a 5 percent interest in Summa Stables, which among other partners included hockey great Wayne Gretzky and golf pro Craig Stadler. One of our horses was Pendleton Ridge, whom we entered in the Kentucky Derby in 1990. Anne and I flew to Churchill Downs, sipped the traditional mint juleps, and watched our horse come in ninth in a field of sixteen on a sloppy track. It was an enjoyable and expensive experience, never to be repeated. I learned that you do not race horses for profit; you race them for pleasure, and pleasure is costly.

St. Martin continued to be a refuge for Anne and me. Anne's mother had maintained and expanded her late husband's business enterprises. Anne had a joint interest with her brother in land inherited from their father, in a Caribbean paradise that was just beginning to open to the wider world of tourism. We selected an ideal site for a home on St. Martin, and we set about creating a tropical haven. As much as I loved La Batterie I did not want to duplicate it. I wanted something with more of a New England feel, unlike the new modern-style Caribbean homes that were springing up on the island. We built the house of blue-green stone, which we found on the site. The house, with sleeping quarters on one side and public quarters on the other, could easily have been built in Massachusetts.

People in St. Martin were happy that Anne and I had found happiness together. Remigia, as well as Remi and Edwina, continued to come to St. Martin, but our paths rarely crossed. In late 1983, I was standing on a sandbar at Maho Beach, when a young woman swam out to me.

"Senator Brooke?" she asked.

"Yes?" I said.

"Your daughter Edwina is on the beach, crying, and wants to talk with you. Will you speak to her?"

I looked toward the beach, and there she was. I knew I had to go and talk with her. As I approached Edwina, I could see her tears. She put her arms around me. She was trembling, and she cried as I had never seen her cry before. "Daddy, I love you, I love you," she said. "I have missed you so much; my boys are growing up without knowing their grandfather. Oh Daddy, I am so sorry. I know I have hurt you. You have always said God forgives, please forgive me and come to see your grandsons. They only know you from the television screen. Please come back to the house with me and see them."

Tears came to my eyes as I held her in my arms. She told me the location of her house, and I said that I would try to come that evening. Still in shock, I went home to tell Anne the news. She said, "You have to go; if you don't you will never forgive yourself."

Around five, Anne and I went to Edwina's house. It was surrounded by a high chain-link fence. Inside were a French poodle and a Great Dane. Edwina came out and held the dogs while we went inside. She brought her sons to me: Vincent, six, who I had last seen as a baby, and Christophe, a toddler, whom I had never met. They were adorable. I hugged and kissed them, and they responded as if we had always been together. It was a memorable moment in my life. Though they were young, I believed it had meaning to them as well.

Edwina's husband, Michel Petit, was the island's only obstetrician/gynecologist and had grown up with Anne. He seemed pleased with this reconciliation. Edwina served tarte tatin, an elegant open-faced French apple pie, and a bottle of chilled Moët & Chandon champagne. At first, conversation was awkward, but after talking about Vincent's schooling, Christophe's first words and steps, Michel's medical practice, and how Edwina occupied her time, we became more relaxed. After visiting for almost two hours, I asked Edwina and Michel to bring the boys to our home and spend the day playing in the pool. On leaving, I told the boys, "I love you." "We love you too, Granddad," said Vincent with Christophe trying to chime in. Ever since that day we have said that to each other many times. When we left I knew this was the beginning of the way back.

My first step toward reconciliation with Remi came not long after that. After work, I stopped at the Watergate garage to pick up my car for my drive out to the farm. Without my knowledge, Remi had resumed contact with my mother and had been upstairs visiting her when she learned that I would be leaving late that afternoon for the farm. She waited for me in the garage. She got out of a chauffeur-driven limousine parked near my car and ran over, hugged me, and asked me to have dinner with her so that we could talk. I told her I had to get home and she asked if she could ride with me to the farm and have the limousine follow. She said she had to talk with me; it could not wait any longer. We rode the forty-five miles or so to the farm as Remi chatted about everything in the world except what had gone on during the divorce and our years of separation. It was as if nothing had happened. On our arrival, Remi cheerfully greeted Anne, whom she knew from St. Martin, and after a few minutes of talk she said, "We wouldn't have done what we did, Anne, if we had known it was you."

Twenty years later, over lunch in Boston in 2003, my younger daughter gave me her answer about her and her sister's actions during the divorce. When I asked, "Why?" Edwina replied, "Daddy, it was greed and love." Then, in 2004, I had another talk with Remi. Our talks were always difficult. There were feelings of guilt on both sides: guilt on my part for not having been with my daughters as much as I would have liked when they were young, and for Remi because of her role in bringing about my defeat in 1978. I had always felt that someone had orchestrated a campaign against me, making statements and leaking documents that the *Globe* used to bring me down. But it was never clear to me exactly who had done what. I felt that Remi had lived a hard life, had often been in depression, and continued to be in denial about what she had done. When we talked in 2004, after so much time had passed, I did not want to cause her pain, but I told her that I thought I finally deserved some answers.

I asked if she had been part of a campaign to discredit me in the media. It was a matter of record that she had called a radio station and made on-air statements that were embarrassing to me. And she did not deny that during 1978 she had been in close touch with an old school friend who had become a reporter for the *National Inquirer*. But she insisted that she had never talked to the *Globe* except when they called her and that she had not been the one who led the attack on me. "You always underestimated Mommy," she said. "She was dysfunctional and she didn't tell the truth. She couldn't help it. She was the one who talked to the press." I took her at her word and resolved to let the matter rest there and to devote my remaining years to love and forgiveness toward my daughters.

There were other developments in my family life. In 1970, after her husband Bun's death, Helene and her daughter Peggy moved from St. Thomas back to Washington. Peggy had been only eight months old when Patsy was killed. Like her mother, she was gifted with beauty and a sweet disposition. But Peggy suffered from all of the pain her family carried for her lost sister. Helene worked for several years as an educational specialist for the Department of Health, Education, and Welfare. After she retired in 1977, Helene and Peggy moved to my house on Martha's Vineyard. Peggy's fine, handsome son David was born in 1986. After Helene's death in 1995, Peggy and David continued to live on Martha's Vineyard, where they were like another daughter and grandson to me. Remigia's brother, Pino, and his wife, Germanna, had moved to New Hampshire. Her sister Mina and her husband Sam Jones had moved to Seattle, where Mina died of cancer in the 1980s.

When Edwina called me in 1994 and said her mother was dying, I hurried to Massachusetts to see her. It was the first time I had been in the house in Newton since Remigia's mother's death in 1977. When I entered the bedroom, Remigia said haltingly, "Carlo, I am sorry." "Remigia, I am sorry too," I told her. Edwina and Remi and I stood at her bedside and wept. The girls left the room and closed the door so Remigia and I could be alone. She asked me to sing "our song," "Trieste il Mia Cor" or "No Greater Love," as it is known in English. I softly sang it to her in Italian. She smiled through her tears. It was sad seeing Remigia gasping for every breath. She gave me her hand. I held it gently, and we prayed silently.

Remigia's funeral service on October 11, 1994, arranged by Edwina, was held at the Boston College Chapel. The archbishop of Boston, Cardinal Bernard Law, officiated, and our grandchildren, Tamara, eighteen; Vincent, seventeen; Christophe, eleven; and Landon, ten, gave eulogies. Remigia, who had too little joy in her life, would have been pleased with the service. She was laid to rest in Newton Centre Cemetery, next to her mother.

19

Private

Citizen

Although I was out of politics, the political world had not entirely forgotten me. Shortly after the 1980 Republican National Convention, I received an invitation to lunch with presidential nominee Ronald Reagan and his wife, Nancy, at the farm they were renting near Middleburg, Virginia. I had first met Reagan many years before when I was attorney general and he was touching base with Republicans around the country prior to his run for governor of California. Although I could not help but like him personally, I was uneasy about what I had heard of his politics. Now he was the Republican nominee for president, and I was trying to find some common ground to justify my support of his candidacy. I had stayed away from the Republican convention in Detroit. But I knew that the Reagan campaign, which was not viewed as supportive of minorities, was actively seeking endorsements. In the weeks before our meeting, the Reverend Ralph Abernathy, Martin Luther King's successor at SCLC, and Charles Evers, mayor of Fayette, Mississippi, had announced their support of Reagan.

The meeting with the governor and his adviser (and later Attorney General) Ed Meese was cordial. We discussed problems facing minorities, including unemployment and the lack of housing. Reagan showed a genuine feeling for people and sensitivity to issues that affected minorities. Meese by contrast was cold and distant. I knew before I arrived that there would be little hope of gaining any concession from them on abortion or tax policy. But I did think I might be able to get Reagan to support equitable access to housing, clearly a fundamental right of all Americans. As we talked, I had the sense that Reagan's natural instinct was to support fair housing legislation, but Meese kept warning him not to make a commitment.

I urged Reagan to support strong enforcement of the Fair Housing Act, an important initiative that protected minorities against discrimination in the renting and sale of homes and apartments. Meese vehemently objected to what he called my attempt to extract a quid pro quo in exchange for my endorsement. He said I should not put the Republican Party's nominee in the position of having to barter for my endorsement. Though I had not put it in those terms, I was in truth trying to do exactly that. This was politics. I was there because they wanted something from me. The question was what I could receive in return. I could not give him my endorsement without some concession on an issue that I thought was important for the country, for the Republican Party, and for Reagan himself.

In the end, Reagan agreed. The meeting concluded. The photographers took pictures, and I made a brief statement to reporters saying I supported Ronald Reagan's candidacy and that I was pleased that the governor was a supporter of the Fair Housing Act. Then Reagan, Nancy, and I sat down to lunch. With politics out of the way, we talked easily, and I came away with an impression of Reagan's charm and affability and Nancy's graciousness. I could see that the Reagans were devoted to one another and that she was a great influence in his life. I did not see Ed Meese again, which was fine with me. After the Reagans and I said goodbye, I drove back to Washington where Anne was eagerly awaiting my report. "Tell me *everything*," she said, and of course I did.

Early in the Reagan administration, the Senate appointed me to the U.S. Commission on Wartime Relocation and Internment of Civilians, a nine-member panel to investigate the damage inflicted on Japanese American citizens who were placed in internment camps at the outbreak of World War II. On February 19, 1942, ten weeks after the attack on Pearl Harbor, President Roosevelt signed Executive Order 9066, which gave to the secretary of war and military commanders the power to remove and detain persons believed to be a security risk. Shortly thereafter, all American citizens of Japanese descent were prohibited from living, working, or traveling on the West Coast of the United States.

Like many Americans, I had at the time been unaware of the injustice done to these patriotic Americans who were taken from their homes, placed in concentration camps, and deprived of their property, economic livelihood, and freedom. One hundred and twenty thousand Japanese Americans living in the western United States were forcibly placed in ten relocation centers scattered from Alaska to Arizona to Arkansas. For many, these bleak camps, enclosed by barbed wire and guarded by armed military police, were home for the duration of the war. In most instances those who were detained lost their homes and property forever.

As a soldier in Italy, I knew firsthand of the valiant Nisei troops in the 442nd Regimental Combat Team who were fighting along the same Italian front as were we. The 442nd suffered horrendous casualties in some of the most vicious battles in Europe. My Senate colleague, Daniel Inouye of Hawaii, who lost an arm in the fighting, was one of the many Japanese American heroes of that campaign. The exploits of the 442nd, one of the war's most decorated units, were celebrated. But most Americans remained unaware of the suffering inflicted on Japanese Americans who were unfairly punished simply because of their racial heritage.

My service on the commission, like my work on the Kerner Commission fourteen years before, was a revisiting of man's inhumanity to man. In twenty days of hearings in eight cities, between July and December 1981, our commission heard testimony from 750 witnesses. Many were Japanese Americans who had been detained for the duration of the war. David Guterson's beautifully etched book, *Snow Falling on Cedars,* and the subsequent film, offers a rare glimpse of what life was like for the internees. But it barely captures the heartbreaking stories of disruption and pain revealed in testimony before our commission. From personal experience I knew the sting of inequitable treatment. But I was not prepared for the agonizing testimony about what our government did to its Japanese American community. I asked a lot of hard questions. I had a real battle with John McCloy, assistant secretary of war in President Roosevelt's administration, who in 1982 was still a defender of the policy. McCloy, an important actor in the displacement of the Japanese Americans, had no apologies.

In December 1982, we released our 467-page report, titled *Personal Justice Denied*. Our strongest recommendations, for which other like-minded commissioners and I fought hard, called for reparations and a formal apology in the form of a joint resolution of Congress, signed by the president, acknowledging the grave injustice done by the acts of exclusion, removal, and detention. We were aware that our government had never before made an apology of this nature. As a result of this grave injustice resulting from "race prejudice, war hysteria and a failure of political leadership," we recommended that $1.5 billion be allocated by Congress for reparations to former internees. The recommended amount of $20,000 each did not begin to compensate for the suffering they had endured.

In September 1987, after years of delay, the House of Representatives approved the measure in a 243–141 vote. Six months later the Senate approved it with a 67–27 vote. On August 10, 1988, forty-six years after Roosevelt signed his initial order, President Reagan signed the bill authorizing redress payments for Japanese Americans. The delays reflected the mixed feelings in Congress. A lot of support for the reparations had come because Danny Inouye was a war hero and a popular member of the Senate. But many members still had reservations about the reparations, and they were slow to come.

The treatment of Japanese Americans was not an isolated event. Although the issue never came before our commission, thousands of German Americans and as many as ten thousand Italian Americans were also interned, and fifty thousand others subjected to curfews and other restrictions during this period. The Japanese Americans were the largest number to be detained, by far, but they were not the only group to suffer. This unjust treatment of American citizens by our government is among the most shameful episodes in our history. Conflicts arouse understandably strong emotions, and an identifiable opponent—especially a minority, ethnic, or cultural group—can easily fall victim to the passions of an aggrieved majority. Regrettably, we are seeing this happening again today as our Muslim citizens are singled out for suspicion and sometimes, senseless attack. As long as discrimination and deprivation of rights can happen to one of us, it can happen to any of us. We must ensure that in the current war against terrorism, these violations of human rights and abandonment of our founding principles are not made again.

As a child of the Depression, and as a soldier in World War II, I shared the veneration of Franklin Roosevelt. But I came to question Roosevelt's judgment in his signing Executive Order 9066, his reluctance to act when Europe's Jews were persecuted by the Nazis, and his failure to desegregate America's armed forces during World War II. These were serious failures in his leadership.

President Reagan, aware of my concern about housing, appointed me to the President's Commission on Housing. The commission was supposed to express his commitment to the issue and his desire to remedy housing problems that affected millions of Americans. It was directed to analyze the relationship between homeownership and the political, social, and economic stability of the nation. It was to review all existing federal housing policies and programs, and to develop housing and mortgage finance options that would strengthen the ability of all citizens to have adequate shelter.

Under the chairmanship of William F. McKenna, a California lawyer, and Vice Chairman Carla Hills, a lawyer and former secretary of housing and urban development, the twenty-eight-member commission and its fifty-member staff spent a year compiling and analyzing research, holding hearings, and taking a hard look at the disgraceful lack of safe, affordable housing for our poorest citizens. We recommended that Community Development Block Grant Programs provide assistance to low-income families to build or substantially rehabilitate additional units under federal housing programs. We also called for the restoration of local management of public housing and recognition of the housing needs of the elderly and handicapped.

Serving on the commission was a frustrating time for me. Most of our recommendations were never implemented. I often found myself fighting against Reagan's Secretary of Housing Samuel Pierce and his officials. I was trying to support and expand housing measures that I had championed as a senator, and they were trying to cut back on them. Far too many Americans continue to live in substandard housing. The problem facing government is how to make good on the post–World War II promise of decent affordable housing for every American. We struggled with that question at the dawn of the Reagan era, and we struggle with it today.

Admittedly, there were advantages to having a Republican in the White House. One night Anne and I were invited by President and Mrs. Reagan to attend an informal White House dinner, which in Washington is the most coveted of invitations. We dined on lobster bisque, veal piccata with saffron rice, and chocolate mousse. Anne looked lovely in the candlelight and was seated next to the president, and I was at another table seated next to Mrs. Reagan. Anne seemed quite under the spell of the president's charm, and I thought he was not unaware of hers. After dinner we joined the Reagans in the downstairs movie theater to see *From Mao to Mozart*, a documentary on Isaac Stern's visit to the People's Republic of China. I noticed that the Reagans were holding hands and eating popcorn just as Anne and I were doing a couple of rows back. It was a family-like evening, which we both enjoyed immensely.

Through most of the Reagan years, Anne and I were busy raising our son. I was finding the practice of law more tolerable and enjoyed my public service work. Politics was far from my mind. Thus I was amused as well as pleased to receive a call in August 1988 from General Colin Powell, who invited me to have lunch with him at the White House. Colin was then a three-star general and assistant to President Reagan for national security affairs. He was also the subject of much media speculation that he might be chosen as the running mate for Vice President George H. W. Bush at the upcoming Republican convention. We met in his modest but comfortable office in the White House, close to the Oval Office. A light lunch with iced tea was served from the White House mess.

I did not know Colin well but admired him and what he had achieved in our military. Over lunch the general brought up the subject of what was being written and said about him being a running mate with George Bush. He asked for my opinion. I told Colin that I thought he would make an excellent candidate for vice president, or president for that matter. "But, as you well know, the realities are that you don't *run* for vice president," I added. "Candidates for vice president are chosen by the presidential nominees. If George Bush makes the offer, you have no choice but to accept. But my frank opinion is that I don't think George Bush or the powers that be in the Republican Party have the wisdom, the vision, or the political courage to take that step."

Colin said, "Senator, I am not seeking the office. I have no clear mind as to whether I would even be interested in elected politics. I'm a military man, not a politician." "Colin, I'll give you the advice I would take myself," I told him. "If I were in your place at this point in time, I would enjoy the moment. But go on and get your fourth star. It will be the culmination of a stellar record of military service. And if I am wrong, and I hope I am, and George Bush does ask you to run, then we ought to have lunch again." We never did. I left the White House trying to imagine a Republican ticket that would include an African American military hero. Regrettably, my prediction was correct. George Bush opted to go with conservative Senator Dan Quayle of Indiana. To this day, I am still convinced that if he had chosen Colin Powell as his running mate in 1992, he would have won a resounding victory in his reelection campaign against Bill Clinton that was his to lose.

In September 1988, I was busy with the practice of law and had paid little attention to the media coverage of an investigation into alleged wrongdoing at the Department of Housing and Urban Development. I therefore thought little of a telephone call from an agent of the department's Office of the Inspector General, asking me for a meeting to discuss the FOOD for Africa Program. I told the agent that I had never heard of the FOOD for Africa Program, but he insisted on coming to talk to me. When we met on September 14 in my office, I repeated that I knew nothing of the program, but did not know what could possibly be wrong with a program that gave food to starving Africans.

He then began to ask me questions about Secretary of Housing and Urban Development Samuel Pierce and about internal activities at HUD of which I had no knowledge. Eventually I saw that he presumed a relationship that did not exist between Secretary Pierce and me and that interested him much more than the FOOD for Africa Program. Just before leaving, he asked me if I had ever lobbied or attempted to pressure a HUD official to allocate units to a public housing authority for award to an owner or developer for whom I was a consultant. My response was unequivocally, "No."

I had no way of knowing that this was the beginning of a ten-year inquiry that would lead to congressional hearings and the appointment of an independent counsel, or that Secretary Pierce and several of his assistants would assert their Fifth Amendment privilege against self-incrimination. The investigation into allegations of wrongdoing at HUD would generate thousands of hours of legal fees, raise unsubstantiated questions, bring negative publicity, damage careers, and invade the privacy of scores of people. It resulted in only a few indictments on doubtful charges at a cost to the American taxpayer of tens of millions of dollars, making it one of the longest and most expensive of all the independent counsel investigations.

The allegations against Pierce were vague, and the questions raised as to my relationship with him and possible influence at HUD were ridiculous. I knew that the secretary was a respected former judge from New York, general counsel of the Treasury Department in the Nixon administration, and the only African American in President Reagan's cabinet. I had met him, but we were far apart philosophically, given his role in implementing the Reagan administration's housing policies. The only thing we had in common, and the reason I think I was questioned in the first place, was that we were both African Americans and Republicans who had achieved national visibility.

My first opportunity to set the record straight was during my voluntary appearance on May 17, 1989, before the Senate Committee on Banking, Housing, and Urban Affairs. I told the committee that never in my consulting work on behalf of clients seeking HUD projects or at any other time was I ever solicited for gifts, bribes, or payments from employees or anyone else at HUD, nor were any ever offered. Nor had I ever lobbied or exerted any influence at HUD. I was prepared to make the same statement before the House Employment and Housing Subcommittee when the subcommittee informed me that my presence was not necessary. However, my photograph appeared several times with newspaper articles on the HUD investigation.

I retained former Assistant U.S. Attorney Paul Knight, who with other members of his firm reviewed the matter, and all agreed that nothing would come of the investigation. They said I should carry on business as usual, ignore the press, and say nothing. It was painful but good advice. Almost ten years later, the Office of Independent Counsel at last concluded that I had never attempted to exert inappropriate influence over the secretary or anyone else at HUD.

Samuel Pierce was never charged with criminal wrongdoing. He acknowledged in 1994 that he helped create a climate in which corruption in HUD had taken place, and he accepted responsibility for the need to launch the independent counsel investigation. In return for that statement, prosecutors agreed not to pursue charges against him. It is a kind of blackmail that prosecutors can enforce, as the price for making them go away. Five lesser figures at HUD were convicted.

In 1999, Congress allowed the Ethics in Government Act of 1978 (which, ironically, I had championed in the Senate) to die a quiet, unmourned death. Congress had come to the realization that the special prosecution process is fraught with peril in the hands of overly zealous prosecutors with unlimited budgets. The law, they concluded, was basically unfair. The unfettered discretion to probe into every aspect of innocent people's lives simply went too far. I would like to think that my own painful experience, along with that of others, contributed to that decision.

I had enjoyed pleasant dealings with George H. W. Bush going back to his Senate race in Texas in the 1970s and his tenure as Republican national chairman during Watergate. For a time his nephew, Hap Ellis, was my press secretary. I saw him occasionally when I was visiting in the White House during the Reagan years and he was vice president. In 1987, when Bush was gearing up to run for president the next year, he called me at my law office and, as I had expected, asked my support for his candidacy. I explained that I was committed to Senator Bob Dole, and that even though we had not always agreed on every issue, I had gone to Kansas to campaign for him when he was in trouble, and he had returned the favor during my 1978 campaign. I felt friendly toward Vice President Bush, and I stressed that if things changed, I would be glad to support him. He thanked me, but we rarely spoke again. However, his wonderful wife, Barbara, continued to be extremely kind to my mother, who visited the White House each year with the Senate wives' organization.

In the fall of 1991, President George H. W. Bush nominated Clarence Thomas to the Supreme Court, and Thomas encountered strong opposition. I had never met the man, but I read some of his opinions as head of the Equal Employment Opportunities Commission and was disturbed by them, as I was by charges made against him during his Senate hearings. During the frenzied days of the hearings, I received a call from a political operative in the White House, who asked if I would make a public statement in support of Thomas. I told him that in good conscience I could not do that. As the world knows, he squeezed by in a close Senate vote.

As the years went on I discovered that the private sector offers its own rewards, the foremost being financial security. In addition to earning enough money through my law firms in Washington and Boston to pay off my debts, I was invited to join several corporate boards of directors that gave me a new perspective on the role of corporate America in the nation's economy.

One of my first invitations came from the Alexander Proudfoot Company, now known as Proudfoot Consultants, through Richard Smith, a close friend and vice president of the company and an expert in management. I was privileged to serve on the board of advisers with Andrew Young, the dedicated civil rights leader whom I admired when he served in Congress, then as the first black mayor of Atlanta and the first African American ambassador to the United Nations.

I was somewhat surprised when Allan "Ace" Greenberg, chairman and chief executive officer of the brokerage firm Bear Stearns in New York, invited me to become a limited partner in his firm. As a member of the Securities Subcommittee of the Senate Banking Committee, I had developed an interest in securities even though I had only a small amount of money invested in stock. As a senator, I had used extra income from speaking fees primarily to invest in real estate. The intricacies of the financial world were a new and exciting experience.

I was also invited to serve on the board of directors of Grumman Aerospace, now Northrup Grumman Corporation. John Carr, vice chairman of the board, invited me to lunch and asked if I would be interested in joining the group. I was a bit surprised, because as a senator I had not been a particular friend of the military industrial complex. Early in my Senate career, while serving briefly on the Armed Services Committee, I became convinced that our nation was not receiving full, dollar-for-dollar returns on our military spending. The Pentagon was flooded with endless cost overruns and failed programs, but when you tried to find out why, rows and rows of generals and admirals would come to testify at our hearings and give their excuses and swear that national survival demanded that we support everything in their budgets. We were overpowered by them. The facts were endlessly complex, and few senators could challenge their arguments. You had to take as gospel whatever they said, and it was politically dangerous to challenge them. Soon I left the committee in frustration, convinced I could do more good elsewhere.

Still, given Grumman's invitation, I visited the corporation's headquarters in Bethpage, New York, where I inspected the huge facility and had lunch with the members of the board. I was impressed, but I also reminded Board Chairman and Chief Executive Officer Jack Bierwirth that I had been a critic of excessive or unwarranted military spending in the Senate. "I would not necessarily be considered a friend of your industry," I warned. "I am an independent thinker and have always tried to call them as I see them."

"We know that," said Bierwirth. "That's exactly why we want you." I accepted their offer, and thus began a six-year relationship during which I served as chairman of the audit committee. I became well versed in the workings of our nation's defense industry and proud of what thousands of Grumman men and women were doing to ensure our nation's preparedness. I must admit that I was thrilled when the movie *Top Gun* highlighted the F-14 fighters designed and manufactured by Grumman for the United States Navy, and used effectively in "Desert Storm" and later in Afghanistan.

My connections in Boston were also drawing me back there. The Unity Bank of Boston was the only African American owned and operated bank in New England and only one of a handful in the nation at the time. The bank was having problems in 1984 when I was asked to become chairman of the board of directors. I believed in the concept of the bank and had great respect for its history and for the men and women who had founded and operated it. I wanted to help, but despite my service on the Senate Banking Committee, I was no banker. So my first recommendation was that the board hire a real professional. In time, with new management and a strengthened board, the bank began to move forward. The bank, now known as the One United Bank under excellent management, is an outstanding example of how much can be gained by extending economic opportunity to minorities.

Another opportunity came in 1985 when I was asked to serve as a member of the board of directors of Mediplex and later Meditrust, a health-care real estate investment trust firm, investing in nursing homes, retirement centers, and later the La Quinta motel chain. I was privileged to serve as chairman of the executive committee and the investment committee until my retirement in June 2000.

My travels in corporate America taught me to respect the intelligence and good intentions of many of the leaders I met there. I was usually appointed as an "outside director," one who is specifically charged with representing the public interest, rather than fixating entirely on the bottom line, and I appreciated the opportunity to express my point of view in a world that did not always hear or share views such as mine. By and large, corporate officials do not understand how Washington works, and they compensate by paying huge fees to lobbyists—often former members of Congress—to guide them through the political jungle. The huge contributions that corporations make to presidential candidates, as well as to members of Congress, and the favors they expect, and often receive, in exchange for their money are vastly detrimental to our democracy and should be of concern to everyone who wants to see social justice in America.

Most people who serve on corporate boards are appointed by the CEOs and are beholden to them. The CEO, most always a man with rare exceptions, is all-powerful. The appointments pay very well and often include pensions, travels on corporate jets, stock options, and other benefits of office. Given all this, too many board members rubber-stamp whatever is proposed by the CEO, without asking the hard questions that they should ask. These realities have led to the many corporate scandals—Enron is only the most publicized—that we have seen in recent years. The CEOs get their huge salaries and bonuses, the board members are handsomely repaid for going along with management, and when trouble comes, it is the ordinary employee who loses his or her pension and the ordinary investor who loses his or her life's savings. The corporate system, with its inadequate safeguards against human greed, has created its own Frankenstein monsters, and to police this system more effectively should be a goal of all who care about good government.

My interest in social policy has not diminished, and I have found great satisfaction in working with feminist leaders Gloria Steinem and Christine Keeler on Voters for Choice, a private entity formed as a countermeasure to the influx of antiabortion money into the political debate about a woman's right to choose. I am alarmed by the increasing vitriol of this debate. I believe that the issue has no rightful place in American politics. Voters for Choice continues to raise funds in support of pro-choice candidates and disseminates information about candidates and issues. I viewed my participation in Voters for Choice as an extension of my advocacy of reproductive freedom for women. I think *Roe v. Wade* was and is good law and I shudder to think that the Supreme Court could ever consider reversing itself on this fundamental American freedom.

Finally, my post-Senate career allowed me to return to my love of the arts. I served as chairman of the executive committee of the board of trustees of the Washington Performing Arts Society, an innovative organization that has brought world-class artists to the nation's capital. Having kept our Watergate apartment, just a stone's throw from the Kennedy Center, Anne and I attended events frequently. We joke that we can have dinner at home, leave five minutes before the curtain, and still be in our seats on time.

As my mother's one hundredth birthday approached in 1992, we teased her about sending her photograph to Willard Scott for display on the *Today* show. She always protested that she did not want everybody knowing how old she was. But when Anne and I arranged a birthday party with one hundred of her closest friends and family members in the Watergate Hotel on April 19, she could hardly conceal her pleasure. "Why are you making such a fuss about my birthday?" she would exclaim, even as she was admiring the new pink and turquoise dress we had selected for her. She was especially touched by the inclusion of one-hundredth birthday congratulations in *The Congressional Record*, at the behest of Senator Fritz Hollings and his wife, Peatsy.

After receiving accolades from her children and grandchildren and an outpouring of love and affection from her family and friends, it was time to take her back to her apartment. She protested I was being overly protective when I said she needed rest. She would have been happier if all one hundred guests had come upstairs with her. I marveled at her energy and her love of people. Even though she was physically unable to do many of the things she once enjoyed, in spirit she could do everything. She never accepted old age. She never believed she was not a young girl. She never felt she was getting old.

Mother attended the Senate Wives Club meetings up until two or three months before she died. She had joined as a stand-in for Remigia back when I was a new senator, and she had rarely missed a meeting. The organization had its origins in the Civil War, when wives of senators would meet to roll bandages. It included the wives of all senators no matter what their husbands' politics. She was the only mother at the time to be included as a member. She was always thrilled to be invited to the White House for lunch when the First Lady would entertain the club each year. She got to know many First Ladies, and liked them all, but Mrs. Nixon, Mrs. Ford, and Mrs. Bush were her favorites. One of her "official duties" was crowning the Massachusetts Cherry Blossom Queen in the annual Cherry Blossom Festival. She loved it all.

Mother always made friends easily. One day, shopping in the Safeway downstairs in the Watergate, she was struggling with her bags when a woman offered to help take her groceries upstairs. Mother gratefully accepted and invited the lady to have coffee and cake with her. This was the beginning of a friendship that was to last until the day she died. Angela Budi, who worked at the nearby State Department, would dine with Mother at least once a week and often spend the night. They would sit up watching television, eating ice cream, and having their little nightcap of Harvey's Bristol Cream. Angela was with Mother the last day of her life, when she walked out of her bathroom and said she was not feeling well. It was Angela who called the ambulance, which rushed Mother to the nearby George Washington University Hospital. Then Angela called me in St. Martin.

When the call came, Anne and I were sitting on the terrace looking at the night sky, where I would often talk to the stars and say goodnight to Mother as a carryover from my army days overseas. We caught the first flight to Washington, and when the Reverend Prentice Kinser, our Warrenton minister and his wife, Mary Ann, were there to meet us at Dulles International Airport, I knew that Mother was dead.

Mother did not die from any particular illness. God was good to her. I think she just decided after she was one hundred years old that it was time. Anne and I went to McGuire's Funeral Home in Washington to make the arrangements. I was at peace. I realized that the body before me was just the vehicle that had carried my mother's spirit all of those years, and that this loving woman who had cared so deeply for me and been a source of unwavering support for me and for so many others, was gone. Although daily in my mind I picture her earthly body, I am far more often aware of her remarkable spirit. She was buried in the dress she wore to her one hundredth birthday party, and her funeral was attended by scores of friends, family, and people who knew and loved her. It was just as I knew she would want it to be. There were tears but more often smiles and laughter as mourners gathered to celebrate her life and acknowledge the gift "Mother Brooke" had given to all of us—the example of faith, love, and charity toward all.

20

Looking

Beyond

In the fall of 1999, my family and I had much for which to be thankful. Anne, Edward, and I were in good health. Edward had graduated from the prestigious Maret School in Washington, D.C., and was preparing for Brown University. Anne and I celebrated our twentieth wedding anniversary on May 12, and with her fifty-first birthday and my eightieth coming in October we decided to commemorate these milestones with a twenty-four-day around-the-world tour on the Air France Concorde. I wanted to "give the world" to the woman who had given a new world to me.

The trip originated in New York City and included stops in Hawaii; Tahiti; Christ Church and Queenstown, New Zealand; Sydney, Australia; Beijing; Hong Kong; New Delhi, Agra and Bombay, India; Nairobi, Kenya; Cairo; and Paris. I had never been to India, Australia, or New Zealand, and despite all of my efforts to bring about better relations between the United States and China, I had never visited the People's Republic of China. Most important, I wanted Anne and me to share this once-in-a-lifetime opportunity to see the world together.

From the Concorde's cruising altitude of sixty thousand feet you can see the curvature of the earth. The impressive supersonic aircraft, which until the tragedy in Paris in the summer of 2000 had an unblemished safety record, was a magnificent testament to human ingenuity and the triumph of technology over the physical world. In cramped luxury, with gourmet meals and attentive service, we whisked across time zones at a top speed of 1,350 miles per hour. I recalled with some amusement that in 1970 I had been an outspoken critic of federal subsidies for Boeing's proposed development of a U.S. counterpart to the British and French Concorde. I had argued that the plane was too costly and was not needed. Yet, here I was in a Concorde, eleven miles above the earth, eagerly visiting faraway cities and natural wonders that as a boy I had known only in the worn pages of *National Geographic* magazines.

Despite the luxury of the Concorde and our accommodations in some of the world's finest hotels, a sense of adventure was part of the tour. In Hawaii we were thrilled to roar through the lush caverns of Hawaii's "Big Island" in electric blue helicopters, hovering like giant hummingbirds over pristine waterfalls and glimpsing paradise from high above. In New Zealand, Anne and I were bounced about like rag dolls in a high-speed jet boat on the Shotover River, which sent our hearts racing and our minds hoping for a quick return to land.

Also in New Zealand, near Arrowhead, Anne thwarted one of my secret ambitions. I was fascinated by bungee jumping, which originated in New Zealand in the 1980s. While Anne took in other sights, I wandered over to the area where would-be jumpers were receiving instructions. After watching several dauntless divers take the plunge from a bridge, held only by a slender cord, I got in line. The dark water of the river swirled 140 feet below me. I was near the front of the line when I heard a commotion behind me. Anne, who never raises her voice, was screaming, "What are you doing? Are you crazy?" I could see her pushing through the crowd, shouting with disbelief. "Don't you know how old this man is?" she demanded of the indifferent attendant. I sheepishly got out of the line. Had she not found me, I would have taken the plunge. To what end, we shall never know.

After all my efforts to build better relations with the People's Republic of China, I eagerly awaited our arrival there. Our guides, however, cautioned us before our landing at an airport in Tianjin, two hours outside Beijing, that the Chinese immigration officials were strict and that we could anticipate delays after our late night arrival. We were strongly advised to keep our seats until we received instructions, and to wait patiently and quietly as each of us was processed individually. We had not received such a warning at any other stop, and we were a little apprehensive.

Unsmiling immigration officials boarded the plane and briskly examined each of our passports. Then, as we descended from the plane and began walking along a red carpet into the bright lights of the airport, we were astonished to hear the sounds of a band. More than one hundred children in red and white uniforms were playing for us. A full moon shone down and the children played until we had all boarded the buses for Beijing. We had been prepared for the worst, only to receive the warmest welcome of our entire trip. Our spirits were high as we drove off into the night with the children waving goodbye.

For the next two hours, however, we bounced unhappily along dark roads, barely glimpsing anything from the scratched windows of the bus. The Chinese would not permit the Concorde to land in Beijing because of its noise, thus forcing us to make the long, uncomfortable ride into the capital. Happily, we were treated to another warm reception at our hotel. The next day we found Beijing all spit and polish, bustling with preparations for the celebration two days later of the fiftieth anniversary of the founding of the People's Republic. Aided by extremely knowledgeable tour guides, who spoke excellent English, we began to explore the city. I was on guard for the "party line," but I did not get the feeling that our escorts had a political agenda. They were candid and even gently critical of their government. We were even astonished to hear one of them say some of Mao's policies were "significant mistakes." By the second day our tour guide was relaxed enough to share with us a Chinese adage: A lucky man has an American salary, a British house, Chinese food, and a Japanese wife. An unlucky man has a Chinese salary, a Japanese house, British food, and an American wife. At least half of us thought the joke was funny.

I was impressed by the vastness of the Tiananmen Square, with its huge posters of Mao and bright bunting for the impending celebration. The square, surrounded by government buildings, was packed with tourists, students in bright yellow jackets, families, children, and soldiers, hardly more than young boys, most of whom were unarmed. The atmosphere was festive, but I could not forget the images of the brutal crushing of the Tiananmen Square uprising on June 4, 1989, and all the young people who died there. Even ten years later, with the square bathed in vivid colors and sunshine, I was overwhelmed by the remembered image of one brave man defying the row of tanks.

When we visited the Great Wall of China, I thought of President Nixon's achievement in establishing relations with the People's Republic in 1971. So much had changed from the days when Americans regarded China as "the yellow peril." The glistening skyscrapers of Beijing and the economic vibrancy of Hong Kong, even after its return to China by the British, testify to the unifying power of commerce.

My former administrative assistant Alton Frye, along with Jan Berris of the National Committee on United States–China Relations, had arranged a dinner for Anne and me with Ambassador Hua Junduo, vice president of the Chinese People's Institute of Foreign Affairs, and his wife. We discussed China's entry into the World Trade Organization, a prospect that was looking doubtful at the time. I was optimistic, however, and tried to give the ambassador encouragement about the WTO and the United States–China relationship in general. We talked about the status of Hong Kong, Macao, and the inevitable question of Taiwan. The ambassador assured me that the Chinese intended to let Hong Kong and Macao continue as they were. However, he was strongly critical of Taiwan's President Lee Teng-hui, and gave no such assurance with regard to Taiwan.

On the morning of September 27, we left by bus for the airport and our departure from China. All of the members of the hotel staff, from its managers to chefs and maids lined the path of our exit from the hotel grounds, shouting and waving farewell. The Hong Kong we arrived at later that day was a much grander city than the one I briefly visited in 1967. From our room at the magnificent Peninsula Hotel, Anne and I looked across the water at the dazzling skyscrapers and the much-improved waterfront, dotted with fewer sampans than I remembered. As we admired this shining emblem of Asia's economic power, I hoped that the ambassador was right when he said his government's plans were to leave it alone. The kind of strict communist rule we had seen on the mainland would destroy the vitality and spirit of Hong Kong.

Soon we were in New Delhi, driving through comfortable neighborhoods with manicured lawns and fountains. The next day we flew to the city of Agra, home of the Taj Mahal, the magnificent monument to a man's love for his wife. We escaped the 105-degree heat by boarding air-conditioned buses that drove through the most harrowing poverty I have ever seen. Inching our way through crowded, filthy streets with the din of constant auto horns, as the drivers tried to blast their way through the mass of humanity, I felt a deep sense of sadness at the conditions in which so many people live their daily lives. Although I was aware of dire poverty in some parts of India, I was not prepared for the reality of such wretchedness. I felt both guilty and grateful that by chance of birth I had lived my life in the United States. Rising out of this chaotic scene filled with people and animals, noise, heat, and overpowering odors is the magnificent Taj Mahal with its delicate towers, one of the world's greatest architectural treasures, and one of the seven wonders of the world.

As stunning as the Taj Mahal is, and as much as I cherish the photographs of Anne and me posing before it, I lament the failure of the Indian government to recognize that to improve the lives of those who live near this monument would not only be a humane act, but a wise economic move as well. With public sanitation, housing, infrastructure, and services, the government could dramatically improve Agra and boost the tourism from whose revenues the improvements could be funded. We left India awed but saddened by the misery we saw there.

In Africa, we found ourselves living in a well-appointed "tent" at the Kichwa Tembo Tented Camp, on the Masai Mara Game Reserve in Kenya. Anne and I rose in the predawn chill and joined others in the tour group on a hot air balloon ride over the endless African horizon. We glided over prides of lions and herds of antelope, wildebeests, gazelles, zebra, giraffes, and elephants on their dusty blanket of native grasses and trees, running as they have for eons on the vast plains. As the bright sun rose, it cast dramatic shadows on the magical landscape on which we glimpsed an occasional hippopotamus and rhinoceros, and saw grazing herds of the deceptively docile water buffalo. I was struck by an all-encompassing awe and wonder at God's natural world and how insignificant are our lives against the vast tapestry of time. We touched down, and the baskets unceremoniously tipped on their side so we could scramble out and enjoy a champagne breakfast. That evening, we watched the sun go down on the Oloololo Escarpment, warmed ourselves by a huge bonfire, and enjoyed a fine dinner on the banks of the Mara River.

Concorde Captain Jacques Chauvin and his efficient crew remained with us for the entire trip. On each of our twenty-eight take-offs and landings one of the ninety-six delightful passengers was chosen by lottery to join the pilots in the cockpit. When the jet neared Paris, Anne, whose charm and command of French had made her a favorite of the Gallic crew, was selected for that honor. She was thrilled as the sleek aircraft circled the city and made its dramatic descent, enabling her to see Paris as few passengers ever have. After a short stay at the Hôtel de Crillon, we returned to our farm in Warrenton, exhausted from the journey, but with indelible memories of this great globe we inhabit and with a renewed appreciation for all of God's blessings and the gift of each other.

Time is a great healer, and over time I reestablished ties to my adopted hometown of Boston. Gone finally were the painful feelings of rejection that I felt so often in Massachusetts in the first years after my defeat in 1978. In 1997, the Massachusetts Commission against Discrimination (MCAD) in commemoration of its fiftieth anniversary established the Senator Edward W. Brooke Scholarship designed to promote recognition and respect for diversity in the state. Each year since, under the inspired directorship of civic leader Marjorie Perry, college scholarships are given to Massachusetts high school students who are chosen to be "Brooke Scholars" under a program funded by the state legislature. The scholarship program is a source of great pride for me, as is the chair established in my honor at Howard University in 2000 and the Boston University Law School and Dunbar High School scholarships in my name, and the Edward W. Brooke Charter School in Roslindale, Massachusetts.

The most dramatic example of my "homecoming" came on the sparkling day of June 20, 2000, when the shining white New Chardon Street Courthouse in the heart of Boston was dedicated in my honor. The six-story building, costing more than $125 million, houses the same family, probate, and land courts before which I practiced in my early days as a lawyer. When told seven months before that it would be the first state courthouse to be named after an African American and possibly the first to be dedicated during the honoree's lifetime, I sent word to Governor Paul Cellucci they had better hurry or the latter record might remain intact.

More than two thousand people had gathered for the ceremony. They included friends, family, and supporters from all over Massachusetts, the nation, and the Caribbean. With Anne seated on the platform behind me, I looked out and saw our son, Edward; my daughters, Remi and Edwina; my grandchildren, Tamara, Vincent, Christophe, and Landon; and Anne's family, including her mother, Yvette; stepfather, Daniel; brother, Louis-Constant; daughter, Melanie; her daughter's fiancé, Vinod; and my niece Peggy and her son, David. I saw my cousins Adelaide Cromwell and her son and my godson, Tony Hill, and my cousin Wilbur Jackson, and his wife, Joanne. I looked to heaven, to my mother, father, sisters, and my friend Roger Woodworth who had helped make this day possible.

I owed this honor in large part to Senate Republican Leader Brian Lees and to Roger Woodworth, who had become his senior legislative and political adviser. Without my knowledge, they had worked to have the Massachusetts legislature name the building for me. Final action on a budget bill containing the provision, which had been added by Democratic Senate President Thomas F. Birmingham, at Senator Lees's request, and supported by Democratic House Speaker Thomas M. Finneran and Governor Paul Cellucci, was taken in the wee hours of the morning of November 16, 1999. Two days later, Roger went in early to open up Senator Lees's office, and on his way to the State House he was struck by a bus and critically injured. After agonizing months, Roger succumbed to his injuries and thus did not live to see me receive the honor he had done so much to bring about. I accepted it as a tribute to him and all those who had worked with me in municipal, state, and national government.

All the Massachusetts political leaders were there, starting with Governor Paul Cellucci, Lieutenant Governor Jane Swift, Attorney General Thomas F. Reilly, and Boston's Mayor Thomas M. Menino. A large delegation from my hometown of Washington included Mayor Anthony Williams, former Mayor and Mrs. Walter Washington, and

Councilwoman Linda Cropp, the first woman and the first African American to be elected president of the District of Columbia City Council. H. Patrick Swygert, president of Howard University and Jon Westling, president of Boston University represented my alma maters. My old, dear friend Al Brothers came in an ambulance and was brought up to the stage sitting upright in a wheelchair by his son Al Junior. Harry E. Johnson Sr., general president of Alpha Phi Alpha, led an enthusiastic and distinguished delegation from my fraternity.

As speaker after speaker hailed my record on civil rights and human rights, I could see pride in the faces of African Americans in the audience. I thought of the days when I began to practice law and how difficult it had been even to get Negroes to retain a Negro lawyer, because when they went to court, almost all they saw were white faces. But now, at the dawn of a new century, to my left and my right were African American clerks, court officers and judges, and politicians. We were represented at all levels, from the guards at the metal detecting machines to judges on the bench.

When I first began my political career, there were few women in public life. Now, a half century later, those participating in the ceremony were a woman lieutenant governor, and later governor, Jane Swift, and two women judges: Chief Justice Margaret H. Marshall of the Massachusetts Supreme Judicial Court, a white South African who spoke meaningfully of her own experience with apartheid, and African American Chief Justice Barbara Dortch-Okara of the Administrative Trial Court. I was moved to hear such distinguished and courageous women speak of the barriers they said *I* had broken.

America's greatness lies in its wondrous diversity. I believe it is our magnificent pluralism that has made this country great and it is our ever-widening diversity that will keep us great. In my remarks, I praised the progress Massachusetts had made in appointing highly qualified women, African Americans, Jews, and representatives of other minorities to the judiciary. I asked that we pledge to work for a nation in which barriers of race, religion, and ethnic origin do not stand in the way of achievement; that we continue to strike down the barriers that divide us; and that we live up to the noble principles that make us strong. I closed with lines from a Unitarian hymn written by William Pierson Merrill a century ago:

God of justice save the people from the wars of race and creed,
from the strife of class and friction make our nation free indeed.
Keep her faith in simple manhood, stronger than when she began,
till she finds her full fruition in the brotherhood of man.

Not long before the courthouse dedication, I had experienced discomfort and occasional pain in the upper right side of my chest. I dismissed this as just another sign of aging. More than two years later, on Monday, September 2, 2002, I awakened feeling a slight but definite pain under my right nipple. I mentioned it to Anne, who, after examining my breast, said that she felt a small lump. She urged me to call our Warrenton family doctor, Trice Gravatte. But the pain went away, and I thought no more about it. Then on the following Monday I had severe pain around my right rib cage. Anne called the doctor and arranged for me to go in right away. After examining me, Dr. Gravatte said it was probably a pulled muscle, but to be on the safe side he would schedule a CT scan for the next day at Fauquier Hospital in Warrenton.

As my visit was about to conclude I mentioned, "Oh, by the way, Trice, my dear wife says that she feels something in my right breast and that I should tell you about it." Dr. Gravatte quickly examined both my breasts and sent me to the hospital for a mammogram. Like most men, I had never thought of men having mammograms. Mammograms were for women. I had always winced at Anne's recounting of what a painful process it is.

The mammogram was much easier to bear than I thought it would be. However, after reading the X-rays, the radiologist sent me to have a sonogram. I returned home and reported to Anne. We tried not to worry, but this new problem was never quite out of our minds. I thought, "Male breast cancer? Come on! I've never smoked a cigarette in my life. I am not a drinker. I eat healthy and I exercise. How could it possibly be?" That afternoon, Dr. Gravatte called with the news: there was a tumor in my right breast just beneath the nipple, and he wanted me to see Dr. John Williams. Soon I was with Dr. Williams in his nearby office, listening to him describe several ways he could find out if the tumor was malignant. He favored a core needle biopsy, which would allow him to obtain tissue from the suspect area and send it to the lab for examination. I asked him where and when this procedure could be done. He said, "I can do it now and here in my office." I glanced at Anne for approval, and then said, "Let's do it." The procedure was painful but not unbearable. When it was over, Anne and I returned home. All this was on Monday, September 9.

Two days later, Dr. Williams reported that the tumor was malignant. I had breast cancer. Anne started to cry. I sat put my arms around her and said, "Please don't cry. It's going to be all right." But I knew that decisions had to be made and soon. My friend for many years, Dr. Lasalle D. Leffall Jr., a celebrated cancer surgeon, the Charles R. Drew Professor of Surgery at the Howard University Hospital and School of Medicine, and former president of the American Cancer Society, was the first person I called. When I told him that I had breast cancer, he said, "Ed, I am sorry to hear the news, but I wouldn't say that it is rare, and, unfortunately, is on the rise, especially in the African American male population." After a few phone calls he recommended Dr. Christine B. Teal, the head of the George Washington University Breast Care Center. We made an appointment with Dr. Teal for two days later, Friday the 13th.

On Thursday, Anne and I stayed overnight at our Watergate apartment, which was only a few blocks from the George Washington University Hospital. On Friday we walked to the Breast Care Center and noted with some amusement that everything was in pink and purple tones. The waiting room was filled with women. I was sure they thought I was there to accompany my wife, rather than the other way around. We were welcomed by Inger Mobley, who was in charge of scheduling, and who had been my neighbor when I lived at Tiber Island in Southwest D.C. in the late 1960s. We met Dr. Teal, who examined me. Later, together with Jean Lynn, program director of the center, we met to discuss my options. Director Lynn was also an authority on breast cancer, including male breast cancer. We were told that it is rare, but that it does occur, because men, as well as women, have breast tissue; she said that more than 1,500 men would be diagnosed and more than 400 would likely die in a typical year from the disease.

We discussed options and settled on a modified radical mastectomy wherein the breast would be removed by excising the nipple and areolar complex and an ellipse of skin with no muscle being removed. For symmetry, we also agreed that my left breast, which had no cancer, would be removed at the same time, limiting surgery to only the breast tissue and trying to save the nipple. Dr. Teal then proceeded to discuss the option of reconstructive surgery in which case, tissue is taken from your back in order to rebuild the breast. The surgery was set for Tuesday, September 24, to allow me time to honor several long-standing commitments. The next evening, Anne and I had dinner with several friends. We mostly talked politics, and no one could have guessed the anguish my wife and I were feeling. We had decided to keep this medical matter private. We believed this was in the best interest of our family and friends, and it was also in keeping with my belief in sharing the joys of life but not the burdens.

On Thursday, September 18, we flew to Boston to make plans for the unveiling of my portrait in the new courthouse. That next afternoon we lunched with my daughter Edwina at No. 9 Park, a restaurant across from the Boston Common. Later, while Anne shopped, I met with Republican gubernatorial candidate Mitt Romney in Senator Lees's office in the State House. After a short meeting, we had a joint press conference at which I enthusiastically endorsed his candidacy—I had, of course, supported the presidential candidacy of his father, Governor George Romney, in the 1960s. The day ended with dinner with our son Edward and college friend, Matthew Balzer, who had come up from Brown. We never mentioned my coming operation.

On September 24, Anne and I walked over to the George Washington University Medical Center where the surgery was to be performed, and where Edward had been born and my mother had died. Soon we were off to "nuclear medicine." The procedure there was by far the most painful of my entire ordeal: a radioisotope was injected into my breast for the purpose of mapping the sentinel lymph nodes. The sentinel nodes needed to be identified in order for Dr. Teal to be able to remove them and have them studied during my surgery. If the two nodes were malignant, then an axillary dissection was to be performed, removing the axillary nodes. Dr. Teal said the surgery would last about four hours, unless the sentinel nodes were found to be malignant, in which case it would last longer.

Next I was prepped for surgery. The anesthesiologist had studied at Harvard and said her parents had voted for me. Finally, I was wheeled off to surgery while Anne retired to the waiting room. In the operating room were seven women, with not a man in sight except the patient, who was soon unconscious. After several hours, the surgeon sent word to Anne that the operation would take longer than planned. The sentinel nodes had proved malignant. To be on the safe side, she had decided to do an axillary dissection, removing thirteen axillary nodes. Fortunately they proved benign. I was kept in the intensive care unit overnight and have only a dim memory of Anne touching my face.

The next day Dr. Teal said I seemed well enough to leave the hospital. Anne drove me to our apartment, where I began the slow process of healing. Every day I got out of bed and sat in the den, my chair piled high with pillows. We devised a strategy to deal with the drains, which resembled grenades dangling at the end of long tubes coming out of holes in my body. They could fit snugly in the pockets of my pajama top. Four times a day Anne drained the grenades by opening the cap and emptying them.

Percocet kept me tolerably comfortable. The worse pain came when I moved about. I did some writing, watched television, read books and the newspapers, and talked on the phone with friends. Although we had agreed to keep this ordeal as private as possible, we knew we would have to tell Anne's mother and the children and grandchildren, but only when it was over and we could see them face-to-face. So I carried on, cheerful on the phone, trying to sound as healthy as possible. Anne would look at me and shake her head, and I would say, "Baby, you do what you have to do!"

On September 30, I had some routine tests to make sure that the cancer had not spread to my bones or other organs. A few days later we went back to see Dr. Teal, who decided, much to my relief, to remove the drains. Anne and I then went to my first appointment with the celebrated cancer specialist Dr. Robert Siegel, director of the Division of Hematology/Oncology at the George Washington University Cancer Center, who would make recommendations for further treatment. I immediately liked this low-key and personable doctor. He discussed with Anne and me the various possible follow-up treatments and recommended the drug Tamoxifen along with a low dose of Coumadin, a blood-thinning drug. He thought that because my breast cancer cells were estrogen receptor positive, I was a good candidate for hormone therapy. He told me that Tamoxifen blocks the effect of estrogen in the body. It was a great relief that no chemotherapy or radiation was ordered; I could keep what thinning hair I had. I was free to return to our farm.

On Saturday, October 5, the First Baptist Church of Warrenton was celebrating its 135th anniversary. I had been asked more than a year before by my friend Deacon John Williams to be the keynote speaker at the banquet that was being held at the Airlie Conference Center, a short drive from the farm. My hosts knew nothing of my surgery. Since the use of my right arm was still extremely painful, Anne devised a strategy by which I would wear a sling on that arm so that I would not have to shake hands with my right hand. It took all my strength of body and mind to dress in my suit and tie, to lace up my shoes, to get in and out of the car, to walk up several flights of stairs and to face a room full of people. With the help of God, I got through it.

On Columbus Day, October 14, 2002, at the height of the sniper attacks in the Washington area, Anne and I drove in for another appointment with Dr. Teal. My incisions were healing nicely, and my X-rays revealed only the normal signs of aging. We started to breathe a little easier. Though I was weak, tired, and still in pain, we left for Boston on October 25. The next day was my eighty-third birthday and the unveiling of my portrait at the new courthouse. My three children were all on hand. My niece Peggy, her son David, and my old friend Georgia Ireland came from Martha's Vineyard. Joe McMahon, Betsy Werronen, and Ralph Neas came from Washington, as did many other former members of my staff. It was another wonderful celebration: Chief Justice of the Administrative Trial Court Barbara Dortch-Okara presided and Chief Justice Margaret Marshall of the Massachusetts Supreme Judicial Court and Republican Senate leader Brian Lees spoke. I spoke about the state of the world but also about my gratitude to Anne, who had commissioned the painting and made the gift to the commonwealth, and about Fabian and Robert Bachrach, who had taken the photograph in 1969 from which the portrait was painted by famed artist Robert Anderson, who became a valued friend.

At the reception after the unveiling, many said how well I looked. They still did not know about my operation. Later that evening Anne and I took the immediate family and several friends for a birthday dinner at McCormick and Schmicks at Faneuil Hall. I could have told them about my cancer, but I still thought it not the right time. The right time did come, however. I had learned that hundreds of men die each year from breast cancer, with an alarming percentage of those deaths among African Americans. As Anne and I basked in my happy outcome, I wanted to take the message to my fellow Americans. I had learned that some men ignore warning signs of breast cancer out of embarrassment, rejecting any possibility of a disease generally thought to strike only women.

I became involved with the internationally known Susan G. Komen Breast Cancer Foundation and the Y-Me organization that promotes cancer awareness. These groups welcome the attention any well-known person can bring to their cause. I was soon being interviewed all over the country and written about on the front page of the *New York Times* and in the *Washington Post*. Keeping a pace of interviews I had not known for more than twenty years nearly wore me out, but the dedication of those who work so hard to fight cancer kept me going. Over and over, people would say, "I didn't know men could get breast cancer." I felt that if I could move only one person to perform a self-examination and seek out a doctor, my efforts would have been worthwhile. Some good could come from this ordeal.

But my life was by no means over. In early spring 2004, I received a call from the White House informing me that President George W. Bush had chosen me as a recipient of the Presidential Medal of Freedom, the nation's highest civil award. I was shocked. I had been a critic of the Iraq War since its beginning. A little flustered, I thanked the young man and told him I would call him back the next day, which I did. I asked him to convey to the president my most humble appreciation for the high honor.

On June 29, at 2 P.M., the award ceremony was held in the East Room of the White House with several hundred guests and families and friends of the honorees, as well as distinguished members of the government including Secretary of State Colin Powell, National Security Adviser Condoleezza Rice, and the president's chief of staff, Andrew Card, a respected longtime friend from Massachusetts. Enormous bouquets of flowers were everywhere, and the Marine band in their smart dress uniforms played beautifully and continually. There was an abundance of delicious food and drink and hosts President and Mrs. Bush could not have been more gracious to us all. It was a memorable event in my life.

During the ceremony, I could not help but appreciate the symmetry of a public career that would place me on the dais along with fellow honoree Gordon Hinkley, president of the Mormon Church, who during the reception remarked on our first meeting in Salt Lake City nearly four decades earlier, which preceded the church's momentous decision to allow African Americans to become leaders in the Mormon Church.

Three weeks before the award ceremony in the White House, President Bush and Mrs. Bush had traveled to Rome to present the Presidential Medal of Freedom to his holiness Pope John Paul II.

Two months after the ceremony, an op-ed piece I wrote for the *New York Times*, titled "A Party for All of Us," was published on Monday, August 30, the first day of the Republican National Convention in New York City. The article was directed to the delegates. I questioned the wisdom of the bloody and expensive war in Iraq and the failure to address the challenges of inadequate health care, equal rights, poorly paid jobs, and the lack of affordable housing on the American domestic front.

I criticized the "new extremism" and chided the Republican Party for its continual failure to reach out to black Americans. I wrote, "If our party writes off black votes in a cynical appeal to voters based on prejudice, it too will fail, both politically and morally. The same is true of the so-called same-sex marriage issue. The majority of the American people oppose a constitutional ban on such marriages, and if our party ignores majority opinion and caters to homophobia, it will once again be wrong both morally and politically."

I cited the alarming parallels between the disastrous Republican Convention of 1964 and the upcoming convention at Madison Square Garden that would nominate President George W. Bush for a second term. I closed the article with a plea for "more candor, more compassion, and more moderation" and my hope that "our party will show a more open mind and a more generous heart and that President [George W.] Bush will reflect this message in his acceptance speech to the nation." He did not. I am ashamed to say the thought entered my mind that I might get another call from the White House asking for my medal back. But it never came.

After twenty-one years, on August 27, 2005, Anne and I sold Edan Farms, our home in the beautiful Virginia countryside, and moved back to Watergate in our two-bedroom co-op that had served previously as my office. The farm was the only home our son, Edward, ever knew. Memories abounded as we said goodbye to our two remaining horses, Dane and Manny, who stayed with the new owners of the property, and to our beloved Labrador Tuff, and cat, Monroe, long ago buried under a tall poplar tree in front of our house. The months before our departure were filled with gathering memorabilia requested by the Moorland-Spingarn Research Center at Howard University, where I had received my bachelor's degree, and the Howard Gotlieb Archival Research Center at Boston University, where I had gone to law school. At their invitation we sent my Senate desk and chair, my 140-year-old Steinway nine-foot concert grand piano, books, awards and papers (other than those already deposited in the Library of Congress), medals, cartoons, and photographs representing highlights of my public career to these venerable repositories. In short order a lifetime of memories were carefully boxed and packed; they lined the bare hallway, ready to be shipped to their new home.

Goodbyes are never easy, but on a beautiful October evening only weeks after we had driven down Edan's gently winding driveway for the last time, Anne and I returned to Warrenton for a "farewell to Virginia" party given in our honor by dear friends Linda and Barry Wright at their charming historic home. Many of our friends and neighbors came and enjoyed the delicious food, spectacular flowers, and delightful chamber music, all arranged by Linda. Barry paid the bill. Anne and I were grateful, happy, and sad. We knew we were closing this significant chapter in our lives.

On September 22, 2005, as part of the opening of a special public exhibition of my political memorabilia, I was invested as a fellow of the Howard Gotlieb Archival Research Center by Boston University President Robert A. Brown, at a ceremony presided over by friend and media star Jack Williams in the auditorium of the impressive George Sherman Union at Boston University. My Senate desk, chair, and flags were placed on permanent display in the Roosevelt Room of the Mugar Memorial Library. After inspirational speeches by Managing Director of the Center Vita Paladino and my dear friends, former colleague Senator Lowell Weicker and U.S. District Court Judge Joseph Tauro, the hundreds of friends, former staff members, and family members who had gathered for the event were treated to a reception with extraordinary food and drink. This was followed by a small dinner at Boston's venerable Algonquin Club, hosted by Dr. Gotlieb, founder of the center, President Brown, and President Emeritus John Silber. I was astonished by how quickly Vita Paladino, the dynamic managing director of the Howard Gotlieb Archival Research Center at Boston University and her able assistants, Alexander Rankin, assistant director for acquisitions; Diane Gallagher, archivist; and Clementine Brown, director of media relations, were able to put together in record time such an impressive exhibit chronicling my political career.

All of these awards and recognition, together with an encouraging prognosis of my cancer are humbling and wonderful in their own way. And, for all of these blessings, I am deeply grateful. But I am deeply saddened that decades since my defeat in 1978 there is still only one African American in the United States Senate. I had hoped that many qualified African Americans would run and be elected to the Senate. It has not happened. Should this be attributed to the African American candidate who does not run for fear of rejection by white voters, who are essential for victory in all fifty states? Or is it the white voter who still, out of prejudice, refuses to vote for a black candidate? No matter what the reason, it is a blight on the American electorate that should be removed.

During the Reconstruction period there were two African Americans elected to the Senate by the carpetbagger Mississippi legislature: Hiram Revels, who served from February 25, 1870, to March 3, 1871, and Blanche Kelso Bruce, who was admitted to the Senate on March 5, 1875, and served a full term. It took nearly a hundred years before another African American would serve, when I was elected in 1966 by the voters of Massachusetts.

When I took the oath of office, I was the only African American in the Senate, and Senator Margaret Chase Smith of Maine was the only woman. Today, there are fourteen women senators. This is progress, but still not representative of the U.S. population. In contrast, African American membership in the Senate has not improved at all. Carol Mosley Braun, Democrat of Illinois, was the only African American in the Senate from 1993 until 1999. And today, Barack Obama, Democrat of Illinois, elected in 2004, holds the dubious distinction, shared with all of his predecessors, of being the only African American in the Senate.

There have been only five African Americans who have served in the history of the United States Senate, and at no time has there been more than one African American senator in office at the same time. I still hope that many qualified African Americans will run and be elected to the Senate. And I have known many who are more than qualified. I also hope that the American voters will cast their votes not on ethnicity, skin color, or religion, but solely on qualifications, character, and integrity. My fervent expectation is that sooner rather than later, the United States Senate will more closely reflect the rich diversity of this great country.

Much work remains to be done to blot out the stain of racism and religious intolerance that still colors our world today—an immoral indulgence that compromises our principles and diminishes our nation's promise. One vital first step in overcoming the heritage of slavery would be a formal apology from our government to African Americans, to be followed by serious consideration of some form of reparations.

Looking to the future of our country and our world, I am deeply concerned about the awesome responsibilities that our children and grandchildren will inherit. So many things need fixing. To name but a few of them, America should seek to achieve the following:

- The elimination of corruption at every level of government and in corporate America as well
- An honest, fair, and simplified tax code

- Protection of our planet with stronger laws and immediate action to prevent irreparable harm caused by man-made global warming
- Action to deal with the reality of global overpopulation
- Enfranchisement of the citizens of Washington, D.C.
- A diplomatic corps trained to be fluent in the language, culture, history, religion, and customs of countries to which they are appointed or assigned
- Decent, safe, and affordable housing for all Americans in keeping with the promise enacted by the Congress in 1949
- A built-in cost-of-living increase in the minimum wage

"Good things come to those who wait," it is said, and my life has been testimony to this adage. I have seen the world move, however slowly, toward increased equanimity and justice. Even though we still have a long, long way to go, I have learned to greet each day with an appreciation of what has gone before.

My life has been a challenging and fascinating journey through the most dynamic century in human history. I have been blessed with more joy than sorrow, more than I could ever have thought possible. In this book I have written about both, because I believe that both are integral to the formation of a full character and a full life. Some of this writing has been painful, and some of it has filled my heart with memories of happy times and inspiring people. I have shared my life in this book as I have lived it—fully, honestly, and gratefully. I hope that this, my last legacy, may inspire some readers, may save some from error, may give comfort and courage to those who have tried and failed and will live to try again, and may give hope and pleasure to all who read it.

Index